SYRIA AND THE
MIDDLE EAST
PEACE PROCESS

SYRIA AND THE MIDDLE EAST PEACE PROCESS

ALASDAIR DRYSDALE
RAYMOND HINNEBUSCH

COUNCIL ON FOREIGN RELATIONS PRESS

NEW YORK

COUNCIL ON FOREIGN RELATIONS BOOKS

The Council on Foreign Relations, Inc., is a nonprofit and nonpartisan organization devoted to promoting improved understanding of international affairs through the free exchange of ideas. The Council does not take any position on questions of foreign policy and has no affiliation with, and receives no funding from, the United States government.

From time to time, books and monographs written by members of the Council's research staff or visiting fellows, or commissioned by the Council, or written by an independent author with critical review contributed by a Council study or working group are published with the designation "Council on Foreign Relations Book." Any book or monograph bearing that designation is, in the judgment of the Committee on Studies of the Council's Board of Directors, a responsible treatment of a significant international topic worthy of presentation to the public. All statements of fact and expressions of opinion contained in Council books are, however, the sole responsibility of the author.

If you would like more information on Council publications, please write the Council on Foreign Relations, 58 East 68th Street, New York, NY 10021, or call the Publications Office at (212) 734-0400.

Library of Congress Cataloging-in-Publication Data

Drysdale, Alasdair.
    Syria and the Middle East peace process / by Alasdair Drysdale and Raymond A. Hinnebusch.
    p.   cm.
    Includes bibliographical references and index.
    ISBN 0-87609-105-2 : $16.95
    1. Syria—Foreign relations. 2. Syria—Foreign relations—Middle East. 3. Middle East—Foreign relations—Syria. 4. Syria—Politics and government. 5. Middle East—Politics and government—1979–
I. Hinnebusch, Raymond A. II. Title.

JX1581.S95Z5 1991
327.5691056—dc20

91-23949
CIP

91 92 93 94 95 96 PB 10 9 8 7 6 5 4 3 2 1

Cover Design: Whit Vye

CONTENTS

FOREWORD

Cyrus Vance

This book grew out of a study group composed of academic scholars and regional specialists convened by the Council on Foreign Relations which I cochaired with Ambassador Richard W. Murphy during the winter of 1989–1990. The group examined Syria's role in the Middle East peace process. Seminar discussions were led by such experts as Farouq al-Shara, Syrian Minister of Foreign Affairs; Daniel Pipes, Director, Foreign Policy Research Institute; Edward Djerejian, U.S. Ambassador to Syria; Vitaly Naumkin, Deputy Director of the Institute of Oriental Studies in Moscow; Itamar Rabinovich, Rector of Tel Aviv University; and Fred Lawson, Professor of Government at Mills College. The entire project, including a research trip to Syria, was made possible by a generous grant from Rita E. Hauser.

Syria and the Middle East Peace Process is an important addition to the scholarly literature on the topic. Professors Drysdale and Hinnebusch delineate the underlying structures and the domestic and external pressures shaping Syrian policy vis-à-vis Israel. They discuss the policies of the United States and the Soviet Union toward Syria, and emphasize the motivations of President Hafez al-Asad. Obviously, when the study was commissioned we had no foreknowledge of President Asad's positive response in mid-1991 to President Bush's invitation to attend a regional peace conference. Although the authors and study group participants claim no credit for these recent developments, we are pleased with the timeliness of the book's appearance.

I first met President Asad in 1977, shortly after I began my service as Secretary of State. The following year, a week after Anwar Sadat, Menachem Begin, and President Carter had signed the Camp David Accords, I called again on him in Damascus. Asad expressed his profound disappointment over the accords. He was convinced that the agreement between Israel and Egypt would block the road to a comprehensive peace with the Arab States and that a separate treaty would not contribute to long-term regional stability. He concluded that "he would sit by the road and observe events," but assured me he would always carefully examine any opportunity that promised an advance along the road toward what he described as real peace.

Asad's agreement to the recent American proposal for face-to-face negotiations with the Israelis surprised many observers. The six weeks of deliberation that Asad spent before replying to President Bush, however, was typical of his cautious, studied style. He had already informed former President Carter in early 1990 of his willingness to talk to the Israelis under specific circumstances. His policies may have evolved, but Asad's manner and decision making process have not changed. One of the most important points addressed by the authors in this volume is that whatever the precise mix of his motivations, Asad has once again reminded us that Damascus must be an integral part of any successful peace process.

Syria has recently moved to end its period of political isolation in the region; Damascus has consolidated its special relationship with Lebanon, reintegrated itself into the Arab community by restoring diplomatic relations with Egypt, and participated in the alliance defending Saudi Arabia against Iraq. Syria has also seen the demise of her client-patron relationship with the Soviet Union. These events, combined with internal economic pressures, persuaded Asad to adopt a new posture—one better directed toward the real peace he described to me so many years ago.

Since my tenure as Secretary of State from 1977 to 1980, Washington has gradually recognized Syria's essential role in regional affairs and the overall peace process. This book correctly conveys the need for strong American involvement to facilitate any movement toward a lasting peace in this volatile region. Active American diplomacy is as essential now as it was then.

October 1991

ACKNOWLEDGMENTS

When we began writing this book, the Middle East peace process seemed moribund. Today, as final arrangements for convening a regional peace conference are being worked out, hopes that the Arab-Israeli conflict may finally be resolved are stronger than at any time in the past forty years. Yet the peace process could still easily be derailed and gloom once again suddenly descend on the region. The obstacles still standing in the path of a comprehensive settlement remain formidable. There has never been a more exciting, or challenging, time to write about Syria and the peace process. At times, the task seemed almost impossible, as we scurried to revise and update our manuscript to reflect the dizzying events of the past year. Three days after we submitted what we hoped would be the final changes to our manuscript, Hafiz al-Asad inconveniently announced that he would attend the proposed regional peace conference (thus proving what all authors know instinctively: there must be something wrong with a manuscript that meets a deadline).

We are, therefore, indebted to David Haproff and Judy Train at the Council on Foreign Relations Press, who patiently awaited our last-minute revisions and were able to turn a messy manuscript into a book in a miraculously short time. We would also particularly like to thank Linda Wrigley, whose careful and sensitive editing confirmed that our manuscript was in the very best of hands: she was consistently prompt, attentive, and thorough in working over a number of drafts. Our special thanks also go to Jim Prince, who was deeply involved in every aspect of this book and tied all of the strings together. Whenever we had a question, Jim was the person we called. Daniel Wolfe, his predecessor as Richard Murphy's assistant at the Council, similarly worked hard on our behalf. The authors' review group offered constructive criticism and support at all stages. Nicholas X. Rizopoulos, the Council's Director of Studies, pushed us when we needed to be pushed, and Richard Murphy, Senior Fellow, offered invaluable insights about Syria. We also owe a large intellectual debt to the many people who participated in the study group out of which this book grew. Our understanding of Syria was greatly enriched by their many hours of discussion and lively debate over several months. However, this book in no sense represents the collective point of view of the study group. On the contrary, many participants may disagree strongly with some of our interpretations and conclusions. Finally, this whole enterprise—the book, the study group, and our fact-finding trip to Damascus in December 1989—would not have been possible without a generous grant from Rita E. Hauser. We hope this book does justice to her dedication to the cause of peace in the Middle East.

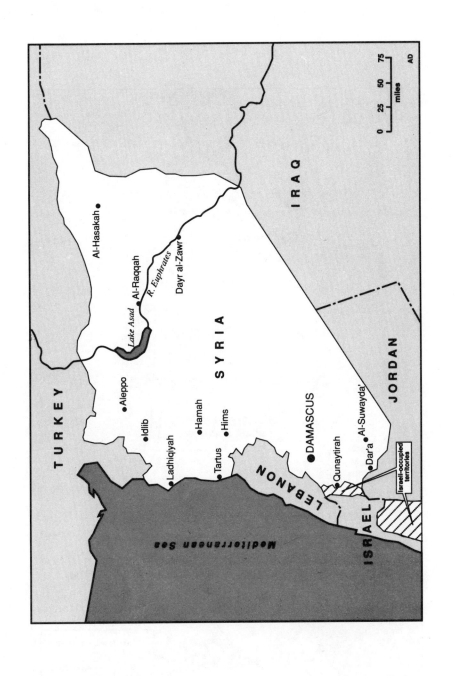

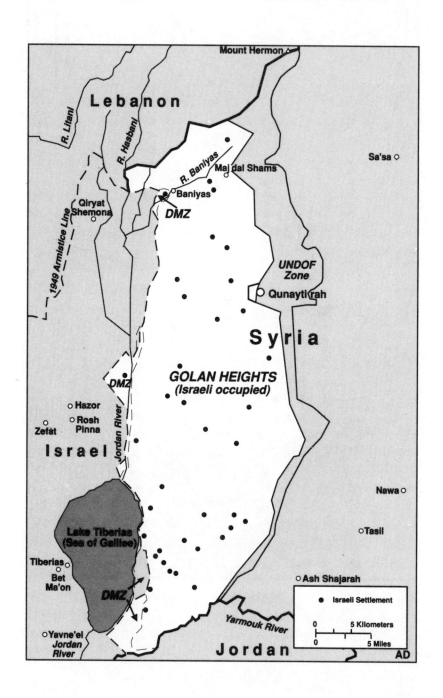

Mount Hermon △

Lebanon

R. Litani

R. Hasbani

R. Baniyas

Maj dal Shams ○

Sa'sa ○

Baniyas ○

DMZ

Qiryat
Shemona ○

1949 Armistice Line

*UNDOF
Zone*

Qunayti rah ○

Syria

*GOLAN HEIGHTS
(Israeli occupied)*

DMZ

Hazor ○

Jordan River

Rosh
Pinna ○

Zefat ○

Israel

Nawa ○

Tasil ○

Lake Tiberias
(Sea of Galilee)

Tiberias ○

Bet
Ma'on

Ash Shajarah ○

● Israeli Settlement

0   5 Kilometers

DMZ

0   5 Miles

Yarmouk River

Yavne'el ○
Jordan
River

Jordan

AD

1

INTRODUCTION

The central thesis of this book is that there can be no comprehensive, lasting, or stable Middle East peace without a Syrian-Israeli peace. This seems so obvious that it may be redundant even to state it. Yet, for most of the past fifteen years or so, the United States has been ambivalent about this reality, and several administrations have effectively excluded Syria from the peace process, or at least not fully involved it, favoring step-by-step separate agreements between Israel and Egypt, Jordan, and the Palestinians over a comprehensive regional settlement. Until recently, the challenge for U.S. policymakers has been not how to engage Syria, but how to shut it out and limit its ability to disrupt the peace process. During the Reagan years especially, Syria was viewed as a truculent Soviet surrogate and as a prime instigator of international terrorism that had to be punished and contained. Before the Persian Gulf War, some even contended that Syria was no longer a key to peace: Plagued by internal economic and political vulnerabilities and the uncertainty of Soviet support, its power was said to be in decline. Thus, it was argued, Syria had lost most of its ability to impede any partial settlement that left it out. The Bush administration's recognition of Damascus's pivotal importance to the Middle East peace process and vigorous efforts to bring Syria and Israel to the negotiating table following the gulf war marked a shift in U.S. policy and, significantly, helped to infuse diplomatic efforts to resolve the Arab-Israeli conflict with new life. Syria's decision, in July 1991, to attend an international conference sponsored by the U.S. and the Soviet Union, and willingness to relax some of its procedural demands, especially concerning the role of the United Nations in any peace talks, raised hopes that a diplomatic breakthrough could be achieved and challenged the prevailing view that Syria does not want peace with Israel. Nevertheless, the conventional wisdom among many in Washington is still that Syria cleaves to a

1

hard-line, maximalist position and has a record of obstructing the peace process. Should the peace initiative that the United States launched in the wake of the gulf war ultimately fail—the obstacles still standing in the way of a comprehensive settlement are formidable—the temptation to exclude Damascus from the peace process in the future may once again be strong.

We contend that Syria is a key player in the Levant and cannot be ignored; that it *is* ready to make peace with Israel under the right conditions; that the kind of peace it wants is realistic and achievable; and that such a peace could be delivered by the regime of Hafiz al-Asad and upheld by its successors. Our thesis is neither new nor original. Henry Kissinger once said that there can be no war in the Middle East without Egypt and no peace without Syria. While the first observation has been proved wrong, the record has so far sustained the second. Why can there be no peace without Syria? The most obvious answer, of course, is that Syria is a major party to the Arab-Israeli conflict, since part of its territory, the Golan Heights, has been under Israeli occupation since 1967. This alone gives Syria a direct and central role in the dispute and a legitimate interest in its outcome. Although the status of the Israeli-occupied West Bank and Gaza Strip and the future of the Palestinians remain the core of the conflict for the Arabs, so long as the Golan Heights are in dispute there will be no peace between Syria and Israel, just as there could be no peace between Egypt and Israel while the Sinai Peninsula was occupied by the Israelis. From Israel's perspective, Syria remains the only frontline Arab state that still poses a serious military threat, although few analysts doubt Israel's ability to defeat Syrian forces decisively in any armed confrontation. The Syrian-Israeli border and the Syrian-Israeli interface in Lebanon remain the main areas of potential military confrontation.

But there are other, equally compelling, reasons why Kissinger's maxim remains largely true. Because of Syria's location at the very heart of the Middle East, bordering Israel, Lebanon, Jordan, Turkey, and Iraq and situated at the crossroads between the Mediterranean and Persian Gulf and between Eurasia and Africa, it enjoys exceptional strategic importance within the region. Few countries have doors that open to so many distinct but interacting geopolitical realms. Asad has expertly exploited this fact, intervening in Lebanon, supporting Turkey's Kurds, blocking Iraqi oil shipments to the Mediterranean, threatening to invade Jordan, interfering with the Palestinians, and forcing Israel to defend its northern borders more thoroughly than its eastern and southern ones. Although Syria does not have the ability to project its power far beyond the Levant, it played a significant, if mostly symbolic, role in the Persian Gulf crisis and offered, in the wake of Iraq's defeat, to contribute soldiers to an Arab security force in the Arabian Peninsula. Syria's geopolitical assets will outlast the present regime. Once Asad has gone, Syria will still occupy exactly the same place on the political map. By virtue of its pivotal geographical location, Syria cannot be ignored in any serious effort to bring peace to the Levant.

Equally important, since 1970 Asad has ruthlessly transformed Syria from a weak and unstable state into a militarily powerful and assertive one (violating human rights on a large scale in the process). Perhaps no other regime in the region has been so resolute in protecting its position and so adept at muscling its way to center stage to ensure that its interests must be accommodated. Syria does not have the political stature of Egypt, the former military might of Iraq, or the wealth of Saudi Arabia, but it is a key frontline state which, for most of the past decade or so, has been Israel's most serious and determined adversary. Because Syria considers itself the "beating heart" of Arab nationalism, it claims to speak and act for all Arabs and characterizes itself, somewhat grandiloquently, as one of the Arab world's twin pillars (Egypt being the other). While these claims are open to debate, it is clear that Syria's imprimatur is essential if a peace agreement between the Arabs and Israelis is to have credibility. With the exception of Egypt, no Arab state has felt comfortable pursuing peace with Israel in the face of Syrian opposition. Syria's historical and political importance within the Arab world, in conjunction with its formidable military strength, shrewd and aggressive pursuit of its goals, and frontline status, have given it power and influence within the region out of all proportion to its size, population, economic potential, and natural endowments. Both geographically and politically, Syria is almost uniquely positioned to facilitate a peace settlement between the Arabs and Israelis or, conversely, to impede one by mobilizing rejectionists, depriving an agreement of legitimacy by withholding its approval, intimidating its Arab neighbors so they will not sign a treaty, or sponsoring terrorist operations to disrupt negotiations. Ultimately, Israel has to deal with Syria, or neutralize its power within the Levant, if it is to settle with Jordan and the Palestinians or enjoy peace along its northern border with Lebanon. To exclude Syria is to repeat past costly mistakes. While Syria may well have lost some of its ability to obstruct any peace settlement that does not include it, the record strongly suggests that it will not let itself be marginalized within the region: Asad has demonstrated a quite remarkable talent for repositioning Syria more favorably within the region's political matrix just when its fortunes seem to be at their nadir.

But what does Syria want? Is Asad a realist who accepts Israel's existence and seeks an honorable settlement, or is he driven by a deeply rooted irredentist pan-Arab ideology that rejects the legitimacy of Israel and envisions no place for it within the region, as many Israelis fear? Throughout most of its history, Syria has rejected the political map of the central Middle East as the most pernicious legacy of European colonialism. In its eyes, the states that the British and the French carved out in the region after World War I—Syria included—were illegitimate entities that artificially divided and weakened the Arabs. From its perspective, Israel was also a product of colonialism, since the British had enabled the Zionist settlement of Palestine during their mandate over the territory. Pan-Arabism, anti-imperialism, and anti-Zionism have constituted the guiding principles of Syria's foreign policy for most of the post–World War II period, as well as the ideological core of the Ba'th party, which came to power in Damascus in 1963. Syria is the bête noire of many Israelis because historically it espoused these ideas more vociferously and more consistently than any other Arab state.

The conflict with Israel remains the central preoccupation of both foreign and domestic policymakers in Syria and is a key source of legitimacy and support for an otherwise narrowly based and repressive regime. However, under Asad, Syria's view of Israel has moderated significantly. Syria has long accepted that Israel is here to stay and has made it clear that it is prepared to negotiate with it under the right conditions. Since 1974, it has explicitly accepted UN resolutions 242 and 338 (to which the United States also officially subscribes) and has indicated its readiness to make peace with Israel if it were to withdraw from the territories it occupied in 1967 and permit the Palestinians to decide their own political future. Syria has repeatedly voiced its support for an international peace conference, to be convened under UN auspices by the five permanent members of the Security Council, or by the two superpowers, and attended by all parties involved in the dispute. In this respect, its position is close to the international consensus on how a comprehensive peace can be achieved and what a final settlement should look like. Asad, in an interview given in 1975, indicated his willingness to have a settlement "formalized with a formal peace treaty." He added: "This is not propaganda. We mean it—seriously and explicitly." Syria has also shown that it can uphold agreements with Israel, scrupulously honoring the 1974 disengagement treaty on the Golan Heights and abiding by the "Red Line" deterrence agreements in Lebanon. For much of the 1970s, Syria was an active, if cautious, partner in the peace process. However, after President Anwar al-Sadat of Egypt opted for a separate peace with Israel, Asad denounced certain specific peace initiatives, such as Camp David, because they were not comprehensive and excluded Syria. Disillusioned with U.S. diplomacy, Asad thereafter refused to countenance negotiations so long as the balance of power seemed to be so much in Israel's favor that the Arabs lacked the bargaining leverage to achieve an honorable peace. Asad has made his basic conditions for peace reasonably clear, although he has not spelled out all of the details.

It has sometimes been suggested that the Asad regime has no genuine interest in a settlement with Israel since its legitimacy is precarious and signing a peace treaty would lead to its certain downfall. Such a minority-based regime, it is said, can survive only by perpetuating the territorial status quo, by exploiting deeply felt nationalist grievances, by mobilizing the population in support of its military preparations, and by using the conflict as a pretext to stifle all internal opposition. An old Arab proverb says that when God wishes to destroy someone, He grants him his deepest wishes. The preceding hypothesis suggests something similar: that peace would undo the Asad regime. We reject this argument. On the contrary, we contend that the Syrian regime believes that an equitable peace settlement is in its own best interests. The evidence suggests that while the Asad regime is unpopular among many Syrians and has pursued many controversial policies—intervening in Lebanon against the Muslim-leftist alliance, supporting Iran in its war with Iraq, and siding with the United States and Saudi Arabia against Iraq in the Persian Gulf crisis—its policies toward Israel have wide backing. In this one area, the regime's position has generally coincided with (and been constrained by) domestic public opinion. There is broad agreement within Syria about what constitutes an acceptable peace settlement. The regime probably would not long survive a separate treaty with Israel that fell significantly short of this consensus. But an agreement that resulted in the return of the Golan Heights and some resolution of the Palestinian problem would enhance Asad's stature within Syria. The regime has far more to gain politically from negotiating an honorable peace than from risking another, even more destructive and expensive, war.

One of the central arguments of this book is that recent changes in the world and the region present excellent opportunities for resolving the Arab-Israeli conflict once and for all. We do not mean to be Panglossian: Such hope has been expressed many times before and has proven misplaced equally often. To make this assertion at a time of high uncertainty, in the aftermath of a war and before arrangements for convening an international peace conference had been completed, may seem nothing short of reckless. Clearly, enormous obstacles still stand in the way of a comprehensive peace agreement. A settlement between Israel and Syria will not come easily. Technically, Israel has already annexed the Golan Heights, and most Israelis consider the area vital to their national security. There is also much to be pessimistic about: the proliferation of chemical, biological, nuclear, and other weapons of mass destruction; the mounting despair among Palestinians in the West Bank and Gaza Strip after 24 years of repressive occupation and four years of a bloody uprising that has not significantly advanced their cause; the present Israeli government's determination to continue building new settlements in the occupied territories; the hardening of opinion among many Israelis in the face of random acts of terror, the spread of Islamic fundamentalism, and widespread Palestinian support for Saddam Hussein, who embodies their deepest fears; and the Arab world's apparent imperviousness to the wave of democratization and change that has recently swept other parts of the world. At a time when many serious conflicts elsewhere are melting away, the Arab-Israeli dispute has proved to be extremely intractable and remains one of the greatest long-term threats to world peace, as well as a main cause of instability and turmoil in the Middle East.

What grounds, then, are there for hope? First and foremost, the end of the Cold War has had a profound effect on the Middle East, which for most of the post–World War II period has been a major arena of superpower rivalry. The United States and the Soviet Union no longer compete in a zero-sum game, so their clients in the region have lost their power to exploit superpower tensions. This increases the likelihood that regional conflicts will be dealt with on their own merits, rather than automatically being refracted through the distorting lens of a bipolar world. The global climate for settling longstanding disagreements has been vastly improved. Indeed, Soviet policy in the Middle East has shifted sharply away from confrontation with the West to active cooperation in resolving the region's disputes, most notably in the Persian Gulf crisis. The United States has already demonstrated its desire to include the Soviet Union in efforts to resolve the Arab-Israeli conflict, a significant reversal of policy. Moscow clearly has a vital and constructive role to play. Israel need no longer fear Soviet encouragement of Arab hostility and can even expect a real Soviet contribution to guaranteeing any peace agreement. The Soviet Union's preoccupation with its own severe internal problems has forced it to disengage from the region and to reassess its relationships with its clients. Perhaps no country has been so affected by this shift as Syria. Moscow has made it clear to Damascus that it will not support Syria's effort to attain strategic parity with Israel and that it strongly opposes any attempt to recover the Golan Heights through military action. Equally important, the Soviet Union has steadily improved relations with Israel. Since the credibility of Syria's military option has rested largely on Soviet backing, these changes have clearly undermined Syria's position vis-à-vis Israel and have forced it to be more receptive to new diplomatic initiatives, to seek better relations with the United States, and to mend fences with moderate Arab states.

Syria's rapprochement with Egypt in 1989—an attempt by the Asad regime to reposition itself within the Middle East in response to the Soviet Union's retreat from the region—represents a historic geopolitical realignment within the Arab world that bodes well for peace. After working hard for a decade to isolate Cairo for signing a separate agreement with Israel, Damascus did an about-face, accepting reconciliation entirely on Egypt's terms. In restoring ties with Egypt, Syria effectively conceded that its tactical rejectionism had failed and clearly signaled its readiness to consider new peaceful approaches to resolving the dispute with Israel. Syria's participation in the coalition against Iraq following the invasion of Kuwait dramatically confirmed its desire to move back into the Arab mainstream. The formation of an Egyptian-Syrian-Saudi axis at the center of the Arab world presents one of the best opportunities in years for peacefully resolving the Arab-Israeli dispute, especially if this coalition is strengthened rather than weakened by the outcome of the Persian Gulf crisis and if the Palestinians can find some way to overcome their present isolation.

Finally, the Persian Gulf crisis has provided some momentum to efforts to resolve the Arab-Israeli conflict, notwithstanding the Bush administration's insistence that the two disputes could not be connected in any way. After fully mobilizing the United Nations and the international community in support of its goals in the gulf, the United States can no longer ignore the global consensus on this other key dispute. Having invested so much energy in securing the withdrawal of Iraq from Kuwait, the expectation among the United States' allies is extremely high that it will now redouble its efforts to settle the Arab-Israeli conflict. Not to do so would jeopardize the United States' position within the Middle East, seriously endanger the friendly Arab regimes that joined the coalition against Iraq, and ensure future crises in the region. Following the conclusion of the gulf war, the United States indicated that it did, indeed, intend to seize the opportunity to resolve the Arab-Israeli conflict through a "two-track" policy of simultaneously encouraging peace between Israel and the Arab states and between Israel and the Palestinians. By early October 1991, the U.S. peace initiative had brought the Arabs and Israelis closer than ever before to direct negotiations, although the peace process could still easily be derailed.

2

THE ASAD REGIME

Syria was once invariably characterized as the most ungovernable, unstable, fragmented, and artificial state in the Middle East. Yet, for most of the period since its independence in 1946, it has been under the rule of a single political party, the Ba'th, which has imposed a measure of stability on the country since it seized power in 1963. Remarkably, some 70 percent of all Syrians have been born during the 28 years of Ba'thi rule and well over half of the population has only ever lived under the rule of Hafiz al-Asad, who assumed power in 1970. This continuity has been purchased at a high cost to human rights and should not obscure the regime's many frailties. Nevertheless, under the Ba'th, Syria has been transformed "from a notoriously weak and vulnerable state" into one which is, in many respects, strong and assertive.[1] In the process, it has ceased being a victim of the designs of neighboring states and has emerged as a major military and diplomatic power in the region—it has, in effect, metamorphosed from a plaything into a player. For much of the period since the mid-1970s, Syria was "the only adversary Israel need[ed] to take seriously."[2] Yet Israel also knows that it can deal more easily with a stable Syria than with an unstable one: The Asad regime has been cautious, pragmatic, and predictable, scrupulously abiding by the 1974 disengagement agreement on the Golan Heights and carefully avoiding provoking Israel in Lebanon. Under the proper conditions, Syria is a country with which Israel can make peace, despite mutual demonization and reciprocal fears about the other's military strength.

The Ba'th has constructed an authoritarian one-party state in which the political center has amassed formidable coercive and bureaucratic power and redefined Syria's national and spatial identities. Once an illegitimate and poorly integrated state that had a flimsy raison d'être, Syria has gradually acquired a certain coherence, despite the persistence of acute sectarian and regional cleavages. The idea of Syria as a separate state has taken root—notwithstanding its involvement in Lebanon, the occasional fears of neighbors that it is pursuing an irredentist Greater Syria policy, and the considerable continuing appeal of pan-Arabism as a legitimating ideology. Syria is now a concrete reality in the mental maps of Syrians, as well as those of its neighbors. Even many Syrians who strongly oppose the regime on a wide range of issues take a certain pride in the fact that, under Asad, Syria has gained an identity and an importance out of all proportion to its size and resource base.

The Ba'thi "revolution" of 1963 brought another important change to Syria: An elite with a strong Alawi minority coloration and roots in small provincial towns and villages replaced a traditional elite that was heavily Sunni Muslim and made up mostly of absentee landowners and urban merchants.[3] These new rulers, through land reform, nationalization, industrialization, and centralized planning, transformed and integrated the Syrian economy and brought new opportunities to regions that had long been neglected. Life in the countryside was revolutionized, giving the regime an important rural constituency. Despite formidable internal problems and many ill-conceived and unsuccessful economic policies, the Ba'thi regime outperformed the ancien régime in the realm of infrastructural development, social planning, long-term investment, and geographically balanced growth.

This is not to deny the regime's egregious deficiencies: Its routine and bloody repressiveness, nepotism, corruption, ideological bankruptcy, economic mismanagement, ossification, and narrow sectarian base are all too apparent. The political system is dominated by one man, Hafiz al-Asad, and the regime owes its longevity primarily to a loyal military and a network of internal security agencies. Possibly no other Middle Eastern government, with the exception of the rival Ba'thi one in Iraq, has a more dismal human rights record. On a number of occasions, opponents have openly challenged the regime, most notably between 1976 and 1982, when the country teetered on the brink of civil war. The absence of large-scale organized opposition since the Hamah insurrection in 1982, when the regime killed thousands of civilians, should not be construed as a sign that there is little discontent within Syria.

In this chapter, after briefly describing the historical context within which the Ba'th party seized power, we examine the nature of the Asad regime—its power base and core constituencies, the instruments through which it mobilizes and controls the population, its performance and vulnerabilities, and the prospects for internal political and economic change. Asad has never been particularly interested in internal affairs, preferring to devote most of his time and energy to the conflict with Israel, the situation in Lebanon, and relations with the superpowers and other states in the region. It would be difficult to understate the extent to which the dispute with Israel dominates his thinking: He sees almost everything, including the internal Syrian situation, through the prism of the conflict. Thus, he has tended to involve himself in internal affairs primarily to the extent that they are a "base for external action." Asad believes that "to be strong abroad he [has] to be strong at home."[4] How strong is he? Is he secure enough to negotiate a peace agreement, or is the legitimacy of the regime too precarious to warrant the risk? What are the connections between the internal political environment and the regional one? To what extent does the regime's domestic standing constrain its foreign policy and affect its ability to seek peace with Israel? Will serious economic problems force a moderation of Syrian policy?

THE TRADITIONAL ELITE

From the late 1940s, when the Ba'th party entered politics, until the early 1960s, when it achieved power, Syrian politics revolved around a struggle between two elites: one dominated by well-established, wealthy landowning or mercantile families from Damascus and Aleppo who demonstrated little interest or competence in nation-building, the other by politically ambitious middle-class elements who saw the urgent need for reform and modernization and who advocated policies that would undermine the exclusive power of the traditional ruling class.[5] As a result of this struggle and the participation of new groups in the political process, the traditional elite's supremacy was challenged and gradually eroded by the Ba'th party, other middle-class groups, and the armed forces. It was not destroyed, however, until after the Ba'thi revolution of 1963.

The legendary "fifty families" constituted the core of Syria's traditional elite. Although these leading families had interests in every sector of the economy and were prominent in every elite profession, the basis for their wealth and power was the vast tracts of land they held, almost always in absentia, throughout the country. In the late 1950s, less than 1 percent of the population owned roughly 50 percent of all agricultural land, while 70 percent of the rural population owned no land at all. Such an inequitable distribution of the resource upon which most Syrians depended for their survival gave a few great wealth and power, but it forced most of the population into a miserable, impoverished existence. Rural landlords consistently formed the largest occupational group in Syria's parliament prior to 1963. Thus, those with the power to effect change blocked land reform, which would destroy their wealth—or at least a part of it—and the very basis of their political power, their stranglehold over an indebted, subservient, and exploited peasantry. In no small measure it was the traditional elite's unwillingness to redistribute land that made certain its eventual downfall.

The traditional elite lacked both the organization and the motivation to solve Syria's most urgent problems in the post-independence era: It demonstrated little genuine enthusiasm for pan-Arabism or for nation-building and showed an almost complete lack of interest in Syria's economic and infrastructural development; it had no desire to widen political participation, reduce social inequalities, or implement land reform; and it seemed unconcerned about the chasm between urban and rural areas and the sharp regional and sectarian cleavages that made Syria one of the most poorly integrated states in the Middle East. Because of this weakness at the political center, from the late 1940s until 1963 Syria experienced almost pathological political instability as various groups jostled for power, usually by means of military coups d'état. It was during this period that Syria earned its reputation as one of the most turbulent countries in the region, with governments following one another in rapid succession. In part, the instability resulted from Syria's humiliating defeat by Israel in 1948–1949, which further discredited the traditional elite. In a deeper sense, Syria's political problems resulted from the illegitimacy of the state, which the colonial powers had arbitrarily created after World War I, despite the strong wishes of its inhabitants to be part of a larger pan-Arab state. Syria's origins ensured that it would become enmeshed in the vortex of regional disputes and rivalries. Throughout the 1950s, Egypt and Iraq actively competed to bring Syria into their spheres of influence, backing rival factions within the country and destabilizing political life even further. The intrusion of the Cold War into the region in the 1950s was also seriously disruptive and resulted in repeated external interference in Syria's affairs. Finally, Syria's deep regional, sectarian, class, and ideological cleavages impeded the development of a stable political community.

THE BA'TH PARTY

It was in this political environment that the Ba'th party emerged and flourished. The Ba'th, as the most active, organized, and articulate proponent of change and modernization, stood for everything that the traditional elite was against. To Syrians who recognized the need for structural reform and were frustrated by the traditional elite's ineffective leadership and bankrupt policies, the Ba'th party's economic and social plans offered hope. Throughout the 1950s, it won growing support, especially in the reform-minded but multifactioned officer corps and among minorities and peasants.

The Ba'th party was formally born in 1947 under the leadership of Michel Aflaq and Salah al-Din Bitar, two Sorbonne-educated teachers from Damascus.[6] Its main goals were succinctly expressed in the slogan: "Unity, Freedom, Socialism." Ba'thists shared a belief that the Arabs had sunk to their nadir as a result of several hundred years of misrule by the Ottomans, the colonial powers, and reactionary indigenous ruling oligarchies. This decline could be reversed and past glories recaptured only through a *ba'th,* or renaissance. The party thus expressed the hopes of many Arabs for rebirth, renewal, and reinvigoration. Its dynamism, optimism, and activism stood in sharp contrast to the lethargy and conservatism of most other political parties in Syria at the time and ensured it support among those committed to bringing about change. Indeed, the Ba'th "excited the minds of a whole generation"[7] and had an enormous impact on the political thought of the Arab world in the 1950s.

The core of Ba'thi ideology was stated in the opening article of the party's constitution: "The Arabs form one nation. This nation has the right to live in a single state."[8] To Ba'thists, it was a self-evident truth that the Arabs were politically, economically, and culturally indivisible, and that any differences among them were "accidental and unimportant" and would "all disappear with the awakening of the Arab consciousness." Pan-Arabism was both the Ba'th party's raison d'être and its primary appeal. It was not by chance that the party emerged in Syria, a state that initially lacked legitimacy and that has always seen itself as the beating heart of Arabism. The second component of Ba'thi ideology, liberation, was inextricably linked to the first, since the Arabs could not unite until they were free, and they could not be free until they were united. Liberation first and foremost meant freedom from all vestiges of foreign political, economic, and cultural domination, for the Ba'th was, and still is, viscerally anticolonial. In a deeper sense, liberation referred to the unshackling of individuals from their restrictive social and intellectual chains. The Ba'th party saw itself as a vanguard (*tali'ah*) of a transformation (*inqilab*) that would sweep away the rotten, the corrupt, and the backward. It distinguished itself from the old political parties, which it viewed as subservient to the imperialist powers and dedicated to serving the political and economic interests of the traditional ruling class. The party, in its constitution, expressed a commitment to "the overthrow of the present faulty structure—an overthrow which will include all the sectors of intellectual, economic, social, and political life" (article 6). Socialism, the final component of the Ba'th's ideological trinity, expressed the party's commitment to social justice, but it was also viewed as "a necessity which emanates from the depth of Arab nationalism itself" (article 4). Ba'thists saw socialism both as a means to destroy the wealth and power of the traditional land-owning and mercantile families who dominated Syria's political and economic life and as a way to create a more egalitarian and integrated society. The party's constitution envisioned a "just redistribution" of wealth and forbade "the exploitation of the work of others" (articles 27 and 28). It also sought state control of industry, utilities, natural resources, and transportation; worker participation in factory management and profit-sharing; regulated wages and working conditions; free medical care; and compulsory education. Most important, it sought to implement land reform and improve the lot of the peasantry. After the Ba'th merged uneasily with Akram Hawrani's Hamah- and peasant-based Arab Socialist party in 1953, the party's socialist orientation and commitment to the agrarian sector became even more pronounced, which gave it a modest base of support in the countryside, especially around Hamah.

Despite the Ba'th's broad appeal and initial dynamism, there were always discrepancies between its aspirations and accomplishments and between its words and deeds. In principle, the party was committed to achieving power through democratic means. However, when democratic machinery functioned, it served primarily to confirm the traditional elite's power, particularly its hold over the peasantry. The Ba'th never achieved major national electoral success: In Syria's freest parliamentary elections, in 1954, it won only 22 of 142 seats. Some Ba'thists recognized that the party would be unable to implement its policies, particularly those such as land reform that would profoundly alter the power structure, without something more than the partial power to which it would have to resign itself if it were to abide by constitutional rules. Given this reality, the Ba'th became increasingly receptive to shortcuts to power through the armed forces, which played an increasingly important role in Syria's political life. Hawrani, in particular, openly tried to recruit officers to the party, recognizing that the struggle for power would probably be played out in the armed forces. This had far-reaching consequences. Real power within the party gradually shifted from its veteran civilian leadership to army officers, who typically had far humbler social origins and were more radical ideologically. As a result of the lowering of entrance requirements to the military academy and the rapid expansion of the armed forces after independence, Syria's officer corps was, by the late 1950s, composed largely of "secondary school graduates of modest means" from the rural hinterland and small provincial towns.[9] Richer Syrians from the major cities, conversely, tended to pursue nonmilitary careers, often buying their way out of compulsory military service. Landed families "despised the army as a profession" and considered the military academy a place for "the academically backward [and] the socially undistinguished."[10] Without question, the modest, usually rural, social origins of most politically active officers during the 1950s were instrumental in radicalizing both national political life and the Ba'th party itself. Since Syrian governments were typically made and unmade by the armed forces, Ba'thi officers increasingly resented and ignored the directives of civilian party leaders.

This civilian-military rift paralleled tensions between the party's leadership and its rank and file. Rural party militants were frustrated that the party's largely urban bourgeois leadership tended to act unilaterally and devoted most of its attention to bringing about Arab unity rather than to the miseries of rural Syria. This growing ideological rift to some extent coincided with, and was reinforced by, class, sectarian, and generational cleavages that emerged in the party in the late 1950s and early 1960s. The Ba'th always appealed to the upwardly mobile offspring of the peasantry. This group grew in size after independence because of the expansion of education in the countryside and the provinces. It was here that Ba'thi membership swelled in the 1950s. Both in relative and absolute terms, the Ba'th's constituency gradually became less urban middle class and more rural and provincial petit bourgeois, even if its leadership did not reflect these changes until after 1963.

From its inception, the Ba'th attracted disproportionate support from Syria's minority communities, particularly the Alawis and Druzes, who played a leading role in the party's formation. As one of the few parties that attempted to establish branches throughout the country, the Ba'th recruited support from a larger hinterland than the traditional Damascus- and Aleppo-based parties. The Ba'th's intense nationalism resonated particularly strongly in Alawi areas, which were deeply affected by France's unilateral ceding of the neighboring Alexandretta region to Turkey in 1939. More important, the Ba'th was explicitly secularist and vociferously opposed sectarianism, tribalism, and regionalism, which in its view impeded Arab unity. The party's constitution proclaimed: "The national tie is the only tie that may exist in the Arab state. It ensures harmony among all the citizens by melting them in the crucible of a single nation and counteracts all religious, communal, tribal, racial, or regional factions" (article 15). To the early Ba'thists, sectarianism and tribalism were among the chief ills of Arab society. Syria's minorities had good reason to concur, for they were its principal victims. They joined the Ba'th in unusually large numbers precisely because it promised to create a society within which their identities would not place them at a perpetual disadvantage. But their support contained the seeds of future conflict, because the Ba'th increasingly came to be seen as a haven for the minorities, especially Alawis, and fell victim to the very sectarianism it originally decried.

The link between the Ba'th and the minorities was especially pronounced in the military. In part, this simply reflected an imbalance in the sectarian composition of the armed forces, a legacy both of discriminatory French recruitment policies during the colonial period and of the obvious appeal that soldiering had to the most disadvantaged sectors of the population. Significantly, the proportional representation of minority officers grew throughout the 1950s, as frequent purges depleted the officer corps of many of the Sunnis who enlisted in the immediate post–independence era and who both led and were the victims of many coups d'état. This enabled minority officers to advance rapidly through the army's emasculated command structure.[11]

The divergence of views within the party widened as a result of Syria's Ba'thi-engineered union with Egypt in the United Arab Republic (UAR) between 1958 and 1961. By 1958, Syria's internal political problems were so severe and its territorial identity and sense of political community so fragile, that a full merger with Egypt seemed to offer the only way to thwart growing Communist strength. In effect, Syria dissolved itself. But the union failed to live up to expectations and many Syrians came to resent Egyptian domination. Socialist reforms, although supported by some Syrians, aroused the opposition of the business and landowning class. In 1961, Syria seceded from the UAR after a coup briefly restored the traditional elite to power. Most of the land reform and nationalization measures introduced during the union were reversed.

Syria's union with Egypt had a profound effect on the Ba'th, whose leaders reluctantly agreed to Gamal Abdel Nasser's demand that the party be dissolved without consulting the membership. Secession also deeply divided the party. Many younger rank-and-file Ba'thists in the provinces grew disenchanted with pan-Arabism, the party's raison d'être, and became increasingly disillusioned with the veteran leadership. Instead, they turned to Marxism for inspiration and plotted ways to assume control of the party. In addition, during Syria's union with Egypt, a group of leading Ba'thi officers formed the secret Military Committee, with the aim of eventually seizing power. Of its five original members, three—including Asad—were Alawi and two were Isma'ili. It was subsequently expanded to include other officers from minority communities or from peripheral provinces. These officers, together with radical civilian Ba'thists from the provinces who had secretly remained active after the establishment of the UAR, formed the nucleus of the so-called neo-Ba'th that seized power with Nasserite and other nationalist officers in March 1963.

Between Syria's secession from the UAR and the coup that brought the Ba'th to power, the officer corps, wracked by acute internal strains following two decades of increasing politicization and factionalization, almost disintegrated. As a result of numerous coup attempts during this period, the army became a swamp of conspiracies and intrigue. Blatant political promotions and extensive purges made rank meaningless. It was in this fluid, uncertain situation—when the army in some respects ceased being a professional organization, its members no longer felt bound by its rules, and mistrust among officers was pervasive—that sectarian, kinship, and geographic ties were activated on a major scale within the officer corps. Ba'thi officers in the Military Committee could not resist the temptation to exploit sectarian ties to cement their alliance and lubricate their climb to power. Communal solidarity gave these Ba'thists a decisive strategic advantage over the many other factions which, given the virtual collapse of military discipline, they could have staged a coup at the time. But the manipulation of sectarian ties was, at this stage, tactical and contextual, a means to an end rather than the end itself.

THE BA'THI REVOLUTION

When the Ba'th seized power in 1963, it bore scant resemblance to the original party, which was virtually defunct. The veteran Ba'thists who had nurtured the party in its early years played no part in the planning or execution of the coup d'état; they were given only a token share of power and ultimately were among the regime's victims. After 1963, the Ba'th in some senses was reincarnated as a new party, both in its leadership and in its constituency and orientation. In a major reversal of priorities, socialism, not Arab unity, became the party's primary goal. Socially, the new rulers were quite unlike those they replaced, with a disproportionate number hailing from rural areas or small towns in remote provinces, particularly Ladhiqiyah, Tartus, and Dayr al-Zawr. Alawis and, to a lesser extent, Druzes and Isma'ilis were heavily overrepresented. Many urban Sunnis resented the newcomers, who exploited sectarian and kinship ties to strengthen their hold over the armed forces and the Ba'th party and thereby consolidate the regime. There were extensive purges in the armed forces, particularly, which were quickly transformed into a Ba'thi- and Alawi-dominated "ideological army." The Ba'th, which in 1963 was a small, poorly organized, and multifactioned party, had to be rebuilt almost from the ground up. Like the army, the party's ranks were flooded with new recruits and packed with friends, relatives, and coreligionists. Party discipline and rules and procedures were widely disregarded in the race to construct a base of support. The symbiosis between army and party, the ruthless purging of opponents, the creation of a one-party state, the imposition of a revolution from above, and the manipulation of sectarian and kinship ties provided the Ba'thi regime with a shield against its opponents, but at a high cost to its legitimacy.[12]

During the Ba'thists' first three years in office, a power struggle was waged between the younger, radical, rural or provincial Ba'thists who had led the coup and the older, more moderate, veteran party leaders, who opposed the regime's doctrinaire socialism and abandonment of pan-Arabism. Generally, the radical Ba'thists had the upper hand within the party, the army, and the state. However, bitter inter- and intrasectarian rivalries, mainly involving Salah Jadid, Muhammad Umran, and Amin al-Hafez, also racked the regime and complicated the struggle between the old and new Ba'th. Despite this internal wrangling, the regime set in motion or advanced the socialist transformation of the economy, expropriating additional farm land and nationalizing most major financial, commercial, and industrial companies. These measures broke the traditional elite's hold over the country's economic and political life and increased exponentially the central government's extractive and distributive capabilities and coercive power. They also reversed the entrenched domination of the countryside by the city and initiated a village revolution of sorts. From the start, the regime's base of support lay in rural areas and small provincial towns at the periphery. The regime's egalitarian and authoritarian impulses and contradictory mix of secularism and sectarianism provoked considerable opposition from the urban merchant class and Muslim fundamentalists, who staged a large uprising in Hamah in 1964.

The Ba'th's radical wing did not emerge fully victorious until February 1966, when Jadid, Asad, and other mostly minority officers staged a bloody intraparty coup and purged whatever remained of the old guard. The regime's rural, provincial, and minority Alawi complexion became particularly pronounced at this point. However, the neo-Ba'thi regime was only slightly more cohesive than its predecessor. In September 1966, a coup attempt by Druze Ba'thi officers was foiled. A more serious problem was the growing personal and ideological rivalry between Jadid and Asad, the two leading Alawi officers in the regime. Syria's humiliating defeat by Israel in 1967 and the loss of the Golan Heights exacerbated the rift and exposed the regime to sharp criticism within Syria. The Ba'th leadership under Jadid blamed the armed forces, which Asad controlled, for the defeat, whereas the army accused the party of crippling it through political purges. The dispute between the two officers also resulted from their different conceptions of the regime's direction. Jadid advocated hard-line socialist economic policies. He also believed that the Palestinians should wage a popular war of liberation against Israel with Syria's support and ruled out cooperation with most Arab governments on the grounds that they were reactionary. Asad thought that Jadid's policies were reckless and economically, politically, and militarily ruinous. He was deeply concerned about Syria's isolation within the Arab world. Because he conceived of the conflict with Israel in classic military terms, he saw an urgent need to build the army into a conventional professional fighting force and to put an end to the intense politicization and factionalization that had distracted it from its main purpose.

THE ASAD REGIME

By 1970, the Ba'thi regime was highly unpopular within Syria and almost totally ostracized within the region. Without Hafiz al-Asad's coup d'état and so-called corrective movement it might not have survived. Asad steered Syria on a more moderate, pragmatic course and attempted to broaden the regime's base of support through political and economic liberalization. During the early years of his rule, the political atmosphere was markedly more relaxed than at any time since 1963. Exiles, whose number had grown dramatically during the harsh early years of Ba'thi rule, were invited to return. Recognizing the importance of the private sector, Asad trimmed state controls over foreign trade and investment and tried to appease the merchants, businessmen, and artisans the Ba'th had so thoroughly alienated. An unconvincing attempt was even made to persuade foreign investors, particularly Syrian emigrants, that they were welcome. Asad's shrewd alliance with the Damascene bourgeoisie significantly changed the regime's complexion and won it new, tentative legitimacy among crucial sectors of the population.

This accommodation was designed not to reduce the regime's hold over Syria but to strengthen it. Asad had no intention of relinquishing control—on the contrary, he has amassed more personal power than any other Syrian leader in the twentieth century. Immediately after seizing power, he centralized political decision making, eschewing the collegial leadership traditionally favored by the Ba'th in favor of authoritarian personal rule. Under Asad, there would be no doubt about who was in charge. In February 1971, only three months after his coup, he assumed presidential powers, and the following month the electorate approved the first of his seven-year terms of office. Asad has placed himself far above anyone else in Syria, forging a kind of despotic presidential monarchy in which he has no serious challengers and in which he controls all of the key levers of power. As president, he has the right to appoint and dismiss cabinets. He can convene and dismiss the People's Assembly, make laws when it is not in session, and legislate over its head if he deems it necessary. Almost all laws emanate from the president's office, and the assembly seldom amends and never rejects them. The constitution specifies only minimal checks and balances to presidential power, and even these have no practical value. The president may assume emergency powers at any time. The judiciary lacks independence, since all judges, including those who sit on the Constitutional Court, are appointed by the president. In practice, the president's power is virtually unlimited. In addition, as commander in chief, Asad controls all appointments to key positions within the armed forces, the regime's main pillar. As secretary general of the Ba'th and chairman of the National Progressive Front (NPF), Asad is also firmly in charge of the only legal political parties in Syria. Although government policies are debated within the Ba'th, Asad clearly has the final word on the party's direction, and no one can advance far within its hierarchy without his approval and backing, elections notwithstanding.[13]

Asad's formal authority is buttressed by a carefully orches-
trated personality cult. Pictures of the president adorn the walls
of government offices, public buildings, places of worship, res-
taurants, theaters, shops, hotels, schools, buses, trains—even
telephone poles. In the state-controlled media, he is omnipres-
ent. Official propagandists depict him as the new Saladin, and he
seems in no hurry to discourage the comparison. In a country
where graven images offend religious sensibilities, statues of the
president tower over many public squares. He is also a source of
new toponyms (Lake Asad) and his name is a safe one for civil
engineers to bestow on their bridges and other unremarkable
structures. There are also signs of an edifice complex: Among
the most conspicuous buildings constructed in Damascus since
1970 are the still unoccupied presidential palace, a massive block
that looms ostentatiously over the city from its hilltop site; the
Asad Tower, the capital's highest skyscraper; and the Asad Library, a peculiar dedication, given Asad's propensity for banning
books—including two biographies, perhaps the only things bearing his name that he has not liked.

Inevitably, Asad's personality, style, and outlook have left a
huge imprint on Syria and its policies. By most accounts, he is
thoughtful, cautious, pragmatic, tough, determined, ruthless,
energetic, patient, astute, calculating, remote, and intelligent.
He towers over everyone else in the elite and is widely respected
for protecting Syria's interests. Even Syrians who detest the
regime reluctantly acknowledge his Machiavellian brilliance.
Asad appears to make all key decisions himself, remaining aloof
and isolated, seldom meeting with his cabinet ministers, and
relying on the telephone as his "preferred instrument of government." [14] Perhaps only three or four security chiefs can call him
directly. His office is small, ill-equipped, and understaffed. Because of his intimidating style, those around him are reluctant to
offer advice or to take the initiative. He lives modestly, unlike
most of those who came to power with him, and works notoriously long hours, seldom leaving his home or office, appearing
in public, or traveling abroad. Ironically, given his provincial
roots and parochialism, Asad has always devoted his energies
primarily to foreign and military affairs, to grand strategy in the

game of nations, for, above all else, he is an Arab nationalist who sees everything, including the internal situation, in the context of the conflict with Israel.

Although Asad concentrated power in the presidency, he also created or strengthened institutions that would give legitimacy, stability, and breadth to his regime. Thus, he expanded the various Ba'thi-controlled popular organizations for workers, peasants, students, and women to mobilize popular support. He also set out to rejuvenate and bolster the Ba'th party, which he considered an essential instrument both for aggregating a constituency and controlling the populace. At the time of the revolution, the party had between one and two thousand members and owed its power entirely to the small group of officers who led the coup d'état. By the early 1970s, the party had recruited some 100,000 members, about 4 percent of the adult population, by relaxing admission standards. Membership increased to 375,000 by 1980 and to between 600,000 and 700,000 by 1990. However, most of these are candidates for membership, not full members, and many are high school students with only a weak affiliation to the party. A special effort is made to reach youth through the Ba'th Vanguard Organization: All school children between the ages of six and eleven are required to attend two classes of ideological indoctrination every week. The party also sponsors the voluntary Revolutionary Youth Federation for students between the ages of twelve and eighteen, which offers summer training camps and a wide variety of activities. To become full party members, candidates must go to weekly meetings for three years and then attend the party's institute outside Damascus for three weeks. Those accepted to full membership must go to weekly meetings.

The party reaches into every village, factory, neighborhood, and public institution. At the base of its hierarchical organization are cells and units, which are combined into sections and then branches. At the national level, the quadrennial Regional Congress brings together hundreds of Ba'thists from all parts of the country to debate party policies and to provide a link of sorts between the leadership and the masses. The congress also selects the party's Central Committee, at least in theory. The top party authority in Syria, and thus a major power center, is the 21-member Regional Command, which serves as a kind of politburo, bringing together the regime's top officers, ministers, and party apparatchiki and officially nominating the president. To the extent that there is a forum for the discussion of foreign and domestic policy, it is here, although Asad, as the party's secretary general, also dominates the Regional Command.[15]

In theory, the party operates according to "democratic-centralist" principles. In practice, party procedures are often ignored and decisions move down through the party, not up. Party congresses are carefully stage-managed and elections are a sham. All key leadership posts are assigned to Asad loyalists. The party does what Asad wants, not the other way around. Furthermore, party discipline is lax and indoctrination superficial. Many Ba'thists are not deeply committed to the party; they care less about its ideology than about the special privileges that membership confers, such as priority in obtaining scholarships, opportunities to travel abroad, easier admission to the military academy, and access to a network of patronage and favoritism. As the ruling party, the Ba'th is the "backbone of the country's establishment"[16] and serves as one of the most attractive means of advancement for opportunists and those with ambition. Moreover, many Syrians are pressured to join the party and face difficulties in their careers if they refuse: Job applications are turned down, promotions rejected, and positions reassigned or transferred. Teachers, physicians, professors, and journalists all report such coercion. Application forms for most jobs in the public sector have a question about party affiliation.[17]

While Asad strengthened the Ba'th party's hold over Syria and ensured that it would continue to dominate the state's political institutions, he also tried to broaden the regime's base, or at least give the appearance of having done so, by bringing non-Ba'thi groups into a ruling coalition, the National Progressive Front, which was formed in March 1972. This Ba'thi-dominated front brought together several like-minded parties from the secular left, including the Communist party and several small Nasserite and socialist parties, such as the Arab Socialist Movement, the Arab Socialist Union, and the Socialist Unionist Movement. Although the coalition's junior partners are represented in the cabinet and the People's Assembly, the front is a transparent attempt to disguise the Ba'th's monopolization of power and to co-opt potential opponents. By joining the NPF, non-Ba'thi parties surrendered their independence in exchange for minimal participation in the political process. They cannot print or distribute their own newspapers, hold public meetings, recruit support in the universities or the armed forces, or establish organizations that might compete with the Ba'th. The NPF's Central Command rarely meets and has no discernable influence over policy formulation—in short, the front is precisely that.

In the seven years after the Ba'th first assumed power in 1963, Syrians were not given the opportunity to vote. Asad, despite his autocratic impulses, recognized that his regime's legitimacy would be enhanced if he received some sort of popular mandate at the ballot box and promised to create a "popular democracy" in which there would be elections. Indeed, Syrians were asked to vote five times during Asad's first three years in power: They ratified his presidency in March 1971, assented to Syria's participation in the Federation of Arab Republics in September 1971, elected local government councils in March 1972, approved a new constitution in March 1973, and elected a new parliament in May 1973. Since then, legislative elections have been held every four years (1977, 1981, 1986, and 1990) and presidential elections every seven years (1978 and 1985). However, the People's Assembly has little real power and is dominated by the Ba'th and other members of the NPF. Seats are reserved for "independents," but the regime controls who gets on the ballot. As a result, voter apathy is widespread and electoral turnout low. The results of the presidential elections are a foregone conclusion: Asad received 99.2 percent of the vote in 1971 and 99.6 percent and 99.9 percent in the two succeeding elections. If nothing else, the magnitude of these victories has inspired many jokes inside Syria: After the last election, an aide congratulated Asad on the result, saying: "You received 99.9 percent of the vote, Mr. President, what more do you want?" To which Asad replied: "A list of the other .1 percent." [18]

After assuming power, Asad, aware of the regime's extreme vulnerability to charges of sectarianism, attempted to change its public face by appointing more Sunnis to the most visible positions and by ensuring that the sectarian composition of government cabinets, the Regional Command, and the legislature was reasonably well balanced. Thus, the prime minster, the defense minister, and the foreign minister have always been Sunnis. Nor have all of Asad's closest associates been Alawi: Muhammad Da'bul, his secretary, is a Sunni; As'ad Elyas, his speechwriter and head of the press office until the mid–1980s, was a Palestinian Christian; Jubran Kurriyeh, his replacement, is a Protestant; Col. Khalid Hussein, his personal bodyguard, who died while saving Asad's life during a 1980 assassination attempt, was a Palestinian.[19] Other non-Alawi members of the inner circle since 1970 have included Mustafa Tlas, the defense minister, Hikmat al-Shihabi, the chief of staff, Abd al-Halim Khaddam, the former foreign minister and vice president, and Ali Abdallah al-Ahmar, Asad's chief aide inside the civilian party apparatus.

Nevertheless, behind the regime's institutional facade, which is generally representative of the population as a whole, an informal Alawi-dominated core controls the main levers of power and almost all the key military, security, and intelligence positions.[20] Members of this Alawi inner circle, past and present, many of whom come from the same tribe or are related, include: Ali Aslan, deputy chief of staff for operations; Hasan Turkmani, deputy chief of staff for logistics; Ali Duba, chief of military intelligence; Muhammad al-Khawli, chief of air force intelligence and perhaps Asad's closest confidant before his dismissal in 1987 for his role in the attempt to bomb an Israeli airliner (the agency is now headed by Khawli's nephew, Ibrahim Huwaji); Ali Haydar, who until 1988 commanded the elite 15,000-man Special Forces, which have often been used to quell internal disturbances; Adnan Makhluf, one of Asad's in-laws and commander of the 10,000-strong Presidential or Republican Guard; Ghazi Kana'an, head of Military Intelligence in Lebanon and another relative of the president; Adnan al-Asad, a cousin who leads the Struggle Companies; Shafiq Fayyadh and Ibrahim Safi, commanders of the Third and First armored divisions, respectively;

and Ali Abdallah Salih, head of the Missile Corps. Before he was sent into exile, Rif 'at al-Asad, the president's younger brother, was a key figure in the regime and commanded the now dismantled, mostly Alawi, 50,000-man Defense Companies, the regime's principal praetorian guard. Mu'in Nassif, Rif 'at's son-in-law, briefly commanded the Defense Companies before they were disbanded. Basil al-Asad, the president's oldest son, heads Presidential Security, a unit within the Presidential Guard; many Syrians believe he is being groomed to succeed his father.

Since the Ba'thi regime ultimately owes its position to the loyalty of the armed forces, Alawis are disproportionately represented within the officer corps. By one estimate, Sunni officers controlled only 25 to 30 percent of all army units between 1965 and 1971. Nevertheless, the charge that the Syrian military is an exclusive preserve of the Alawis is false and simplistic. The regime recruited many Sunni officers with peasant or lower-class origins, and from small towns and villages, who support the Ba'th's goals. Some of these have risen to senior positions within the armed forces, although they are mainly assigned to professional functions in noncombat units. In addition to the defense minister and chief of staff, some 60 percent of General Staff Command officers are Sunni, as are some 45 percent of senior officers. Sunnis reportedly account for over half of the wing commanders and senior officers in the air force and command several armored or infantry brigades and divisions. Christian, and especially Circassian, officers are also disproportionately represented. The Asad regime is well aware that it cannot field an effective, professional army against Israel if it is rent with sectarian cleavages and unrepresentative of the Syrian population. However, Alawis are overrepresented at all levels within the armed forces and control the key personnel, security, and intelligence networks which can block a coup d'état. Alawi officers also occupy senior and sensitive positions in all armored, mechanized, and infantry brigades and divisions. All but one of nine divisions are said to be commanded by Alawis. According to one estimate, Alawis account for some 60 percent of the officer corps and roughly half of the senior echelons. A majority of cadets in the military academies are also thought to be Alawi.[21]

Although the regime clearly has an Alawi core, it would be a grave error to reduce all of Syria's political life to simple sectarian terms. Sectarian identities are important, but not universally or consistently so. Their salience is fluid and contextual. Certainly they do not preclude other affiliations that can serve to bring people together or drive them apart—intra-elite cleavages and struggles have arisen over personality, ideological, generational, occupational, and class differences. There are Alawis who oppose the regime, as well as Alawis who support it.

INTERNAL PROBLEMS

The early 1970s were the Ba'thi regime's best years, with political and economic liberalization and the military's creditable performance in the 1973 war greatly enhancing its legitimacy. Nevertheless, Asad faced opposition almost from the start. The idea of having an Alawi president was intolerable to some Syrians, so deeply entrenched were their prejudices against this long-despised and underprivileged minority. The publication of a revised constitution in 1973 provoked protests, particularly in Hamah, because, in a sharp break with precedent, it did not specify that the president should be a Muslim. Asad backed down on this issue and, to answer doubts about whether an Alawi could legitimately be considered a Muslim, persuaded Imam Musa Sadr, the influential Lebanese-Iranian Shiite cleric, to issue a *fatwa* stating that the Alawis were Shiites.[22]

By the mid-1970s, the regime once again found itself in serious trouble. Its Achilles heel has always been its sectarian complexion, so much so that many of its critics refer to it as an Alawi regime. Some Syrians have always seen the Ba'thi revolution as a revanchist minority conspiracy against the Sunni majority. Those whose influence and wealth were destroyed by land reform and nationalization dismissed the regime's secularism and socialism as a way to dress the transfer of power to the minorities and the countryside in more ideologically acceptable garb. Many Syrians also saw a contradiction between the regime's pronouncements about the irrelevance of sectarian identities and the role such identities manifestly played in appointment to sensitive positions, especially in the military and in the *mukhabarat,* the intelligence and state security apparatus. The regime's minority Alawi coloration created a chronic legitimacy problem. For various reasons, criticism of the Alawi role widened and intensified after the mid-1970s.

Many Syrians resented the Alawis' growing prominence, which they attributed to favoritism. Since 1963, the position of the Alawis within Syria has improved beyond recognition. Once the country's poorest and most exploited area, the Alawi region (the coastal zone and the mountains immediately behind it) has experienced a dramatic economic transformation that has lifted it out of its poverty. Ladhiqiyah and Tartus, the main cities, boomed because of port and industrial development. Furthermore, Alawis have eagerly taken advantage of the expansion of educational opportunities and the favorable political climate under the Ba'th; they are the most upwardly mobile group within Syria, and thousands have became doctors, lawyers, engineers, academics, writers, and other professionals.

Another serious complaint against the regime was the spread of corruption after Asad came to power. In part, this accompanied the steady deterioration of Ba'th party organization and discipline. Because party membership became a means of getting ahead, it attracted many opportunists, who neither knew much nor cared about the party's original aims. A report to the party's Regional Congress of 1979–1980 criticized the "inadequate ideological education" of party cadres and the "growing tendency toward dissipation" among younger members. It observed that the party was suffering from "indifference . . . lack of enthusiasm and party spirit [and] opportunism."[23] A degenerating party, the growth of a huge, inefficient public sector, increased government spending, the influx of Arab aid, and the easing of restrictions against local capitalists created a climate in which corruption could flourish at all levels. Indeed, it became so deeply rooted and widespread that many Syrians were skeptical that it could be eliminated without bringing down the regime. Many top Ba'thists, including Rif'at al-Asad, enriched themselves during the 1970s and openly flaunted their wealth, abandoning all pretense of socialist ideals. This new bourgeoisie, made up of men from the top ranks of the officer corps, the security agencies, the party, and the government had "legal or illegal access to state revenues" and "were distinguished by their ability to buy what they wanted and behave as they wanted without regard to public opinion or state regulation." Over many years, they "milked budgets, [took] cuts on government projects, put their sons into private business, struck percentage deals with agents of foreign suppliers, placed protégés in public sector companies, speculated in property, and made money." Their activities were so flagrant, and their patronage networks so extensive, that some spoke of the emergence of a huge "merchant-military complex."[24] By the late 1970s, Syria bore scant resemblance to the austere, socialist state that the Ba'th had constructed in the mid-1960s. As the economy slowed down and inflation soared, the gap between those who had benefited and those who had suffered from Ba'thi rule widened and nourished mounting discontent with the regime. The widespread, and not entirely unjustified, belief that Alawis had gained the most under the Ba'th and had cashed in on their ties with those in power unquestionably aggravated sectarian tensions.

The Ba'thi regime also frittered away the political capital it had accumulated during the 1973 war by intervening in the Lebanese civil war in 1976. The dispatch of 30,000 troops to restrain the leftist-Palestinian alliance was highly unpopular among elements of the regime's core constituency and seriously endangered its Arab nationalist credentials. To many Syrians who supported the regime, the intervention seemed a betrayal of everything the Ba'th stood for. Other Syrians who had always disliked the regime viewed the intervention in crude sectarian terms. The Alawis were heretics, not Muslims, who were suspected of having shady theological links with the Christians. Didn't they permit wine drinking? Didn't some of them have fair coloring? Hadn't they cooperated with the French during the mandate? The intervention, to protect Christians from Muslims, drew renewed attention to the Alawi origins of many of Syria's rulers and underlined the differences between ruler and ruled. The regime's subsequent attempts to reel in Israel's Christian allies improved its image only marginally.

It was inevitable, given the close geographic, cultural, and historical links between the two countries, that sooner or later some of Lebanon's sectarian problems would spill over into Syria. The rotation of thousands of Syrian soldiers accustomed to relative austerity into the freewheeling atmosphere of Lebanon exposed the armed forces to new stresses. There were frequent reports of checkpoint extortion, gratuitous brutality, and extensive involvement in smuggling. As Syria's goals shifted, some Lebanese Christians tried to foment sectarian strife among Syrian soldiers to weaken the Asad regime's resolve. Maronite radio broadcasts gave the widest possible coverage to real and imagined sectarian incidents within Syria. One of the worst offenders in Syrian eyes was Saad Haddad, Israel's puppet in southern Lebanon. In one appeal to his "brother Syrian Sunnis and Christians," he said: "I tell the Sunnis that the Alawi intend to destroy you, and I remind the Christians that the Alawi is using you to kill the Christians in Lebanon. . . . We are prepared to receive any Syrian Sunni or Christian soldier who kills an Alawi."[25] The war was costly in other ways, too. The Syrian economy slowed down as Saudi Arabia and the other Persian Gulf states sharply reduced their financial aid to protest Syria's attack on the Palestinians. In addition, the expense of keeping a large expeditionary force in Lebanon became a significant economic burden.

Beginning in 1976, the regime was rocked by a wave of bombings and assassinations of prominent Alawis. The attacks were believed to be the work of the Muslim Brotherhood and related fundamentalist organizations. The regime's intelligence agencies and praetorian guard responded with heavy-handed repressive measures. The assassination campaign was probably designed to polarize Syrians along sectarian lines. That, at any rate, was one of its consequences: Alawis drew together, their differences evaporating in the face of the common peril, and Sunnis, many of whom had little real sympathy with the Muslim Brotherhood's goals or methods, added the regime's growing repressiveness to their already long list of complaints. One of the bloodiest incidents occurred in June 1979, when gunmen slaughtered as many as 60 Alawi cadets at the Aleppo artillery school. A more serious broad-based challenge to the regime was mounted between late 1979 and early 1980 in Aleppo and Hamah, traditional opposition strongholds. Demonstrations, strikes, and escalating violence paralyzed both cities. In March 1980, Aleppan merchants protesting price controls declared a general strike, which quickly spread to other major cities. Organizations representing lawyers, doctors, engineers, academics, and other professional groups soon issued manifestos demanding democratic rights, the release of political prisoners, and an end to sectarianism. The disturbances were explicitly anti-Alawi, with the authenticity of the Alawis' Muslim credentials a key issue in the Islamic movement's war against the regime. Underground opposition newspapers openly referred to the "infidel Nusayris [i.e., Alawis] who are outside Islam" and who had "made Islam their traditional enemy."

The regime, nervous that a popular, Iranian-style revolution was brewing, dispatched 10,000 troops to Aleppo and cordoned it off. In the process of reasserting control over the city, it may have killed as many as 2,000 people, and it arrested an estimated 5,000. In June 1980, the Defense Companies reportedly massacred as many as 500 political prisoners at a prison in Palmyra in retribution for an assassination attempt on President Asad. Membership in the Muslim Brotherhood was made a capital offense the following month. Despite the regime's brutal display of force, the opposition's campaign continued. Between August and November 1981, several massive car bombs exploded in Damascus, which increasingly resembled an armed camp, with troops and checkpoints everywhere.

The bloodiest challenge to the regime occurred in Hamah, where an uprising by the Muslim Brotherhood erupted in February 1982. The regime dispatched 12,000 troops to the city, sealed it off, and then systematically pummeled it, employing heavy artillery, tanks, and helicopter gunships. In three weeks of savage fighting, between 5,000 and 10,000 civilians were killed and large sections of the old city were razed.[26] The ruthlessness and ferocity of the regime demonstrated with alarming clarity for all Syrians the lengths to which it would go to defend itself, and it has not been confronted with any serious display of opposition since 1982. The armed forces also demonstrated that their loyalty to the regime could be counted upon in even the most extreme circumstances.

The regime's public explanation for its troubles was simple: Syria was at the forefront of those countries which rejected the Camp David framework for peace with Israel. In the words of Prime Minister Abd al-Ra'uf al-Kasm: "This does not please Sadat and Israel, or the United States. . . . So it is natural for [them] to fight us and try to overthrow the regime."[27] The Syrian government also repeatedly accused the Maronites, Iraq, and Jordan of playing a major role in the disturbances, not without good cause. Asad was convinced that he was confronted not simply with an outburst of internal dissent, but with "a large-scale conspiracy to unseat him. . . . He saw himself as the victim of a 'terrible alliance' of external and internal enemies."[28] Although the regime's external foes unquestionably exploited its difficulties and assisted the opposition, dissatisfaction with the regime within Syria was the driving force behind the outburst of anti-Ba'thi sentiment.

Since the Hamah uprising, the only time the existence of the regime has looked precarious was in early 1984, following President Asad's heart attack. While he was recuperating, a power struggle erupted among his would-be successors, including Rif'at, his younger brother.[29] More than anything else, the crisis demonstrated the extent to which Asad dominated the country's political life and the flimsiness of Syria's political institutions in his absence. The regime's leading officers tried to settle matters in the streets of Damascus and came close to exchanging blows. The crisis not only exposed the praetorianism that lurks close to the surface in Syria, it also revealed that Asad had not appointed a successor. Patrick Seale likened Asad to the pole holding up the tent: When he was removed from the scene, the whole structure threatened to come tumbling down.[30] Nevertheless, there were also powerful centripetal forces at work within the regime; ultimately these outweighed the centrifugal ones. Fears that the regime would collapse and the country descend into chaos were enough to force the key figures to rally and discipline those who threatened their survival. In the end, the regime demonstrated its resilience.

Although it became clear that there was no one in Syria with the stature or ability of Asad waiting in the wings, the crisis also suggested that his death would not necessarily change the basic nature or orientation of the regime, whose future would still probably be determined by its top Alawi officers. The possibility of the regime being overthrown by Sunni officers still seems remote seven years later, so well positioned are Alawis to block a military coup d'état. It is much more likely that a successful putsch in Syria will be an intra-Alawi affair: Alawis still hold the keys to change. In the event Asad dies in the near future, the most likely outcome would be some sort of collective Alawi military leadership, possibly with a Sunni facade or some Sunni participation. If the past is any guide, factional disputes and power struggles would weaken, distract, and eventually even destroy such a collective leadership. The longer Asad survives, the more orderly and planned the succession will likely be. Many Syrians believe that the president is preparing Basil, his eldest son, to succeed him. Nor has everyone written off Rif'at al-Asad as a candidate to lead Syria, despite his unpopularity among many Syrians. An Asadian dynasty is no less plausible than some other outcomes and would satisfy the hunger for stability, order, and continuity that coexists uneasily with the thirst for change within Syria. For while many Syrians look forward to the day when Asad is gone, there are others who are apprehensive about what Syria will be like without his strong presence.

PROSPECTS FOR POLITICAL LIBERALIZATION

The upheaval within the Eastern bloc in the past two years has highlighted the Asad regime's own considerable deficiencies and vulnerabilities and encouraged new calls for political liberalization. Significantly, shortly after the overthrow of President Nicolae Ceausescu, graffiti began to appear in Damascus alluding to the similarity between the corrupt and repressive Syrian regime and the deposed Romanian one. One wall slogan simply said: Shamsescu (Sham being the Arabic name for Damascus).

The resemblance between the hated Securitate, Ceausescu's vicious praetorian henchmen, and Asad's various predacious palace guard units, particularly the disbanded Defense Companies of Rif'at al-Asad, must have been noted by critics of the Ba'thi regime. Syrians, who fear the *mukhabarat*, the ubiquitous intelligence agencies, must have taken vicarious pleasure when East Germans seized control of state security offices and began burning secret dossiers fattened by the tattling of legions of favor-seeking informants. Tales of pervasive corruption and of fabulous illicit wealth being surreptitiously enjoyed by ruling elites who railed against the evils of consumerism, preached the need for sacrifice and hard work, and always seemed to have explanations for this or that shortage must also have sounded familiar to many Syrians. The willingness of the successor regimes in Eastern Europe to simply tell people the truth, admit mistakes, and be openly challenged contrasted sharply with the situation in Syria, where the closely controlled official media still fed people vapid propaganda. The sudden disintegration of ruling parties that had once seemed omnipotent raised the question in many Syrians' minds whether the Ba'th party was just as flimsy and bankrupt as its Eastern European counterparts. Would its rank-and-file membership also desert the party in droves if there was a whiff of crisis in the air? The close links between the reviled and rejected regimes of Eastern Europe and the Asad regime inevitably impelled many Syrians to wonder what conclusions the Ba'th might draw about its own future. The complete and astonishingly swift collapse of Eastern Europe's socialist governments could not have failed to impress and inspire Syrians yearning for political and economic change after a quarter century of virtually exclusive Ba'thi rule.

Just as important as what is occurring in Eastern Europe is what is happening elsewhere in the Middle East. Democratic reforms in neighboring Jordan have made a big impression on Syrians, who are able to watch the proceedings of Jordan's relatively freely elected parliament broadcast by Jordanian television. Syrians are also closely watching events in Algeria, which, like Syria, has been under single-party socialist rule since the early 1960s. The rout of Algeria's National Liberation Front in free local elections in 1990 served to remind many Syrians that the Ba'th rules without their consent and lacks a real popular mandate.

Nevertheless, the short-term prospects for political liberalization in Syria are bleak. *Perestroika* in the Soviet Union, the sweeping away of socialist regimes in Eastern Europe, the humiliating defeat of a like-minded regime in free elections in Algeria, and democratization in Jordan have certainly triggered serious discussions within the ruling elite about Syria's future direction, but these have not resulted in any substantive changes. There have been hints of some ferment within the Ba'th about where to go next—the party's ideologically influential Damascus University branch, which is reputedly a key forum for discussing new ideas and the place where the party's diminutive intellectual vanguard resides, was rumored to have been purged late in 1989 and packed with Ba'thists who favored reform. One indication that the party may be in ferment is the repeated postponement of the long overdue quadrennial party congress, last convened in 1985. The delay may have been engineered to keep the lid on things a bit longer and prevent deep divisions from surfacing before some sort of consensus can be built at the grass-roots level. Another possibility is that the party is paralyzed and simply does not know what to do.

The regime has taken a number of steps to open up the political system in response to rising demands for liberalization in the wake of events in Eastern Europe and elsewhere in the Middle East, but these have been meager and mostly cosmetic. Martial law regulations, in place since Syria's union with Egypt from 1958 to 1961, have been abolished with great fanfare. However, the practical consequences of these moves will not amount to much so long as the various agencies of the *mukhabarat* remain virtually unaccountable and fundamental human rights are so blatantly disregarded. In the spring of 1990, some opposition figures were invited to return to Syria and two minor new political parties—the Nasserite Democratic Arab party, led by Muhammad al-Sufi, a former minister of defense, and a moderate Islamic party led by Muhammad Sa'id al-Buti, a professor of Islamic law at Damascus University—were allowed to operate.

However, these can in no sense be regarded as viable opposition parties, with credible platforms and organized constituencies. An exiled leader of the Syrian opposition belittled Sufi's party with the observation that "all its members combined do not amount to one row of people lined up for prayer in the Umayyad Mosque." He went on to say that Buti's party was led by "elders of religion who sell themselves to any buyer." Both groups were "a form of decoration that the authorities adorn[ed] themselves with and hid behind."[31]

President Asad has demonstrated little sympathy for democratic reform, asserting that the political system is fundamentally sound and needs only minor adjustments. His only apparent concession to those seeking political liberalization was an announcement that he intended to "develop, enrich, and reinforce"[32] the ruling National Progressive Front, within which the Ba'th party is by far the dominant party. However, few regard the NPF as anything more than a cover for Ba'thi control of the state. The junior parties in the front lack real constituencies and do not have the right to recruit within the armed forces or universities, which are reserved exclusively for the Ba'th. Persistent rumors circulated early in 1990 that the regime might allow non-Ba'thi members of the NPF to publish their own newspapers, but these would probably not differ much from the regime's organs. It is hard to imagine a regime that has monopolized the mass media for 28 years surrendering control over the flow of information.

One common (and disingenuous) argument put forth by the regime is that Syria does not need to change its political system because it already had its *perestroika* when Asad seized power in 1970. As the president recently said, "We have been practicing democracy for some time"[33]—practicing it so discreetly, it seems, that many Syrians are unaware of the fact. The official position is that Syria was simply ahead of everyone else: The upheaval in the Eastern bloc demonstrated the great foresight and wisdom of Hafiz al-Asad and vindicated his so-called corrective movement. Whether this line is the worst sort of cynicism about what Syrians can be persuaded to believe, or reckless denial of the regime's failings—all dictatorial regimes are prone o such myopia—remains unclear. As a result of the corrective movement, Asad claims, Syria has enjoyed "a multiparty system and political pluralism," with free elections for representatives to the People's Assembly and several political parties represented in the NPF. He added: "We are satisfied with [the political system] and we have not built it to be despotic."[34]

Asad put to rest whatever hopes still remained of a Syrian *perestroika* in a May 1990 speech:

> Despite the fact that in many countries elections are held on a party basis; despite the fact that many in the world consider this method to be more advanced, more effective, more democratic, and more conducive to national unity; [and] despite the fact that many in Syria are convinced that this is the best method . . . we are of the opinion that the phase through which our country is passing is not the most suitable for implementing this electoral system.[35]

However, as a sop to those pressing for a more open political system, the number of seats in the People's Assembly was increased from 195 to 250 in the May 1990 elections in order to increase representation by independents. Of the 250 contested seats, NPF candidates won 166, or 66 percent, and independents took 84, or 33 percent. Predictably, the Ba'th won the largest bloc of seats—134, or 53 percent of the total. Turnover from the previous assembly was high, with 133 members elected for the first time. Only 49 percent of the electorate cast votes, an indication of low interest in the outcome. The relatively good showing of independents should not be misconstrued: They do not constitute an organized opposition able to constrain Ba'thi power and effectively challenge key government policies. Moreover, the regime closely monitors who gets on the ballot and, through its control of mass media, who gets heard. These elections were neither fair nor open, despite Asad's assertion in his speech inaugurating the new parliament that balloting had been conducted in a "free and democratic atmosphere" and that the results indicated that "the march of popular democracy . . . [had] achieved great strides on the road to progress and entrenchment."[36]

A significant opening of the political system beyond what has already occurred seems unlikely because Asad recognizes the risks of further liberalization. The regime certainly has learned a lesson from the recent experiences of the Soviet Union, Eastern Europe, and Algeria, but the lesson is not that it must give Syrians more political freedom if it is to survive. On the contrary, Asad has grasped more clearly than ever before that substantive or structural reform might unleash uncontrollable forces that could threaten the regime's very existence. Asad is, by temperament and instinct, a deeply cautious man who likes order, stability, and predictability. He genuinely cannot understand how Gorbachev could let things unravel so in the Soviet Union and he clearly has little sympathy for *perestroika*. In his words, "We benefit from the experiments of others, but we never copy what others do."[37] He believes that freedom is disruptive and must be constrained:

> Regulating the practice of freedom means protecting it. . . . Freedom and its regulations belong side by side. If they are separated, anarchy and despotism will prevail. . . . Freedom needs order. . . . Freedom disappears if its orderliness disappears. . . . And when the order is completely disturbed, freedom will be completely absent.[38]

The striking imagery in some of his recent speeches underlines how threatened he feels by the changes occurring around him:

> What is coming seems to be more dangerous and far more destructive. And those who do not prepare themselves to counter the approaching deadly monsters will be destroyed by these monsters. . . . There is something new in the world that we must not ignore or neglect. . . . The world is in turmoil, and no one knows how long this will continue or what the final outcome will be.[39]

Asad has good cause to fear political liberalization. In Jordan and Algeria, recent free elections demonstrated the popularity of Muslim fundamentalism, the Ba'th's old bête noire. While religious parties would probably not do as well in Syria, a comparatively secular country by Middle Eastern standards, the Ba'th would almost certainly be repudiated in genuinely free elections. Asad and his supporters also know that if they relinquish power, either voluntarily or because they are forced to do so, many of those who have enriched themselves at the public's expense or who have dealt harshly with their critics over the past quarter-century would be called to account for their misdeeds. There are many scores to be settled. Since the end of Ba'thi rule would also likely mean the end of Alawi ascendancy—one reason why the regime's demise is so earnestly desired by some Syrians—there is a grave possibility of a sectarian bloodbath in a post-Ba'thi Syria. For this reason, the regime would fight a popular uprising, just as it has done in the past. The violence that accompanied Ceausescu's downfall in Romania would probably pale in comparison with the blood that would be shed if the regime had to fight for its survival, this time in Damascus rather than Aleppo or Hamah. However powerful the Romanian Securitate was, it had neither the firepower nor the sectarian survival instincts of Asad's praetorian divisions. So long as the Syrian military remains at the center of political life and its upper echelons continue to be heavily Ba'thist and Alawi in composition, the obstacles to regime-directed political liberalization may be insurmountable. Even if the regime had no fears about a sectarian backlash and a settling of accounts if it were to open up the political system, its preoccupation with the struggle against Israel, and its impulse to control society and mobilize all its resources, does not favor democratic reform. Syria considers itself an embattled country that is surrounded by enemies and that must be hypervigilant in countering externally instigated plots against it. The regime always asserts that its enemies in the region have had a hand in fomenting whatever discontent is displayed within Syria; it fears that a more open political system would inevitably expose it to external threats no less than internal ones. So long as the state of war continues, the regime has a convenient excuse for stifling dissent.

Since the destruction of Hamah in 1982, large-scale organized opposition to the Asad regime within Syria has been absent, although there is still considerable discontent beneath the surface. The Islamic Brotherhood and the League of Communist Action are probably the most active opposition organizations inside the country. The exiled opposition is ideologically diverse, splintered into many rival factions, and geographically scattered, with the main concentrations in Paris and Baghdad. For most of its twenty years, it has been disorganized, isolated, deeply penetrated by Syrian intelligence agencies, dependent on Iraqi or other state sponsorship, and singularly ineffective.[40] The most active dissidents have been former or current Ba'thists, Muslim Brothers, Nasserites, and Communists. Many of the regime's opponents united to form the National Alliance for the Liberation of Syria in March 1982, immediately after the destruction of Hamah, but this front accomplished nothing. In February 1990, a new, supposedly more broad-based opposition grouping, the Iraqi-backed National Front for the Salvation of Syria (NFSS), was formally established in Paris. The NFSS's composition closely resembles that of its predecessor and brings together a disparate collection of opposition parties and personalities: dissident Ba'thists, the Muslim Brotherhood, the Nasserite Socialist Unionist party, the National Democratic party, and various independent former cabinet ministers and commanding officers, including former president Amin al-Hafez. The front's charter calls for the establishment of a democratic, constitutional, and parliamentary republic in which Syrians can openly and safely express their religious and political beliefs. However, the front will have no impact at all if it is unable to recruit followers within Syria and build links with opposition groups working inside the country.

THE ECONOMY

By many measures, Syria is better off materially than it was when the Ba'th came to power in 1963. The regime can claim some credit for a number of accomplishments over the past quarter-century, including the laying of an extensive transportation network, the construction of ports, the building of the Euphrates dam, the expansion of irrigation, the modernization of agriculture, the initiation of numerous industrialization projects, the development of the energy sector, the provision of state services throughout the country, the extension of electricity to rural areas, and the reduction of urban-rural and center-periphery inequalities. Nevertheless, the country faces severe structural economic problems and the regime's economic performance remains one of its greatest points of vulnerability. Asad has never been overly concerned with economic matters. His closest associates have military or foreign affairs backgrounds, while his economic appointees lack stature within the elite and do not have easy access to him.

The economy has not always performed poorly. In the three years after Asad came to power, the GDP grew by almost 10 percent annually in real terms, largely because of the economic liberalization measures he introduced. After the 1973 war and the explosion of world oil prices, Syria benefited from a large inflow of Arab capital, which fueled even higher levels of growth. Between 1973 and 1977, real GDP grew at an annual rate of almost 13 percent. Foreign aid, mostly from Arab oil-producing countries, climbed from $50 million annually before the 1973 war to $600 million annually afterward. Syria was also increasingly successful in securing loans and grants from the World Bank, Western Europe, and the United States. Moreover, Syrians working in the Arabian Peninsula, which was awash in new wealth following the runup in oil prices, began to remit their earnings of several hundred million dollars annually. Finally, between 1973 and 1974 the value of Syria's own oil exports climbed tenfold to $700 million; oil replaced cotton as the country's chief export. As a result of this influx of capital, some sectors of the population began to enjoy real prosperity. In addition, the government was in a better position than ever before to finance its ambitious development plans. Under the Ba'th, an integrated, modern national economy emerged, albeit one beset with problems.[41] Life in rural areas improved as a result of land reform and the establishment of a network of cooperatives that provided peasants with seeds, fertilizers, technical and financial assistance, and marketing facilities.

Toward the end of Asad's first decade in power, economic growth slowed to about 7 percent annually—still double the rate of population increase. In the early 1980s, however, as the regime faced mounting internal discontent and a war in Lebanon, growth declined to less than 5 percent annually. Between 1983 and 1987, GDP contracted almost 3 percent annually, sliding over 9 percent in 1987 alone. In fact, real GDP (in 1980 prices) was roughly the same in 1988 as it had been in 1982. With the population growing by 3.8 percent each year, real GDP per capita fell substantially. Recently, the economy has experienced an upturn, growing by 11 percent in 1988. In 1990 GDP grew by an estimated 9.5 percent in real terms.[42]

Sudden changes in Syria's GDP reflect the vagaries of weather more than anything else. Industrialization notwithstanding, the economy remains agriculturally based and is extraordinarily vulnerable to sharp annual fluctuations in rainfall. Despite efforts to expand irrigation, about 80 percent of the cultivated land is rainfed. Therefore, the severe droughts that regularly strike the country can have a devastating effect on the economy. This is what happened in 1987, when GDP fell precipitously. Conversely, heavy rains the following year allowed the agricultural sector to grow by 31 percent, which in turn boosted GDP by 11 percent. Winter rains in 1988–1989 were about 40 percent below average, the main reason why the economy grew so slowly in 1989.[43] Whereas in 1988 Syrian farmers produced a record 2.8 million tons of wheat, by far the most important crop, in 1989 they harvested only 1.02 million tons. As a result, Syria had to import 1.7 million tons of grain in 1989, almost twice as much as the previous year. Wheat purchases cost the country almost $300 million in 1989, equivalent to 14 percent of all imports.[44]

Syria's massive military expenditures, which reflect its frontline status with Israel and Asad's regional ambitions and preoccupation with maintaining internal security, have been an enormous economic burden, averaging 30 percent of GDP. Patrick Clawson estimates that $51 billion was spent on the military between 1977 and 1988. In the late 1970s, the regime launched an arms buildup that, by 1985, had nearly doubled the size of the fully mobilized army to 570,000 men and increased the number of tanks from 2,300 to 4,050. As a result, the military budget doubled between 1976 and 1983.[45] Since then, it has declined in real terms. According to published figures, defense and security spending accounted for almost 30 percent of total outlays in the 1990 budget, but the actual figure may be closer to 60 percent. While overall spending increased 7.8 percent in nominal terms over 1989, defense outlays declined 0.4 percent. This represented a substantial real decline in military spending, given an estimated inflation rate of 40 percent.[46]

Clearly, Syria's military ambitions far exceed its economic capacity and domestic resource base. Asad has always recognized that Syria's relatively small and poorly performing economy cannot sustain his strategic and foreign policy goals without considerable external assistance. Because Syria has depended so heavily on Soviet and Arab support, and cannot generate internally the resources it needs to purchase arms, its status as a regional power is fairly fragile. Clawson argues that "massive foreign aid has enabled Asad to acquire a world-class military without making Syrians pay for it."[47] But Syrians have, in fact, paid dearly through the diversion of scarce domestic resources into military consumption. On the other hand, they have not paid the whole bill: Between 1977 and 1988, Syria received an estimated $22 billion in military aid and $20 billion in civilian aid, primarily from the Soviet Union, the Arab states, and Iran.[48] Without this help, Syria would not have been able to play such a pivotal role in the region, and its economy would be in far worse shape.

Recently, Syria's dependence on external assistance has highlighted its economic vulnerability. The Soviet Union, faced with its own economic crisis, has insisted that Syria pay off some of its estimated $15-billion military debt. In addition, there are indications that future Soviet arms deliveries will be on a cash-only basis—most of the arms Moscow has supplied in the past have not been paid for. The World Bank, which puts Syria's total external debt at roughly $5 billion, stopped financing development projects in 1988, after Syria fell $210 million into arrears on its loans from the bank. Worst of all, between November 1988 and August 1990, when Iraq invaded Kuwait, Syria reportedly received no Arab aid at all. After Egypt signed the Camp David Accords, the Arab states pledged at the 1978 Baghdad Summit to grant Syria $1.8 billion annually for ten years. The donor states generally kept within a few hundred million dollars of their commitments until 1982, when aid dropped off because of anger over Syria's support for Iran in the Iran-Iraq War, Iraq's competing need for Arab assistance, the decline in Arab oil revenues, and opposition to Syria's policies in Lebanon and toward the Palestinians. Transfers peaked at $1.8 billion in 1981, falling to $1.3 billion in 1982 and to $1 billion in 1985. Between 1986 and 1988, Syria received only $500 million annually, and almost all of this came from Saudi Arabia. When aid pledged at the Baghdad Summit officially ended in November 1988, the Asad regime lamely asserted that this was an excellent opportunity for Syria to become more self-sufficient and to live within its means. Healthy or not, the regime did not welcome the loss of revenue, which had disguised the severity of some of the country's economic problems. In 1988, Syria actually paid back to Arab states and lending agencies $9.6 million more than it received, compared with net receipts of $580.8 million the year before.[49] The loss of Arab aid was undoubtedly one of the reasons why the Asad regime dispatched troops to Saudi Arabia after the Iraqi invasion of Kuwait. King Fahd immediately rewarded Syria with $500 million and promised more later on. Asad is also banking that Kuwait will richly reward Syria for its stance. By early 1991, Syria was reported to have received as much as $2 billion in windfall aid from the Arab gulf states. Syria stands to benefit enormously from being one of only two Arab states that can counter Iraqi military power in the region. Thus, the Asad regime has once again demonstrated its talent for finding ways to supplement its own meager financial resources.

One of Syria's most serious structural economic problems is the existence of a bloated public sector, which the regime is reluctant to dismantle both for ideological reasons and because this would undermine one of its main constituencies. Since the socialist reforms of the 1960s, the state has controlled a major part of the economy. Currently, it employs over 450,000 Syrians—one-fifth of the labor force. However, since 1988, the government has not guaranteed university graduates government employment, suggesting a desire to shrink the public sector. State industries are notoriously inefficient and a significant drag on the economy. Many operate at below 50 percent of capacity, unable to import raw materials and crucial spare parts because of the severe shortage of foreign exchange.[50] Others lie idle altogether. The regime has not shown any willingness to privatize public sector industries or to introduce a full market economy, but it has expressed a commitment to giving the private sector a larger role. According to Muhammad Imadi, the minister of the economy and an energetic advocate of liberalization, the regime has made it a top priority to encourage the private sector. Changes have been piecemeal and ad hoc, however, and there is no sweeping or comprehensive reform program. Indeed, the regime has been talking about relaxing controls over the economy for the past twenty years, so, understandably, there is some cynicism about whether it is any more serious about liberalization this time.

The small but vigorous private sector has traditionally controlled retail trade and owned and operated the smaller industries, but bureaucratic and economic controls have long left it fettered and unwilling to risk large-scale investment. Syrian entrepreneurs have an extraordinary amount of capital at their disposal, but most of it is deposited overseas or has been sunk into speculative real estate. To improve investor confidence and attract expatriate capital, the government now allows exporters to keep 75 percent of the hard currency they earn, and it is under considerable pressure to let them keep all of their export earnings. Since 1986, the regime has also encouraged the formation of mixed private-public investment companies, particularly in agriculture and tourism. Because of these and other measures, the private sector's share of exports has risen dramatically. To reduce spot shortages, private entrepreneurs have also been allowed to import items like rice, sugar, paper, timber, steel, and tires, which previously were handled by the state. In addition, a variety of austerity measures have been introduced to reduce the role of the state. Subsidies for bread, electricity, gasoline, sugar, tea, and other basics have been decreased. In 1989, for example, the government introduced a higher quality loaf that cost twice as much as the traditional one; now, the more expensive loaf accounts for almost half of all bread sold. The regime is also moving away from rationing basic foodstuffs like sugar and rice by making them available on the free market at a higher price. However, until the government further eases currency controls and introduces a unified and realistic exchange rate, the private sector will harbor doubts about how far economic liberalization can proceed. There have been some positive signs. In May 1991, the People's Assembly passed a new Law for the Encouragement of Investment (Law Number 10) to stimulate domestic and foreign private investment by lifting restrictions on foreign exchange transactions and by providing tax and customs incentives. The new law will reportedly end harsh penalties for illegal foreign currency deals.[51] In 1990, the official rate of exchange for the dollar was £Sy 11.2, while the black-market rate was roughly £Sy 45. Consequently, scarce dollars have been siphoned off into the underground economy. (Syrian expatriate workers in the Arabian Peninsula, for example, remit pounds that have been exchanged at the offshore rate.) The government is also reportedly studying a draft amendment to the income tax laws that would sharply reduce the top tax rates—currently, income over £Sy 100,000 ($8,900) is taxed at a rate of 92 percent—to encourage private investment.[52]

Syria's economy is probably not as unhealthy as official figures suggest because of a thriving "black" economy, without which life would be much harder. Virtually everything—German automobile parts, French cheese, Italian toiletries, Swiss pharmaceuticals, American cigarettes, and Japanese electronics—is available outside official channels, smuggled in through Lebanon. It is a measure of the regime's economic mismanagement that the Lebanese, who have been battered by years of civil war, are selling luxury goods and necessities to the Syrians, not the other way around. Between the Lebanese town of Shtaura in the Bekaa Valley and the border with Syria, and in the Akkar region of northern Lebanon near Tripoli, businesses have sprung up to serve the Syrian market. Lebanon has been described as the lung through which Syria breathes.[53] Some of the regime's leading officers are said to be deeply involved in this thriving trade. While the black market diverts exchange from the official treasury and subverts the government's control over the economy, it also provides badly needed goods and basically keeps the economy afloat. There are no reliable measures of how large Syria's off-the-books economy is, but by all accounts it is huge.

One bright spot in the economy is the energy sector. Since the early 1970s, fields in northeastern Syria have been yielding a heavy grade of oil, some of which has been exported and some of which is mixed with less sulfurous oil at refineries in Homs and Baniyas. The light crude needed for blending was imported from Iraq before 1982 and from Iran between 1982 and 1988. During the mid-1980s, therefore, Syria was a net importer of oil products. However, since 1987 American and other Western companies have produced high quality light oil from the Dayr al-Zawr area. As a result, total oil production has climbed from 162,000 barrels per day (b/d) in 1985 to 270,000 b/d in 1988, and to 470,000 b/d in 1991—enough both to supply Syria's needs and to make it a net exporter of petroleum. In 1989, oil exports were worth $811 million, or 26 percent of all exports.[54] This barely made up for the loss of Arab aid and the cost of increased grain imports. However, Syria was a major beneficiary of the sharp, but temporary, increase in oil prices following Iraq's invasion of Kuwait. The windfall could not have come at a better time. In addition, Syria has significant potential as a gas producer. Estimated reserves have repeatedly been revised upward following several promising recent discoveries, particularly by Marathon, a U.S. company, near Palmyra. The government intends to substitute gas for oil in generating electricity, freeing more oil for export. Gas generation will also reduce Syria's dependence on hydroelectric power from the Euphrates, a notoriously erratic source because the water level in Lake Asad has at times fallen to the point where turbines cannot be driven. The end of Syria's chronic power shortages is in sight.

By 1990, Syrian government officials were expressing optimism about the economy. In February, the minister of economy and foreign trade announced that there had been a trade surplus of almost $1 billion in 1989—the first time the trade account had been in the black in over 30 years. According to official data, exports more than doubled. The government attributed the surplus to a rapid increase in oil exports, a sharp rise in private-sector exports of food and textiles, and strict controls over imports of commodities and capital goods. Most analysts are skeptical about the government's trade figures since it is unclear which of the three rates of exchange were used for computing private sector exports, which accounted for roughly half of all non-oil exports. Depending on the rate used, the surplus may have been as low as $220 million. More important, official trade figures grossly underestimate imports because they do not record goods smuggled in from Lebanon. The scale of these illegal imports is astonishing: When a government committee established to combat smuggling invited Syrians to register illegally imported televisions and pay a small duty in exchange for immunity from prosecution, some 155,000 illegally imported sets were declared.[55]

Prime Minister Mahmud al-Zubi, citing the trade figures, the booming energy sector, and the imminent end to electricity shortages, asserted: "We have never been more satisfied with our economic situation than we are today."[56] Not many Syrians would agree. In fact, Syria's economy is neither as healthy as some official statistics suggest nor as unhealthy as other ones indicate. By 1991, the country's economic prospects looked more promising than at any time since the 1970s, despite some severe problems. The nominal trade surplus grew to an estimated $1.8 billion in 1990. One analyst predicted a "gradual improvement" in the economy because of the oil sector's strong performance and the "steady implementation of major structural reforms." The resumption of Arab aid and the rapid increase in the price of oil after this forecast was issued add weight to its author's optimism. Most significant was the assertion that the regime "appears to have scored considerable success domestically in convincing important elements of the business sector of the seriousness and practicality of the reform programme, in return for which private sector cooperation is growing."[57] Should this prove to be correct, the regime can expect to face even stronger demands for political reform. Whatever Syria's short-term prospects, over the long term it faces a serious demographic crisis that will adversely affect its economic performance: The population, at current rates of growth, is expected to double within eighteen years to 25 million—five times higher than in 1963 when the Ba'th came to power.

•

It has been suggested that the Asad regime's economic problems are so severe that it must soon seek peace with Israel. Alternatively, it has been argued that because of its economic woes,

Syria can no longer block the peace process and can therefore safely be excluded from it. For example, Clawson, noting that Syria's main vulnerability is its economy, contends that the reduction in Arab and Soviet aid upon which the regime depends so heavily has forced Asad to moderate his policies in the region. "Economic pressure has succeeded where diplomacy failed: Asad has not recently trumpeted rejectionist policies in part because he lacks the means to make good on his ambitions."[58] This conclusion seems premature. While Syria's economic predicament is serious, its prospects are far better now than they were even in 1989 because of a temporary oil price increase during the Persian Gulf crisis, the resumption of Arab aid, and the gradual revival of the private sector. Asad is a realist: He knows that Syria is weak economically and cannot, on its own, afford the weapons it needs to compete with Israel. But there is scant evidence he will be more or less amenable to peace with Israel because of Syria's economic circumstances.

It has also sometimes been suggested that the Asad regime cannot afford to settle with Israel because of its Alawi base and fragile legitimacy. According to this argument, the regime, in order to survive, must constantly prove its suspect nationalist credentials, and the most effective way to do that is by opposing Israel. Only by mobilizing the population against an external adversary can the regime maintain its control. Those who subscribe to this view argue that Asad is neither motivated enough to negotiate a peace agreement nor strong enough to deliver one and knows that if he tries, the regime will be overthrown. It is true that the regime has a narrow base of support and a precarious legitimacy, but it has weathered many internal challenges and demonstrated its strength and longevity, if not its popularity. In intervening against the left in Lebanon, opposing the PLO, supporting Iran in the Iran-Iraq War, and siding with the conservative monarchies of the Arabian Peninsula against Iraq, Asad has frequently pursued policies that have raised questions about his nationalist credentials and met strong opposition domestically. When Asad has wanted to pursue a controversial policy, he has shown he is strong and determined enough to do so. In any case, the evidence suggests that while Syrians may disagree with the regime on a wide range of issues, they back its policies toward Israel by a wide margin. In this one area, at least, the regime's actions have been congruent with public opinion. There is a consensus within Syria about the shape of an acceptable peace settlement. Asad could not easily settle for less than he is demanding without risking the regime's survival, but if he got what he and most Syrians want—an Israeli withdrawal from all of the occupied territories and some recognition of Palestinian rights—his position within Syria would be strengthened. Asad is strong enough to deliver a peace treaty, if it is perceived to be equitable, and there is no reason to believe that his successors would not honor such an agreement.

3

ASAD'S REGIONAL STRATEGY

Asad's regional policies can best be understood in the context of Syria's view of itself as the birthplace and guardian of Arab nationalist ideals, its frontline status with Israel, its location at the heart of a region with no deeply rooted tradition of statehood, and its injured sense of territorial identity, a product of the arbitrary way in which the colonial powers drew the Middle East's political map after World War I. As a result of these factors, anti-imperialist, anti-Zionist, pan-Arab, pan-Syrian, and residual irredentist sentiments are stronger in Syria than anywhere else in the Middle East. In this chapter, we look at the interplay between Syria's origins and identity as a state, its regional policies, and its conflict with Israel.

THE PAN-ARAB CONTEXT

Asad's regional policy reflects a set of inherited perceptions and motivations shaped by the pan-Arab context within which Syria is embedded. Syria has always thought of itself as the beating heart of Arabism and as the state where pan-Arab sentiment is most deeply and consistently felt. Historically, it was at the forefront of most Arab unity schemes and saw itself as an important component, if not the nucleus, of a larger Arab state. Syria is a state within which "the diffuse idea of pan-Arabism has remained perhaps the most widely and intensely held symbol of political identification."[1] One consequence of this has been the tendency of Syrian governments to equate Syrian interests with those of Arabs generally, occasionally to the irritation of Arabs elsewhere. Fouad Ajami notes a national consensus of sorts within Syria that her "mission transcends her boundaries."[2] The sense that Syria has a responsibility to speak and act for all Arabs runs deep, at least in Syria. Asad, unrestrained by any sense of modesty, has remarked that "Syria is the only hope of the Arab world."[3] Hikmat al-Shihabi, his chief of staff, has described the Syrian army as "the Arab nation's army," asserting that it represented "the Arab nation's aspirations."[4]

Another consequence of pan-Arabism's intense appeal has been Syria's almost unique difficulty in coming to terms with its own existence. For most of its history, it has rejected the political map that the region inherited from the colonial powers as altogether deficient and temporary. From its perspective, the partition of the Arab world into a number of states was the result of imperialist *divide et impera* policies designed to weaken the Arabs. Syrians, more than other Arabs, portrayed the boundaries that separated the Arabs as wholly artificial and arbitrary. In their eyes, the states themselves lacked legitimacy because of their origins and were destined to be replaced in the future with an Arab state that would extend from the Atlantic to the Indian Ocean. By definition, there could be no Syrian, Iraqi, Egyptian, or any equivalent nationalism, because these were not distinct nations but components of a single Arab nation (*qawm*). Loyalty to the individual states, to the extent that it existed, was "tacit" and "surreptitious" and Arab unity was the "sole publicly acceptable objective of statesmen and ideologues alike."[5]

At its birth, Syria had no authentic national identity, having been created by the French after World War I. As a colonial artifact, it originated through no felt need by those who lived in it, and its hastily drawn boundaries ignored fundamental cultural, historical, economic, and geographic relationships within the Levant. If its inhabitants identified with a Syrian entity, it was with an ill-defined space, *bilad al-Sham,* which included the newly created Palestine, Lebanon, and Jordan. However, this Greater Syria was generally conceived of as a region within the Arab homeland, not a discrete political entity that precluded other, less parochial attachments. Syrians viewed their state as a makeshift rump. Nowhere else in the Arab world was the sense of territorial violation and dismemberment so keenly felt: The French had detached Lebanon in the 1920s, depriving Syria of its traditional port outlets in Beirut and Tripoli and sundering the Levant's natural geographic unity; they had unilaterally ceded the mostly Arab Alexandretta region to Turkey in 1939,

reducing Syria's coastline; and they had carved what was
.to sectarian mini-states—one for the Alawis, one for the
.zes, and, briefly, even one for Damascenes and one for
.eppans. Most important, the British had detached Palestine,
where they facilitated Zionist colonization and the creation of an
alien, settler state. To Syrians, this intrusion went hand in hand
with the Arab world's Balkanization—both had to be reversed.
Pan-Arabism and anti-Zionism therefore became the twin guiding principles of Syrian foreign policy.

From Syria's inception there was almost universal agreement among its inhabitants that, within its arbitrary and colo-
nially demarcated boundaries, it was an amputated state. Many
of its political leaders felt obliged to reject its very existence, since
to do otherwise would be to acquiesce in an imperialist fait
accompli and accept the partition of the Arab world. One Syrian
president in the mid-1950s disparagingly referred to Syria as
"the current official name for that country which lies within the
artificial boundaries drawn up by imperialism when it still had
the power to write history."[6] Many of Syria's early postindepen-
dence rulers went out of their way to avoid the appearance of
accepting the territorial status quo and were reluctant to cultivate a specifically Syrian centripetal iconography. This is exem-
plified in a communiqué issued after one of the many coups
d'état: "Arab Syria and its people have never recognized the
boundaries of its [*sic*] country and only acknowledge the fron-
tiers of the greater Arab homeland. Even Syria's national an-
them does not contain the word Syria but glorifies Arabism and
the heroic war of all the Arabs."[7] Because of the allure and resilience of pan-Arabist ideas, loyalty to Syria as an independent
political entity was long equated with betrayal of the pan-Arab
suprastate idea, and those who appeared to put the interests of
Syria, or any other state, above those of the Arab nation were
accused of regionalism (*iqlimiyyah*).

Syrian patriotism (*wataniyyah*) is far better developed today
than it was two or three decades ago. Most Syrians cannot remember a time when their boundaries were any different and
have naturally come to identify with the state, despite its imper-
fect origins—states have a way of acquiring their own justifica-

tion. The failure of so many Arab unity schemes, particularly Syria's merger with Egypt between 1958 and 1961, has also had a sobering effect: Syrians, like other Arabs, are far readier to admit that there are real differences among the states that cannot be wished away and to accept that loyalty to the individual states can coexist with pan-Arab ideals, especially when Arab unity is seen primarily in terms of solidarity rather than complete integration. Notwithstanding public rhetoric to the contrary, pan-Arabism has ceased being the foremost determinant of Syria's foreign policy, which is now shaped primarily by assessments of how best to defend and enhance the power and prestige of Syria within the existing regional state system—in short, by conventional raisons d'état.

Nevertheless, there is still some ambivalence about the state's identity. Syrians still have a somewhat blurred view of its territorial coordinates. Leaders often refer to Syria as a region (*qutr*) rather than a state. The preamble to the constitution states that the "Syrian Arab *region*" (emphasis added) is a part of the Arab homeland and that its people "are a part of the Arab nation which strives . . . for . . . complete unity." In addition, Syrians, when they look at the region around them, still do not perceive a classic state system comprising distinct national entities; what they see are artificial states that are part of an Arab nation with an overriding interest that ought to shape their foreign policies. To the extent that Syria has a defining identity, it is as the most Arab of Arab states. Its foremost sustaining myth is still that it is the main champion of the Arab cause and the most steadfast and self-sacrificing defender against Zionist expansion. Since it assumes such a heroic role, it can claim the right to define the higher Arab interest, which of course always coincides with Syria's best interests. Because of this blurring between what is good for Syria and what is supposedly good for the Arabs as a whole, Syrian regimes have felt entitled to become deeply involved in the affairs of other Arab states, particularly within historic Greater Syria.

Pan-Arabism has also not lost its importance as a legitimating ideology for the Asad regime, particularly in view of its narrow sectarian base and repressive instincts. Shakespeare's observation seems especially appropriate: "For how can tyrants safely govern home / Unless abroad they purchase great alliance?"[8] No Syrian government could survive for very long if it gave up all public pretense of acting in the best interests of the Arab nation, even when it manifestly is not doing so. Thus, the Asad regime justified its intervention against the Palestinians in Lebanon and its support for Persian Iran against Arab Iraq in the Iran-Iraq War, policies that could not, by any objective standard, be characterized as being in the Arabs' best interests in precisely those terms. Similarly, the regime's righteous opposition to the Iraqi invasion of Kuwait was couched entirely in terms of loyalty to the greater Arab good—there was not even a hint that Asad's hatred for Saddam Hussein had anything to do with Syria's position. Despite the rise of the Syrian state and the declining importance of pan-Arabism, no Syrian regime could settle with Israel over the Golan Heights alone—resolving the Palestinian issue is at least as important. In this respect, Syria is not at all like Egypt, which was willing to sign a peace agreement in exchange for the return of the Sinai Peninsula. Syrians perceive Israel as an imperialist-backed colonial settler state implanted in the heart of historic Syria at the expense of their Palestinian cousins and to the detriment of Arab unity.

It is not by chance, then, that the Ba'th party was born in Syria and has been in power there continuously since 1963. No other party expressed Syria's sense of territorial amputation and incompleteness as vigorously or as convincingly as the Ba'th. Above all, the party captured and articulated the deep yearnings within Syria for a reconstituted, revived Arab nation and for a redressing of past territorial wrongs, particularly the establishment of Israel. The Ba'th viewed the Middle Eastern state system and the existence of an expansionist Israel as a "mutilation" of the Arab nation. Its "eternal mission" was to overcome this dismemberment, to redraw the political map so that national space and political space were congruent, and to liberate Palestine; in this scheme, Syria was not a national unit but a base for this national mission.[9]

REGIONAL STRATEGY AND THE STRUGGLE
WITH ISRAEL

Although Syria's policies are conditioned by the dream of pan-Arabism, the immediate factor shaping them is the need for a credible strategy in the struggle with Israel. Asad sees almost everything in terms of the Arab-Israeli conflict. This is particularly true of his regional policies, which have largely evolved in the context of what he believes can best serve Syrian and Arab interests vis-à-vis Israel. Thus, he opposed Iraq's war against Iran primarily because he viewed it as a waste of Arab resources that could be used against Israel and because Iran could be an ally in this struggle. Among other reasons, he was dismayed by Iraq's invasion of Kuwait because he saw Israel as the main beneficiary. Syrian media lamented that "when Arab countries invade each other Israel will celebrate"[10] and complained that the Iraqi invasion had "strengthen[ed] Israel's case for retaining occupied Arab land."[11] Asad likewise sees events in neighboring Lebanon through the filter of the Arab-Israeli conflict. He moved into Lebanon initially because he did not want to see a leftist Muslim-Palestinian victory, which might provoke Israeli intervention and a war he was not ready to fight. Syria's continued presence in Lebanon is partly designed to block an Israeli invasion through the Bekaa Valley. Asad's policies toward Jordan are similarly shaped by fears of an Israeli flanking attack on Syria through northern Jordan. His policies toward Egypt and the Palestinians all begin with Israel as a main reference point.

The fundamental premise of Asad's regional policy has been that the Arabs can neither fight a war with Israel nor negotiate a just or favorable peace agreement with it from a position of weakness or inferiority. He has opposed all partial or separate settlements with Israel because, in his view, these can only confirm Israeli hegemony in the region. To defend themselves, the Arabs must act together and strive for a comprehensive peace on all fronts. This conviction lies behind many of his regional policies. However, he has been singularly unsuccessful in stitching together a unified Arab front. For most of the past decade or so, the Asad regime, faced with a fragmented Arab world—whose leading states have had very different priorities from its own—has acted defensively, trying to hold the Arab fort by building Syrian power within the immediate region to the point at which Syria could confront Israel on its own.

After Egypt and Iraq removed themselves from the military equation, the former by signing a peace treaty with Israel, the latter by getting bogged down in a war with Iran, Asad unsuccessfully pursued what has sometimes been characterized as a "Greater Syria" policy, that is, an attempt to bring Lebanon, Jordan, and the Palestinians into his orbit in order to block Israeli designs in the region. Although the idea of Syria as a discrete political space has gradually taken root among its citizens, there is a lingering belief among Syrians that Jordan, Palestine, and Lebanon were carved out of historic Greater Syria and that these "lost" territories should fall within Syria's special sphere of influence and interest.[12] The Greater Syria concept long preceded Asad, who expressed a sentiment shared by virtually all Syrians when he said: "In the recent past Arab Syria extended from Sinai to the Taurus Mountains. Who divided this Syria? Where is this Syria now? Why did they dismember Syria? Reaction, allied with colonialism, did all of this."[13] Asad has claimed that Syria and Jordan "are one country, one people, one thing."[14] A reader of a Syrian newspaper would not find anything remarkable about the assertion that "Jordan is a natural part of Syria. History has never recognized the presence of an international, even administrative, entity separate from Syria."[15] Asad speaks for many Syrians when he claims that the Syrians and Lebanese "are one single people, one single nation. We may be divided into two independent states, but that does not mean we are two separate nations. . . . The feeling of kinship . . . runs deeper than it does between states in the United States."[16] Similarly, Asad once reportedly told Yasir Arafat, "There is no Palestinian entity. There is Syria. You [Palestinians] are an integral part of the Syrian people."[17] A typical Syrian editorial asserts that "from the viewpoint of history, geography, and struggle, Palestine is southern Syria."[18]

Rhetoric notwithstanding, Asad's objective was not the territorial annexation of Syria's neighbors. Rather, recognizing that

Syria, on its own, was no match for Israel, he sought to create a new regional power center that could compete effectively against Egypt and Iraq, his two main rivals in the inter-Arab political arena, and that could challenge Israeli supremacy in the region. Not only did Asad fear that, with Egypt out of the game, Israel might strike Syria through Lebanon and Jordan, he was also afraid that a powerful Israel which no longer feared Egypt might extend its influence over Jordan and Lebanon and, with American encouragement, compel them to sign separate peace agreements, further isolating and neutralizing Syria.

Asad's Levant strategy provoked charges that he was actually trying to reconstruct historic Greater Syria with Damascus at its center. Some even accused Asad of being a closet member of the pan-Syrian Syrian Social Nationalist Party (SSNP), the Ba'th's traditional ideological rival. The growth of Syria into a powerful state, and Asad's pursuit of regional policies that violated pan-Arab principles, seemed to confirm the suspicions of his critics. However, Asad's primary goal was to build Syria into a major regional power; his strategy was rooted in geostrategic considerations and was not a product of some atavistic and irredentist ideological imperative. It was natural that he would seek alliances with neighboring states which shared a border with Israel (Lebanon and Jordan) or with those who also had a stake in rolling back Israel's occupation of the territories it captured in 1967 (the PLO and Jordan). Inevitably, Asad's regional policies focused on Syria's immediate environs, where it faced special security threats. He never considered his Levant strategy to be a substitute for or incompatible with pan-Arabism—he always conceived of historic Greater Syria as an integral part of the Arab world.

The Asad regime has shown an uncommon ability to survive, maneuver, and even flourish in a hostile regional environment by deftly exploiting its limited assets to the full and by vigorously, and sometimes ruthlessly, asserting its interests. By 1990, the collapse of the Eastern bloc, the failure of the Greater Syria strategy, the reassertion of Egyptian leadership within the Arab world, and the end of the Iran-Iraq War had seriously undermined Syria's position and left it isolated within the region.

Its recent rapprochement with Egypt, its strong opposition to the Iraqi occupation of Kuwait, and its military backing for Saudi Arabia underlined its diplomatic agility and phoenix-like ability to move back to center stage within the region just when it seemed most powerless and marginal. Time after time, Syria has been prematurely written off as a declining regional power. But Asad has transformed Syria into an outwardly strong state whose interests in the region must be accommodated to some degree. Syria does not have the political stature and human resources of Egypt, the former military might and oil wealth of Iraq, or the financial assets and global influence of Saudi Arabia, but it is a key frontline Arab state which, for the past decade or so, has been Israel's most serious and determined adversary. Its dubious claim to represent the interests of all Arabs, in conjunction with its formidable military strength, the shrewd and aggressive pursuit of its goals, and its location, has given Syria power and influence within the region out of all proportion to its size, population, economic potential, and natural endowments. Nevertheless, Syria cannot stand alone, and its many intrinsic weaknesses "dictate alliances with others to provide for its defenses and its regional influence."[19] Its recent détente with Egypt must be seen in this context.

EGYPT

Despite its intense pan-Arabism, Syria has only united with another Arab country once, between 1958 and 1961, and that was a bitter experience that will probably not be repeated. The fact that its integration partner was Egypt, rather than an immediate neighbor, is significant: With pan-Arabism and anti-Zionism its overriding, interrelated foreign policy goals, Syria naturally sought to merge with the Arab world's most important, influential, and powerful state. Syria has long recognized that neither Arab unity nor victory over Israel could be achieved without Egypt's participation. Whatever power Syria has accumulated in the past twenty years and whatever its progress toward achieving strategic parity with Israel, Asad knows that Syria cannot fully defend itself on its own, let alone recapture the

Golan Heights. To this day, Syria favors an alliance with Egypt, whether in war or in peace, as the best way to accomplish its objectives vis-à-vis Israel. Yet from the mid-1970s until the late 1980s, Syria's regional policies were dominated by one objective: to isolate Egypt within the Arab world and prevent other Arab leaders from following Sadat in signing a separate peace treaty with Israel. Syria also views Egypt as a natural counterweight to Iraq, its chief Arab competitor in the Middle East. Throughout history, rival Nile- and Mesopotamian-based states have vied to bring Syria into their orbit to shift the balance of power within the region in their favor and to preempt the other from becoming too powerful. This triangular dynamic—one of the most enduring geopolitical patterns within the region—has been played out repeatedly as the center of political gravity has shifted back and forth between Cairo and Baghdad.

Israel's humiliating defeat of the Arabs in 1967 had an enormous impact on Asad, who made it his priority, after he assumed full power in 1970, to reverse the outcome of that war and recover the Golan Heights and other lost territories. To have any chance of accomplishing these goals, however, he had to end the regional and international isolation that the radical Ba'thi regime of Salah Jadid had imposed on Syria. Within days of seizing power he flew to Cairo, where he announced Syria's intention to join Egypt, Sudan, and Libya in the proposed Federation of Arab Republics (FAR). Although he also improved ties with Saudi Arabia, Lebanon, Morocco, and Tunisia, Asad most wanted to rebuild the alliance with Cairo, since Syria could not wage war successfully against Israel without Egypt's involvement. Asad believed that a Syrian-Egyptian axis was imperative for both geopolitical and military reasons. It is an article of faith to Asad that Syria and Egypt are the two main pillars of Arab unity: When Cairo and Damascus are aligned, the Arabs can triumph; when they are not, the Arabs are weak and vulnerable to outside pressures. Although the FAR went the way of so many other Arab unity schemes, the intense diplomatic activity among its member countries provided Asad and Sadat with the cover they needed to prepare for war against Israel.

The October 1973 war was a major disappointment for Asad, although it catapulted him to even greater international prominence and improved his standing among Syrians and other Arabs. Asad and Sadat had different aims when they went to war. The former hoped to liberate the Golan Heights, the latter wished to reactivate peace diplomacy. Sadat reportedly misled Asad about his war plans, suggesting that he sought to recover all of the Sinai Peninsula through military means. In reality, Sadat's intention was to launch a limited attack. After crossing the Suez Canal, Egyptian forces dug in, allowing Israel to turn its attention to the Syrians on the Golan Heights. The strategy of fighting Israel on two fronts quickly collapsed. In addition, the Syrian-Egyptian alliance was severely tested by postwar diplomacy. Asad was convinced that Secretary of State Kissinger hoped to drive a wedge between Cairo and Damascus in order to facilitate the negotiation of a separate Egyptian-Israeli peace treaty. Despite all his talk about Arab solidarity, Sadat did not want to be constrained by Syria and showed great willingness to enter into bilateral negotiations with Israel under U.S. auspices. Thus, Egypt attended the Geneva Conference in December 1973, while Syria refused to do so. Egypt also signed an American-mediated disengagement agreement with Israel in January 1974, arousing Asad's fears that Sadat wished to go it alone. These fears were confirmed in September 1975, when Egypt and Israel signed a second American-mediated disengagement agreement. Egypt effectively removed itself from the military equation, leaving Syria to face Israel more or less on its own. But worse was in store. After Sadat's trip to Jerusalem in November 1977, Egypt and Israel began direct talks, which resulted in the Camp David Accords in September 1978 and a separate peace treaty in March 1979. Asad, feeling betrayed, angrily denounced Sadat's peace initiative and, less than a month after the Egyptian president's trip to Jerusalem, played a leading role in mobilizing Arab opposition to Egypt in the Front for Steadfastness and Confrontation. In addition, he sought a reconciliation with Iraq, although the détente between the two Ba'thi regimes was delayed until October 1978 and proved to be short-lived. It was in the context of Egypt's moves to make peace with Israel, Iraq's continuing hostility, and the ineffectiveness of the Steadfastness and Confrontation Front that the Asad regime initiated a policy of bringing the Levant under Damascus's control. For more than a decade, the regime's policies in the region would be shaped largely as a reaction to Egypt's uncoupling from the rest of the Arab world.

Egypt's ostracism within the Arab world was unnatural in view of its political power, military might, cultural influence, and demographic weight. One by one, the key Arab states restored relations with Egypt, much to the annoyance of Asad, who strongly opposed anything that suggested Arab acquiescence to the Camp David framework. Yasir Arafat turned to President Hosni Mubarak in 1983, following his expulsion from Tripoli by the Syrians, and Jordan resumed diplomatic ties with Egypt in September 1984. Iraq, which taunted Syria from 1974 to 1978 with charges of treachery and defeatism for accepting UN resolutions 242 and 338, gratefully accepted Egyptian assistance in its war with Iran: Egypt sold Iraq over $1-billion worth of Soviet arms from its stockpiles early in the conflict, and over a million and a half Egyptian peasants and workers helped to keep the Iraqi economy going during the war (some Egyptians even fought in the Iraqi army). Despite its shrill criticism of the Camp David Accords and the Egyptian-Israeli peace treaty, Iraq was one of the first major Arab countries to seek improved relations with Egypt (the Iraqi foreign minister visited Cairo in July 1983).

Syria could not afford to forgive and forget so easily, however, since any reconciliation with Egypt while its peace treaty with Israel remained in effect would signal to other Arabs that the political costs of making separate deals with Israel were small. Nevertheless, Asad met with Mubarak—for the first time since the Egyptian president assumed office in 1981—at the Islamic Conference Organization Summit in Kuwait in January 1987. Despite some progress in repairing relations, the meeting did not produce a rapprochement. In November 1987, the Arab League, at a summit meeting in Amman, adopted a resolution allowing member states to restore full diplomatic relations with Egypt, which the Arabs viewed as an important counterweight to Iran at a time when many feared an Iraqi defeat in the Iran-Iraq

War. However, Syria worked to postpone discussion of Egypt's readmission to the Arab League at an emergency summit of Arab leaders convened in Algiers in June 1988 to discuss the *intifadah,* the Palestinian uprising in the West Bank and Gaza Strip. In February 1989, Mubarak's efforts to end Egypt's isolation within the Arab world without sacrificing its peace treaty with Israel received a major boost when Egypt joined with Iraq, Jordan, and the Yemen Arab Republic to form the Arab Cooperation Council (ACC). The ACC's members announced they would not attend any Arab League meeting to which Egypt was not invited. In the face of Arab pressure, Syria dropped its objections to Egypt's readmission into the league, and Mubarak was invited to attend an extraordinary Arab summit in Casablanca in May 1989. At this stage, relations between Syria and Egypt were not yet cordial, and during the meeting Mubarak openly called for the departure of all Syrian and other foreign troops from Lebanon. Nevertheless, Egypt's readmission to the Arab League, after a ten-year absence, opened the door to warmer relations with Syria and Libya, the only two Arab states with which Egypt still did not have diplomatic links, Lebanon having resumed ties in June 1989. Flights between Damascus and Cairo resumed in mid-December 1989, after a twelve-year hiatus, and full relations were restored at the end of the year.

After the rapprochement between Syria and Egypt, their relationship was hailed as if their estrangement had never occurred. Damascus radio cooed that the two countries "constitute the heart and strength of the Arab body" and suggested that it had been the "enemy's strategy" to divide them.[20] Abd al-Halim Khaddam, Syria's foreign minister, described the two countries as "an impregnable fortress" that had defended the Arabs against the Mongols, the Tartars, the Crusaders, the French, and the Zionists. Any disagreements between them had been mere "passing clouds."[21] Asad met with Mubarak again at the end of March 1990 in Libya, paving the way for a visit by the Egyptian president to Damascus two months later. Many Arabs in the region hoped that the reconciliation between Syria and Egypt would lead to an Egyptian-mediated end to the quarrel between Asad and Saddam Hussein, but Mubarak was unsuccessful in his efforts to persuade the Syrian leader to patch up his differences with his Iraqi counterpart or to attend the emergency Arab summit conference that took place in Baghdad in May 1990.

In mid-July, Asad sealed the rapprochement between Damascus and Cairo and signaled a major geopolitical realignment within the Arab world by traveling to Egypt for the first time in almost fourteen years. The fact that the reconciliation occurred entirely on Egypt's terms was enormously significant, and could only be construed as a defeat for Asad's tactical rejectionism. Indeed, the rapprochement provided more evidence that Syria was interested in new approaches to resolving the dispute with Israel. Lately, Asad has restated his readiness to negotiate with Israel, if the conditions are right, and his reconciliation with Egypt is consistent with that desire. Although Asad has been less flexible than Mubarak over what constitutes an acceptable peace process, he will be reluctant to criticize Egyptian dealings with Israel so long as Syria and Egypt remain allies. Close relations between the two countries also make it more likely that they will coordinate their positions with respect to any peace proposals.

Syria's reconciliation with Egypt grew out of the Asad regime's increasing isolation in the region after the other Arab countries welcomed Egypt back into the fold. The end of hostilities in the Persian Gulf in 1988 had left Syria exposed to Iraqi retaliation for supporting Iran in the war—particularly in Lebanon, where Baghdad openly backed efforts by Gen. Michel Aoun's Christian forces to expel the Syrians. The only way Syria could rejoin the Arab mainstream and counter Iraqi power was by aligning itself with Egypt, an approach that had succeeded many times in the past. Thus, Syria and Egypt were in complete agreement about the necessity for an Iraqi withdrawal from Kuwait after the August 1990 invasion, and both sent troops to Saudi Arabia as part of a joint Arab force. The crisis underlined the extent to which Egyptian and Syrian interests in the region had converged.

Syria's repositioning within the region must also be seen in the context of important global changes. As will be discussed more fully in chapter five, the Soviet Union's retreat from the

Middle East and open opposition to Syria's goal of achieving strategic parity with Israel raised doubts about its reliability as an ally and sharply reduced Syria's military options. Concerned about the Soviet Union's dramatic decline as a superpower and Arab disunity and apparent unreadiness to meet the challenges of a rapidly changing world, Asad once again views Arab solidarity as the solution to Arab problems. As Syrian and Egyptian leaders and commentators remarked over and over again, nothing serves the Arab world's interests so well as strong relations between these two countries. But the reconciliation between Syria and Egypt, one of Washington's principal Arab allies, also signaled Asad's strong desire for improved relations with the United States, which, as he recognizes, holds the key to peace in the region.

JORDAN

Asad has always been concerned that Jordan would be drawn into a separate peace with Israel and forced to settle on unfavorable terms, leaving Syria to face Israel alone. He is well aware that Jordan is the weak link in his regional strategy: King Hussein has held secret talks with Israeli leaders on numerous occasions over the years and has shown far greater willingness than Asad to explore a variety of peace proposals. For the past twenty years, Syria has tried to block Jordanian attempts to steer an independent course in the region, sometimes by cultivating friendly ties and at other times through intimidation. Asad also views Jordan, by virtue of its location and long boundary with Israel, as an immensely important potential strategic ally; he has repeatedly tried to bring it into a military alliance. Hussein, conversely, resents Syrian attempts to limit his maneuverability and to influence Jordan's regional policies. He has been reluctant to get too close to Syria, lest he be drawn into a military confrontation with Israel, which could have catastrophic consequences for the kingdom.

Differences between Syria and Jordan were particularly pronounced after the neo-Ba'th came to power. The radical Syrian regime accused Jordan of backing an attempted coup d'état in September 1966 and retaliated with a massive car bomb at a border crossing post in May 1967, prompting Hussein to sever diplomatic relations. In the late 1960s, relations deteriorated even further as the Syrian regime backed Palestinian guerrilla organizations in their struggle with the Jordanian government. When the inevitable showdown between the PLO and King Hussein occurred in September 1970, Jadid ordered Syrian ground forces into northern Jordan to support the Palestinians. Asad's role in the invasion remains unclear, but it is generally believed that he opposed Syrian military intervention. As minister of defense and commander of the air force, he reportedly denied air cover to Syrian armored units, which were forced to withdraw in the face of Jordanian attacks and a threatened Israeli intervention. Six weeks later, Asad ousted Jadid and assumed full control of Syria. Asad, placing grand strategy above ideological purity, quickly restored relations with Jordan and other moderate Arab states, whose help he deemed essential in the confrontation with Israel. (He had advocated the creation of an eastern front with Iraq and Jordan since 1968.) But he was not willing to pay any price for improved relations with Jordan, severing diplomatic ties in July 1971 when Hussein once again moved against the Palestinians.

Syria resumed relations with Jordan in 1973 in an effort to close Arab ranks before initiating the October War. Asad also tried to persuade Jordan to open a third front along the Jordan River valley, but Hussein, fearing he would lose his kingdom altogether, decided to send only two brigades to the Golan Heights, and carefully avoided provoking Israel. Other basic differences between the two countries emerged after the war. In December 1973, Jordan agreed to participate in the postwar Geneva Conference, which Syria refused to attend. Tension also arose over Syria's support for the PLO as the sole legitimate representative of the Palestinians at Arab summit meetings in Algiers in November 1973 and in Rabat in October 1974. Despite these differences, Asad tried to bridge the gap between Jordan and the PLO and even broached the idea of forming a tripartite Syrian-Jordanian-Palestinian federation, an arrangement that had little chance of success because of the intense animosity between Hussein and Arafat.

Asad's efforts to bolster relations with Jordan were largely inspired by his fear that the Syrian-Egyptian war coalition was collapsing and the suspicion that Sadat was seeking a separate deal with Israel. In April 1975, Asad and Hussein agreed to form the Joint Supreme Leadership Council to coordinate their policies. In June, Asad made the first visit by a Syrian head of state to Jordan in eighteen years, and in July the two countries agreed to establish the Higher Jordanian-Syrian Joint Committee to plan the political, military, economic, and cultural integration of the two countries. Although talk of unification was chimerical, the two countries formed a close relationship in the mid-1970s based on their common fear that the second Egyptian-Israeli disengagement agreement had lessened their chances of regaining their respective occupied territories. This led Hussein to openly support Syria's unpopular military intervention in Lebanon in 1976.

Syrian-Jordanian relations began to deteriorate in 1977, however, in the wake of Sadat's trip to Jerusalem. Hussein, who ostensibly opposed Sadat's peace initiative, did not react with Asad's extreme alarm over this move, and he refused to join the Syrian-led Steadfastness and Confrontation Front formed in December 1977. As Sadat moved toward signing a separate peace agreement, Asad grew increasingly concerned that Hussein would be drawn into the Camp David framework and begin negotiations with Israel. In 1979, reacting to Syrian pressures, Hussein allowed the Syrian Muslim Brotherhood, which was waging a bombing and assassination campaign against the Asad regime, to operate from Jordan. Asad was enraged, and in December 1980 Syria massed 35,000 troops and hundreds of tanks along its border with Jordan, threatening to march in and destroy opposition bases unless Hussein stopped harboring and abetting the Muslim Brotherhood. This crisis, which only ended with Saudi mediation, was followed by others. In February 1981, Jordan accused Syria of attempting to assassinate its prime minister, Munir Badran, and lashed out against the Asad regime with inflammatory sectarian propaganda.

It was largely to counter Syrian and Israeli threats that Jordan sought the protection of Iraq after the short-lived reconciliation between Damascus and Baghdad collapsed in mutual recriminations in 1979. United in their animosity toward the Asad regime, and by a land bridge that served the economic interests of both countries, Jordan and Iraq created one of the most durable Arab alliances of the 1980s. King Hussein openly supported Iraq in its conflict with Iran and played a major role in the war effort. After Iraq's ports in the Persian Gulf were closed, Aqaba became the Baghdad regime's lifeline. Thus, Syria and Jordan found themselves on opposite sides of the Iran-Iraq War, and this became a significant source of tension between the two countries in the 1980s.

In September 1982, President Ronald Reagan unveiled a new Middle East peace plan that called for Palestinian self-government "in association with Jordan." Asad feared, correctly, that the war in Lebanon, in weakening the PLO, had created an opportunity for the United States to draw Jordan into the peace process. King Hussein, who had long favored a Jordanian-Palestinian federation as a solution to the Palestinian problem, welcomed the Reagan proposal and tried to persuade Arafat to empower him to negotiate on his behalf. In December 1983, shortly after Arafat's expulsion from Tripoli by the Syrians and his reconciliation with Mubarak, Hussein invited the Palestinian leader to Amman. In addition, the king restored diplomatic relations with Cairo and hosted the seventeenth Palestine National Council. Asad's old fears of being left out quickly resurfaced. To his consternation, Hussein and Arafat signed an agreement in February 1985 that gave the king the mandate he sought to negotiate on behalf of the Palestinians. Asad was determined to prevent Hussein from entering into separate talks with Israel from what he considered to be a position of weakness. From late 1983 to mid-1985, therefore, Syria unleashed a wave of terrorist attacks on Jordanian embassies, airline offices, and other targets around the world. Jordan responded in kind, but by late 1985—because of the combination of Syrian threats, the failure of the Labor party to win the elections in Israel, U.S. lack of interest in its own plan, and, most important, opposition from the PLO's Executive Committee, which rejected the February 1985 agreement between the king and Arafat—Hussein had backed down.

In September 1985, the Syrian and Jordanian prime ministers met in Saudi Arabia and declared a truce. In November, King Hussein, in an extraordinary open letter to his prime minister, admitted that Jordan had supported the Muslim Brotherhood's war against the Syrian regime. His apology paved the way for improved ties between the two countries. In December 1985, Hussein traveled to Damascus for the first time since 1979, and two months later, to Asad's great satisfaction, he publicly renounced his agreement with Arafat. Asad visited Amman for the first in nine years in May 1986, sealing the reconciliation. After the collapse of U.S. efforts to draw Jordan into a separate peace with Israel, Hussein renewed his call for an international conference that would include the five permanent members of the UN Security Council and all parties involved in the Arab-Israeli conflict—a position essentially identical to Syria's. With the outbreak of the *intifadah* in December 1987, the renunciation of all Jordanian claims to the West Bank in July 1988, and the PLO's declaration of a Palestinian state in November 1988, Syrian concerns about a joint Jordanian-Palestinian separate deal with Israel receded even further. As a result, Syria and Jordan have recently maintained correct diplomatic relations, in spite of a number of important differences still dividing them. With the Iraqi invasion of Kuwait, Syria and Jordan once again found themselves on opposite sides of one of the most bitter rifts to open up within the Arab world. Undoubtedly, one of King Hussein's concerns at this juncture was that the collapse of Saddam Hussein's regime would leave Syria free to exert pressure on Jordan.

THE PALESTINIANS

The Syrian-Palestinian relationship is a complex mixture of alliance and conflict and exemplifies Syria's drive both to advance the Arab cause and to subordinate other Arab actors to its strategy. Syria regards Palestine as a lost part of itself and Palestinians as southern cousins. Championship of the Palestine issue, which is considered to be the heart of the Arab cause, is a major component of regime legitimacy. Syria sees itself as having made the heaviest sacrifices in the conflict over Palestine and as having played the major role in supporting the Palestinian resistance, in keeping the Palestine cause on the world agenda, and in preventing any solution to the Arab-Israeli conflict that ignores it. In the 1960s, the Ba'th was committed to the liberation of all Palestine, but under Asad this evolved into the lesser demand that "Palestinian rights"—essentially the right to a state in the West Bank and Gaza Strip—be satisfied.[22]

Yet, Syrian-Palestinian relations have been characterized by conflict as much as by solidarity. Syria has claimed tutelage over the PLO, insisting that Palestine is an Arab and Syrian cause as much as a PLO one and that Palestinian interests be pursued in concert with the Arab interest the Ba'th claims to represent. Syria has also sought to "play the Palestinian card" in the peace process, recognizing that its leverage would be enhanced if it could veto any resolution of the Palestinian problem that left Syria out and if it could "deliver" the Palestinians into an acceptable settlement. However, the PLO has insisted on pursuing an independent policy, regardless of Syrian interests, and has tried to preserve its autonomy by cultivating relationships with Egypt, Jordan, Iraq, and Saudi Arabia, all of which have been rivals of the Asad regime at one time or another.

Many specific issues have also divided the two parties. Palestinians have often questioned Syria's commitment to their cause, fearing that it might settle with Israel separately. Some suspect that Ba'thi ideology and pan-Syrian dreams might be better satisfied by the incorporation of liberated Palestinian territory into some larger Arab entity than by the formation of an independent Palestinian state. The two parties have also differed on tactics: Syria has challenged Palestinian rejectionism when this has diverged from its own accommodationist policies, but it has also tried to counter Palestinian moderation when this threatened Asad's own rejectionist tactics. Asad has regarded Palestinian guerrilla activity as a useful means of pressuring Israel but as far less effective than Syrian power and diplomacy.

Whenever such activity invited Israeli retaliation, and thereby threatened Syria's own security, he has restricted it. Thus, Syria has eliminated Palestinian guerrilla operations on the Golan Heights and curbed them in southern Lebanon. Syria's ever more intrusive and heavy-handed efforts to control the PLO have widened the gap between them. Damascus long tried to exert influence inside the PLO through Palestinian surrogates, such as the Syrian-sponsored guerrilla movement, al-Saiqa. It used alliances with Arafat's rivals to challenge his policies and, in the 1980s, attempted to depose and replace him with the rival Palestinian National Salvation Front. The deep personal animosity between Arafat and Asad has aggravated and intensified Syrian-Palestinian frictions.

LEBANON AND THE PALESTINIANS

Since Syria's intervention in 1976, Lebanon has represented Damascus's second main foreign policy front, subordinate only to the confrontation with Israel. The Asad regime's turbulent relations with the PLO have been largely played out in Lebanon. Syria's policy toward its neighbor has been shaped by a number of considerations. Above all, Damascus considers Lebanon, a part of historic Syria, to be within its sphere of influence, a "sisterly" country whose Arabness Syria must protect. Lebanon was also a component of the anti-Israeli alliance that Asad tried to construct among Syria's immediate neighbors. Asad has always considered Lebanon's security to be indistinguishable from Syria's. He believes Syria faces special security threats in Lebanon, which is vulnerable to Israeli penetration because of the civil war and the large Palestinian presence. An Israeli offensive through the Bekaa Valley, outflanking the Golan defenses, could split Syria and encircle Damascus. Moreover, since Camp David, the Asad regime has been afraid that Israel would exploit Lebanon's extreme weakness by trying to impose a peace agreement on it, which would further isolate Syria. For years, the conventional wisdom in Israel was that if Lebanon was not the first Arab state to sign a peace treaty, it would certainly be the second. Asad evidently believed this too. Control of Lebanon was also essential if Syria hoped to dominate the PLO and use it for its own ends. PLO guerrilla operations could draw Israel into Lebanon and involve Syria in a confrontation it did not want, but if carefully timed and calibrated, they could be used to show Israel and the United States the costs of failing to pursue a comprehensive peace settlement.

Syria's involvement in Lebanon's politics has a long history. In the mid-1960s, Ba'th radicals tried to stimulate revolution and turn the country into a fedayeen base. Asad preferred to maintain Lebanon as a buffer state, but he sent Palestinian reinforcements into the country when its government sought to crush the PLO in 1973. However, it was the outbreak of civil war in 1975 that led to a massive Syrian intervention and the occupation of large parts of the country. In the conflict between the Maronite rightists and a Muslim-leftist-Palestinian coalition over the distribution of power and the PLO presence, Syria initially supplied arms and support to the latter, its traditional allies, while also trying to restrain its clients, put together a national unity government, and engineer agreements to reduce the fighting. In early 1976, when rightist Maronite forces launched an offensive that threatened the country with partition, Syria warned that "Lebanon can stay united or it will have to return to Syria." It also dispatched Palestinian Liberation Army units to curb the rightist advance and impose a cease-fire. Syria, seeming to hold the balance between the warring parties, offered a peace plan that provided for a moderate redistribution of power in favor of the Muslims and the disengagement of Palestinians from Lebanese politics. In effect, Syria was trying both to contain the civil war and use it to establish itself as the arbiter of Lebanese politics.

The Lebanese left rejected the Syrian plan, however, demanding a completely secular state and a more radical redistribution of power. Muslim factions of the Lebanese army backed the left, threatening a breakdown of order. They were joined by radical Palestinians seeking to turn a revolutionized Lebanon into a base for struggle against Israel and, after some hesitation, by the mainstream PLO under Arafat, who feared that Syria's intervention threatened Palestinian autonomy and saw an opportunity to consolidate an independent base in Lebanon. A

Palestinian-leftist counteroffensive soon put the Maronites in jeopardy. Syria tried to restrain and intimidate its allies by cutting off supplies and launching military probes into Lebanon. When Syria's forces met stiff resistance, putting Syria's prestige on the line, Asad decided to chastise the Palestinian-Lebanese leftist coalition. Syria began to support a Maronite war of attrition against its former allies, and, in the fall of 1976, launched a massive offensive that swept deep into Lebanon and involved major fighting with Palestinians. Only after inflicting a defeat upon them did Asad accept Arab mediation to end the conflict.

There were numerous reasons for this radical departure from traditional Syrian policy. Asad believed that a leftist military victory could not succeed and would only embitter the Maronites against other Arabs. Such a victory might have triggered Lebanon's partition, which might, in turn, have endangered the cohesion of Syria, where sectarian tensions were close to the surface. Asad also hoped to forestall Maronite moves to draw Israel into the conflict on their side by guaranteeing, and thereby attaching, Maronite security interests to Damascus and the Arab world. Syrian empathy for the Christian position may have been reinforced by Asad's personal ties to the Lebanese president, Sulayman Franjiyyah, the Alawis' own experience of Sunni Muslim hostility, and Asad's perception that leftist leaders, such as Kamal Junblatt, were engaged in sectarian vendettas. But none of these factors counted as much as Asad's belief that the Maronites, as the core of Lebanese society, were better conciliated than alienated. Asad also sought to prevent the emergence of a "rejectionist," Palestinian-dominated, pro-Iraqi Lebanon from which guerrilla attacks could be launched against Israel. Asad feared that this would give Israel an excuse to avoid making peace and to seize southern Lebanon. He was also concerned that Israeli intervention, whether in response to Maronite distress or against radical forces, could drag Syria into a war on unfavorable terms and threaten its western flank. For Syria, a Lebanon in which it could balance the two rival communities, establish its own dominance, and impose a Pax Syriana was far preferable to one dominated by radical forces. Syria also wanted to deprive the PLO of its autonomous Lebanese stronghold, from which it could evade Syria's pressures for strategic "coordination." At a time when the peace process still seemed viable, Syria could not tolerate being sandwiched between rejectionist regimes in Iraq and Lebanon, and it had a strong interest in showing itself to be the key to regional peace and stability. Some Palestinians, especially rejectionists, were afraid that Syria aimed to "deliver" the PLO into an unacceptable peace. However, after its victory, Syria never tried to make the PLO settle for less than a Palestinian state. Nor were Ba'thi dreams of incorporating Lebanon into Syria operative in the intervention; such an objective would have required that Asad smash, not protect, the Maronite militias.[23]

The outcome in Lebanon briefly appeared to be a Syrian victory. Syria's "peacekeeping" role was accepted, and its army settled in to guard its western flank. The pacification of Lebanon won Syria American recognition as an important power; President Jimmy Carter signaled that he wished to draw the Syrians into his peace initiative. But the Pax Syriana was soon stalled. If the Asad regime believed its defense of the Maronites would win their acceptance of a lesser role in a Lebanon under Damascus's influence, it had miscalculated. The Maronites continued to insist on their traditional dominant role in a Lebanon distinct from its Arab hinterland or, failing this, on an autonomous ministate backed by the West and relying on Israel to balance Syrian power. Syria aimed to reconstruct the Lebanese state and army under Syrian tutelage, but the Maronites had no desire to cede their power on the ground to imperious Syrian occupiers or their influence in the army to a Syrian-dominated central government. They resisted deployment of Syrian "peacekeeping" forces in Christian areas and pressed ahead with the consolidation of an autonomous Maronite entity. While the fighting ended for a period, Lebanese governmental authority could not be restored against de facto partition. Syria wanted permanent agreements that would legitimize the deployment of its forces in strategic areas, such as the Bekaa Valley, and bind Lebanon to its foreign policy, but the rightists opposed all such infringements on Lebanese sovereignty. The Maronites demanded that the Palestinians be disarmed and removed from their last remaining stronghold in southern Lebanon, and, in the spring of 1977, they began a campaign, through the Israeli-backed militia of Saad Haddad, against leftist and Palestinian positions there. Syria, however, wanted to satisfy minimum Palestinian interests and to preserve a Palestinian guerrilla option—under sufficient control to avoid provoking Israeli intervention—in the south. It tried to nip growing Maronite-Israeli collaboration in the bud through the July 1977 Shtaura Agreement, under which the PLO pledged to respect Lebanese sovereignty and refrain from guerrilla attacks on Israel. But the rightists demurred, demanding the expulsion of all Palestinians from Lebanon as a condition for national reconstruction.

In 1978, the Syrian-Maronite marriage of convenience broke down and the "right" decided to throw in its lot with Israel. The new warmth in Syrian-Palestinian relations resulting from their common opposition to Sadat's trip to Jerusalem, the dwindling Maronite need for Syrian protection from a declining Lebanese left, and the decision of Israel's new government under Menachem Begin to build a close Maronite alliance set the stage for a realignment of forces. Israel's 1978 "Litani" invasion of Lebanon cemented this realignment. The invasion consolidated the southern zone under Haddad, apparently sealing the border against the fedayeen, and emboldened the Maronites in the north, who stepped up their challenge to Syrian control of the strategic positions they needed to consolidate their mini-state in the mountains and in East Beirut. Syria, aroused, responded with force, seeking to punish the Maronites for their Israeli connection and force the acceptance of a Pax Syriana. Syria insisted that the army be reformed along nonsectarian lines, Haddad be purged, and the state's authority be extended to the south. It also demanded that the Maronites cooperate in the reconstruction of the state, end their collaboration with Israel, and recognize the Arab character of Lebanon. In sporadic heavy fighting throughout 1978, Syria struck at the Christian militias but, deterred by Israeli threats, heavy casualties, and Saudi pressures, it could not bring them to heel. Eventually, Syria accepted a cease-fire that left the Maronite militias in control of the Kesrawan-Jubayl-East Beirut area. Thus, two Maronite enclaves, overtly aligned with Israel, stubborn obstacles to the reconstruction of the country, and a threat to Syrian security, emerged in central and southern Lebanon. Israel, as much as Syria, had become the arbiter of Lebanon.[24]

Thereafter, Syria made the reconstruction of Lebanon a lower priority. It redeployed some of its forces to defensive positions in the Bekaa Valley and abandoned its policy of balancing the rival sides in favor of a rebuilt alliance with leftist, Muslim, and anti-Phalangist Christian forces. With the breakdown of the Middle East peace process, Syria had less motive to show it could pacify Lebanon and some reason to stir the pot in the south. For their part, the Christian "Lebanese Forces," now led by Beshir Gemayel, continued to challenge Syria. In 1981, seeking to precipitate an Israeli-Syrian clash, they contested Syrian control of Zahlah before they were driven back. The following year, the Israelis invaded Lebanon with the aim of establishing Gemayel in power and driving out the PLO and the Syrians.

Syria's effort to bind the PLO to a strategic alliance, as part of its grand design for Arab leadership, was dealt a setback by the bloody 1976 conflict between the two parties. Indeed, the mistrust created by that confrontation was never to be fully overcome. Nevertheless, after 1978 Syria—thwarted in its effort to break the Israeli-rightist control over southern Lebanon, and calculating in the wake of Camp David that controlled conflict in the south could demonstrate the futility of a Middle East peace effort from which it was excluded—supported Palestinian efforts to establish a military threat to Israel from the south, entangling it in increasingly violent clashes with Israel throughout 1979. Syria also calculated that, in the post–Camp David era, a "strategic alliance" with the PLO was more crucial than ever. So long as the PLO acted in concert with Syria, the Camp David approach to "solving" the Palestinian problem and the vindication of Egypt's separate peace could be prevented, and any Jordanian bargaining over the West Bank would lack the PLO blessing it needed to be credible. Many Palestinians thought their interests coincided with Syria, since they also opposed a disposition of the West Bank that denied them an independent state and were as vulnerable as Syria in a fragmented Lebanon, where they believed forces seeking to destroy opposition to Camp David were most likely to strike. In 1981, the Palestine National Council stressed the need for an alliance with Syria and radical Palestinian factions, such as the Popular Front for the Liberation of Palestine (PFLP) and the Democratic Front for the Liberation of Palestine (DFLP), and hailed Syria as the last bulwark against Camp David "capitulation." Arafat and the more moderate Palestinians remained wary of Asad, however, and belittled the importance of a strategic alliance with Syria. Arafat, fearful that Asad was seeking to replace him, and mindful of the clashes of 1976 and of Syria's failure to fight with the PLO during the 1978 Litani invasion, was determined to preserve PLO autonomy. He also refused to burn his bridges with Egypt, thus threatening Syria's ability to prevent the legitimation of the Camp David Accords. In fact, Arafat pursued various diplomatic initiatives, including contacts with private Israelis, which undermined Syria's bid to control the "Palestinian card" at a time when Asad considered this a crucial asset.

The 1982 Israeli invasion of Lebanon precipitated a seemingly permanent rupture between the mainstream PLO and Syria. Syria had insisted on establishing a kind of protectorate over the PLO but, in seeking to avoid a confrontation with Israel and in agreeing to a cease-fire while the PLO was still under assault, it evaded the responsibilities of such a role. Arafat openly blamed Syria. Asad was infuriated by this lack of gratitude for Syria's sacrifices on behalf of the Palestinians and at Arafat for distancing himself from Damascus after the PLO's evacuation from Beirut. Deprived of his Lebanese base, Arafat became convinced that the struggle now had to focus on the West Bank, where Israeli settlement threatened. He began to explore the Reagan peace plan—even though it did not provide for Palestinian statehood—with King Hussein, whom he saw as a counter to Asad. Syrians believed that the Reagan Plan, which made no provision for the Golan Heights, was the second prong of the Israeli-American offensive against them that had begun in Lebanon. Thus, while Asad was engaged in a deadly struggle to ward off the Israeli domination of Lebanon, Arafat was contributing to his isolation. When a rebellion against Arafat broke out inside the PLO, Syria saw a golden opportunity to depose the Palestinian leader and reshape a pro-Syrian PLO. Anti-Arafat Palestinians led by Abu Musa and Ahmad Jibril and, at times, the PFLP and DFLP were grouped in the Damascus-based Palestine National Salvation Front (PNSF). Syrian forces supported the rebels in expelling Arafat loyalists from the Bekaa Valley and then in the siege that drove Arafat from Tripoli. Yet, this only rallied the majority of Palestinians, who were appalled at Syrian encouragement of intra-Palestinian fighting, to their leader. It also pushed Arafat into the arms of Syria's rivals. His visit to Cairo was a first step in breaking Egypt's isolation in the Arab world. In 1985, Arafat once again explored the possibility of participating in peace negotiations in partnership with King Hussein. The PLO, Asad declared, no longer spoke for the Palestinian cause; henceforth, Syria would lead the struggle. Nevertheless, Asad was not prepared to support the resumption of armed struggle by Palestinian radicals, which might have made their strategy a credible alternative to Arafat's diplomacy.

Even though the 1985 Arafat-Hussein partnership did not last, Asad continued his vendetta against Arafat. After Arafat reestablished a foothold in Lebanon and began to cultivate anti-Syrian alliances there, Syria, to punish him, backed the Shiite Amal militia's drive against the PLO in the "War of the Camps." This campaign drove a wedge between the major Palestinian radical groups and Damascus, precipitated a closing of Palestinian ranks, and gradually undermined the PNSF. It was also profoundly delegitimizing: Fighting Palestinians vitiated Syria's status as the champion of the Arab national cause, which was the basis for Asad's claim on the support and cooperation of other Arab states.

In 1988, with the Palestinian uprising in the Israeli-occupied territories, Arafat's "moderate line" prevailed within a virtually reunified PLO. Arafat carried the vast majority of the Palestinian movement with his argument that the *intifadah* had given the Palestinians the leverage to bargain by themselves for a West Bank state. To win international and American support, the PLO recognized Israel and renounced terrorism. Once again, the PLO insisted on its right to make independent decisions irrespective of the pan-Arab interests Syria claimed to represent. Most of Asad's Palestinian allies deserted him. Syria lost much of the leverage it had over the PLO as the organization shifted its political base from Lebanon to the West Bank, where Syria had little influence, and as it abandoned the strategy of armed struggle, which required a Syrian patron. Syria continued to insist that the PLO's claim to independent decision-making did not give Arafat the right to Sadat-like treason and that Syria could speak equally well for the Palestine cause. But it seemed to have lost its bid to play the Palestinian card.

The growing alliance between the PLO and Iraq, Syria's foremost Arab rival, also drove a wedge between Damascus and the Palestinians. Both the PLO and Syria's one-time allies in the Palestine National Salvation Front, the PFLP and DFLP, sided with Iraq after its invasion of Kuwait in August 1990, while Syria joined the anti-Iraq coalition. But in the wake of the Persian Gulf War, Syria and the PLO, realizing a common front would strengthen their hands in any revived peace process, began to move toward reconciliation. The two seemed to commit themselves to the joint pursuit of a comprehensive peace and to eschew separate deals. The PLO needed Syrian protection against efforts to exclude it from the peace process because of its support for Iraq. To Syria, the PLO's vulnerability seemed to present a new opportunity to play the Palestinian card. In addition, Asad saw the reconciliation as an opportunity to polish his Arab nationalist credentials, which had been tarnished by his position in the war against Iraq.

In Lebanon, Syria spent much of the 1980s trying first to thwart Israel's ambitions and then trying to put the country back together under its tutelage. In its drive to counter the Israeli presence, it mobilized the National Salvation Front, a coalition of Muslim militias, leftist parties, and pro-Syrian traditional politicians. As Israel withdrew from Lebanon, President Amin Gemayel acknowledged that the Maronites had to return to the Arab fold, and invited Syrian forces to Beirut to restore order. In 1984, at the Lausanne Conference on National Reconciliation, Syria sponsored a national unity accord providing for a more equitable distribution of power among Christians and Muslims.

However, Syria could find no Maronite leader able to deliver the community. Gemayel proved an unreliable partner, and the Maronite hard-liners obstructed implementation of the Lausanne Agreement. Syria struck a deal with a Maronite militia leader, Elie Hobeika, who, with his Shiite and Druze counterparts, acknowledged a Syrian "protectorate" over Lebanon. But a Maronite revolt against Hobeika showed that the community still preferred cantonization to relinquishing some of its power and accepting Syrian tutelage.

Syria's position eroded further when its post-1983 conflict with Arafat's PLO began to split the pro-Syrian Muslim camp, with Lebanese leftists and the Druzes backing the PLO against Amal. There were even signs of a budding PLO-Maronite alliance against Damascus. As Lebanon's growing fragmentation made it increasingly ungovernable, Syria relied on a "balance of weakness" to maintain hegemony, playing off various sides, working through proxies, and cutting down to size any faction that got too strong. The combination of such heavy-handed domination with an inability to establish security in the country exhausted much of Syria's political capital with the Lebanese.[25]

Nevertheless, Syria continued to undertake initiatives apparently aimed at reconstructing a reformed and unified Lebanese state. Its interest in stability in the south was manifest in its role in giving Amal responsibility for security there at the expense of Hizbullah, the Iranian-backed Shiite party, which wanted to carry on a guerrilla war with Israel. As the Lebanese presidential elections of 1988 loomed, Syria pushed to make them contingent on Christian acceptance of reform. But Syria's attempt to impose a single candidate was rejected by the Christians, and Lebanon was left without a president and divided between two rival governments. This opened the door for Michel Aoun's 1989 attempt, with Iraqi backing, to challenge the Syrian presence. General Aoun miscalculated the willingness of outsiders to rescue him when his plans went awry, however, and he was forced to accept a cease-fire. The failed challenge unwittingly set in motion the Arab-mediated Taif Agreement, which even many Maronite factions accepted. The accord provided for many of the reforms Syria had long advocated, including a reduction in the power of the Maronite president and a more equitable sectarian distribution of power in parliament and the cabinet. Syria agreed to withdraw its forces to the Bekaa Valley within two years, contingent on the restoration of Lebanese government authority. A pro-Syrian president, Elias Hrawi, was elected, but Aoun rejected the accord and Hrawi's authority. Syria held back from launching a military offensive against Aoun, which it feared might provoke Israeli intervention, cause heavy casualties, drive the Maronites to rally around Aoun, and delegitimize Hrawi. Furthermore, Syria felt constrained by the lack of a green light from the Arabs and the United States for such a drastic move. But the Taif Accord and the devastating internecine Maronite fighting set off by Aoun's attempt to control the Lebanese Forces militia gravely undermined the general's legitimacy. The Asad regime's opposition to the Iraqi invasion of Kuwait won it a free hand to strike against Aoun, whose downfall restored Syria's dominant position in Lebanon. Subsequently, the Hrawi government made significant progress in establishing its authority against the unruly militias.

The Treaty of Brotherhood, Cooperation, and Coordination signed by the Syrian and Lebanese governments on May 22, 1991, crowned Syria's hegemony and institutionalized Syrian tutelage over Lebanon's foreign and security policies. Although they were resentful of this unequal treaty, most Lebanese accepted it as the price of peace and a reduced Syrian military presence. Until Lebanese stability is consolidated and Israel's proxies and presence in its southern "security zone" are removed, however, Syria is certain to retain a military presence in eastern Lebanon. The Lebanese government's drive to extend its authority to the south in July 1991, notably over Palestinian guerrillas, seemed to be a first step in a diplomatic campaign to end the Israeli presence there.

SAUDI ARABIA

Syria's relations with Saudi Arabia should be seen primarily in the context of Asad's drive to mobilize all available Arab resources to sustain his strategy toward Israel. His radical predecessors regarded Riyadh as a center of reaction and Western influence—and therefore an impediment to the mobilization of Arab resources for the struggle against Israel—and sought, without success, to encourage the regime's overthrow. Asad, subordinating ideological disputes to Arab unity, buried the hatchet with the Saudis in exchange for financial aid. After the October War, Syria felt itself entitled to a share of the Saudi oil windfall, arguing that it had borne the brunt of the fighting while Saudi Arabia reaped the advantages in increased oil prices. Since 1978, when the oil-rich Arab states established a fund to assist the frontline Arab states in the wake of Camp David, Saudi Arabia has been by far the largest contributor of financial aid to Syria. Asad believes that Saudi Arabia's stake in its American connection has deterred the Saudis from using the oil weapon against the United States, but he recognizes Saudi Arabia's unique influence in Washington as potentially useful in countering Israel's influence. In return, the Saudis have expected Syria to refrain from reigniting the Arab ideological war and to restrain radicals, whether leftist Palestinians or pro-Iranian extremists. Yet Saudi Arabia has been wary of the growth of Syria's influence and deplored its alliance with Iran. The Syrian-Saudi relationship remains uneasy. The Saudis use Syria's economic dependency to moderate its radicalism and ambition. Syria tries to counter Saudi leverage by raising the specter of instability, which the Saudis so fear. The dispatch of Syrian troops to bolster Saudi Arabia against Iraq, however, is likely to initiate a new closeness in Syrian-Saudi relations. The formation of a Syrian-Egyptian-Saudi coalition at the center of the Arab world, which Iraq's invasion of Kuwait strengthened, is one of the most significant, and potentially most stabilizing, geopolitical alignments in the region in many years.

IRAQ

The enmity between the Ba'thi regimes of Syria and Iraq is the most inveterate and perplexing within the Arab world. The quarrel has lasted over twenty years, broken only occasionally by brief, and ultimately futile, attempts at reconciliation. A denouement of sorts was reached after Iraq's invasion of Kuwait. Yet the two regimes are similar in many respects, especially structurally and ideologically. Both claim to uphold the Ba'thi goal of Unity, Freedom, and Socialism—and neither has done so. The origins of the two states are also alike: Both emerged after World War I, the product of arbitrarily drawn colonial boundaries, and both traditionally had a profound sense of political geographic impairment. Each has grappled with questions about the nature and identity of the Arab state and its relationship to the broader Arab world. Notwithstanding their behavior to the contrary, no other states have expressed their commitment to Arab unity so insistently, and their sense of kinship has prompted several unsuccessful attempts at integration. They complement one another economically and have strong incentives to cooperate: Both rely heavily on the Euphrates River for irrigation, and the most direct route for Iraqi oil exports is across Syria to the Mediterranean. Were Syria and Iraq to overcome their differences—an unlikely prospect—the balance of power in the Middle East would be significantly altered. Were they ever to unite— an even less likely prospect—the resulting state would be a formidable military power, and the political and strategic maps of the Middle East would be radically redrawn. Indeed, Israel fears a Syrian-Iraqi axis more than any other in the Arab world.

The antagonism between the Syrian and Iraqi regimes originated in a complex dispute between two wings of the Ba'th party, each of which correctly claimed that the other did not adhere to Ba'thi principles. After the 1966 coup in Syria, Michel Aflaq, the Ba'th's co-founder, and other veteran party leaders were ousted. The Ba'thists who came to power in Baghdad in 1968 were Aflaqists. They claimed to represent the true party and rejected the ruling Syrian Ba'thists as impostors who had hijacked the party to serve narrow sectarian interests. Moreover, the new Iraqi regime welcomed Ba'thists who had fled or been expelled from Syria after the 1966 coup. Damascus and Baghdad quickly became havens for one another's exiles and opponents.

Nevertheless, during the 1960s Asad, as Syria's defense minister, sought close ties with Iraq in order to build an eastern front against Israel. After seizing power in 1970, he continued to pursue this goal without success, although relations improved slightly. At Asad's request, Iraq sent two armored divisions and one infantry division to the Golan Heights during the 1973 war, but these were withdrawn immediately after Syria accepted UN resolutions 338 and 242, which implied recognition of Israel. Iraq vehemently rejected both resolutions and accused the Asad regime of betraying the Arab cause and of seeking a peaceful settlement. Between late 1973 and the Camp David Summit in 1978, Iraq refused to cooperate with Syria unless it repudiated the UN resolutions. Nonetheless, Asad persisted in his efforts to settle all differences with the Iraqi regime, visiting Baghdad and frequently offering to unite the two countries. In April 1975, he again invited Iraq to join an eastern front. Before long, however, relations had soured so much that the two regimes were slandering one another over the air waves. Syria's intervention in Lebanon against the leftist Muslim-Palestinian alliance confirmed Iraq's belief that the Asad regime was "fascist." The regime's attempts to bring Lebanon, Jordan, and the Palestinians into its orbit aroused fears in Baghdad about the emergence of a rival regional power center in Damascus.

Despite their deep differences, the two Ba'thi regimes came together briefly in 1978, united in their opposition to Egypt's efforts to seek a separate peace with Israel. Historically, Syria has tried to exploit the rivalry between Egypt and Iraq, the Arab world's two most powerful states, by playing one off against the other, aligning itself with Cairo when Baghdad seemed threatening and building ties with Baghdad when it wished to counterbalance Cairo. Sadat's trip to Jerusalem in 1977 deeply alarmed Asad, who recognized that, without Egypt, Syria was no match for Israel militarily. Iraq was the only possible counterweight. Therefore, on the day that the Egyptian president addressed the Knesset, Asad appealed to Iraq to resolve the differences between Damascus and Baghdad. His plea initially fell on deaf ears. However, the Camp David Accords galvanized the Iraqi regime. Both Ba'thi governments feared that Saudi Arabia and Jordan might follow Egypt if they did not join forces to mobilize the Arab world against Sadat. After an exchange of messages, Asad traveled to Iraq in October 1978 to seal the Syrian-Iraqi rapprochement by signing the Charter for Joint National Action, in which the two regimes announced their intention to unite. He returned to Baghdad in November for a key Arab summit meeting.

Given the history of the relationship between the two Ba'thi regimes, few were surprised at the brevity of the rapprochement. In mid-July 1979, Saddam Hussein replaced Ahmad Hasan al-Bakr as president of Iraq. Before the end of the month, Baghdad announced that it had uncovered a plot against the new regime and hinted at Syrian involvement. Syria vigorously denied any complicity and appealed to Iraq not to scuttle the alliance. Relations quickly deteriorated, however, and, in August 1980, Iraqi authorities entered the Syrian embassy in Baghdad and removed large quantities of explosives. All Syrian diplomats were ordered to leave the country immediately.

Without question, the two Ba'thi regimes have been deeply involved in subversive plots against one another. Damascus has provided covert backing for Iraqi Kurdish groups, while Baghdad has been a haven for Syrians trying to unseat the Asad regime. By the early 1980s, this interference in one another's affairs had poisoned relations irreversibly: Asad accused Iraq (as well as Israel, the United States, Jordan, and the Lebanese Maronites) of supporting the Muslim Brotherhood's insurrection within Syria. By this point, the deep personal antipathy between Asad and Saddam Hussein certainly equaled, and may have eclipsed, ideological differences and geopolitical rivalry as the main driving force behind the feud. Asad tried repeatedly throughout the 1970s to heal the breach with Iraq, but by the end of the decade he had clearly given up any hope of a lasting reconciliation and adopted a much more aggressive position toward his neighbor.

Two other issues have aggravated relations. To date, no formal international agreement has been signed to allocate water from the Euphrates River, which rises in Turkey and flows through northern Syria and central Iraq to the Persian Gulf. An informal, tripartite understanding has failed to prevent disputes over riparian rights. All three states have built or are building dams to generate electricity and provide water for agriculture to serve the needs of their rapidly growing populations. Iraq, far-thest downstream, is both most dependent on the river and most vulnerable, since it receives what water is left after Turkey's and Syria's requirements have been met. Syria and Iraq are justifia-bly anxious about the massive Ataturk Dam under construction in Turkey, but Iraq has also suffered as a result of Syria's dam at Tabqa, which was completed in 1974. In April 1975, as Lake Asad filled, Iraq, after two consecutive years of drought, accused Syria of blocking the river and threatening the livelihood of millions of peasants downstream. Only Saudi Arabian mediation averted a military conflict. Since then, the two countries have generally avoided confrontations over the Euphrates. Syria is aware that blocking the flow of water to Iraq would be a casus belli and has been careful about how it exploits its position upstream to punish the Iraqi regime, despite the absence of virtually all ties for over a decade. In 1990, the two countries, faced with a sharply reduced discharge when Turkey began filling a reservoir behind the Ataturk Dam, reportedly signed a water-sharing agreement, demonstrating their ability to tran-scend political differences when their vital interests are at stake.

A far more serious irritant in their relations has been Syria's frequent disruption of the flow of Iraqi oil across its territory to the Mediterranean. Historically, most Iraqi oil was exported by pipeline from Kirkuk, via Hims, to Baniyas in Syria and to Tripoli in Lebanon. Transit fees were an important source of revenue for Syria. Because Iraq lacked alternative outlets for its oil, in January 1973 it was forced to agree to Syria's demand for higher royalties. But the Iraqi regime immediately sought to reduce its dependence on Syria by building pipelines to Turkey's Mediterranean coast and to its own Persian Gulf coast. These pipelines enabled Iraq to bypass Syria altogether in 1976 when it stopped pumping oil to Baniyas and Tripoli, ostensibly to protest the Asad regime's intervention in Lebanon, but in reality be-cause of a complex payments dispute and deep political differ-ences. Iraq signed an agreement to reopen the pipeline to Baniyas early in February 1979, pumping only 200,000 to 300,000 b/d, however, well short of the line's 1.1 million b/d capacity, to underline its determination never again to become so dependent on trans-Syrian routes.

Whatever disagreements existed between the two regimes, they paled in comparison with the one that arose during the Iran-Iraq War, when Syria backed Iran against Iraq. Whereas Asad welcomed the overthrow of the shah, an ally of Israel and the United States, Saddam Hussein viewed the Iranian revolution with apprehension, fearing that religious fervor would spread to Iraq's own majority Shiite population. When Iraq attacked Iran in September 1980, after months of border skirmishes and frequent Iranian sabotage and assassination attempts in Baghdad, Asad was quick to condemn the invasion. He opposed the war as a waste of Arab energy and resources that could be used against Israel. Asad and Saddam Hussein had fundamentally different ideas about where the main danger to the Arabs lay because of their countries' locations and respective geopolitical orientations: to Syria, Israel was the enemy, whereas to Iraq, Iran was the immediate threat. In October 1980, Iraq broke off diplomatic relations with Syria, whose backing for Iran became more open in spite of Arab criticism. Although Asad opposed the war, after it began his primary goal was to prevent an Iraqi victory, which would boost his adversary's power in the region immeasurably. Asad undoubtedly also relished the fact that, while the war was underway, Iraq posed no threat to Syria, allowing him to pursue his policies in the Levant more freely and to assert his leadership within the region. Similar calculations led Israel to provide arms to Iran: While the war raged, Iraq, a potentially formidable foe, was not a threat and squandered the Arabs' oil wealth.

In 1982, Syria shut its border with Iraq and closed the pipelines through which Iraqi oil was pumped to the Mediterranean. Since Iraq depended on oil exports to finance its war effort, and fighting had blocked its gulf terminals, Syria's action was a severe blow. As a result of the closure, Syria lost $600 million annually in transit fees and no longer had access to the light oil it needed to blend with its own heavier crude for refining. By way of compensation, Iran agreed to provide Syria anually with one million tons of oil—worth $200 million—free of charge and to sell it additional oil at concessionary rates. Syria's closure of the border and the pipeline ensured that a reconciliation between the two regimes would probably be impossible so long as either Asad or Saddam Hussein was in power.

To Asad's dismay, Saddam Hussein was able to claim a victory of sorts in the Iran-Iraq War following the 1988 cease-fire and, freed from a conflict that had consumed his energies for eight years, immediately set about reasserting his leadership within the region. Punishing Asad for supporting Iran was high on Saddam Hussein's agenda, and the easiest way to do this was in Lebanon, where Iraq openly backed the forces of Michel Aoun. However, Asad and Saddam Hussein encountered growing Arab pressure to resolve their differences: Jordan, Egypt, Saudi Arabia, and Libya all tried to mediate an end to the Arab world's most intractable quarrel. Throughout the first half of 1990 there were frequent reports that a reconciliation was imminent, particularly before the Arab League summit in Baghdad in May. But evidence of how difficult it would be to heal the rift also abounded. Saddam Hussein indicated in February 1990 that there could be no reconciliation unless Asad apologized to all Arabs and Iraqis for "positions and acts that have harmed the [Arab] nation." He noted that Asad had "backed Iran in the Gulf war, blocked the transfer of Iraqi oil through Syrian territory . . . and diverted the waters of the Euphrates River." In addition, he demanded that Syria withdraw its forces from Lebanon.[26] Asad's response was restrained. He observed in May 1990 that, much to his regret, the rift with Iraq was "wide" and that bridging it would need "much time and effort." A reconciliation was "not within reach" because the two countries had conflicting opinions over a wide range of issues. In fact, their "points of agreement [were] so few that they [were] almost nonexistent."[27] Asad vigorously opposed the May 1990 Arab summit in Baghdad on the grounds that it was ill-prepared and accused Iraq of putting its own narrow interests above those of the Arab nation. Despite a formal invitation from Saddam Hussein to participate, the first official visit by an Iraqi envoy to Damascus in over ten years, and considerable Arab pressure, Syria refused to attend the conference, which it loudly denounced. Speculation about a Syrian-Iraqi rapprochement nonetheless continued, especially during Asad's visit to Cairo in July 1990.

Iraq's invasion of Kuwait ended all hope of a reconciliation and offered Asad new opportunities to reposition Syria within the region at Saddam Hussein's expense. Syria immediately and forcefully condemned the attack. Two days after the invasion, the Syrian Foreign Ministry demanded the "immediate, unconditional withdrawal" of Iraqi forces from Kuwait. Syrian media blasted Iraq for providing the pretext for a massive foreign intervention in the Persian Gulf and for playing into Israel's hands. The Arabs' "decline and bleeding" was accelerating "through disputes and squabbles." Because of Iraq's recklessness, the Arabs were "going astray in a whirlpool of subsidiary conflicts, . . . drowning in a tunnel of marginal concerns, and . . . dissipat[ing] their efforts and energies."[28] Syria played an important role at the subsequent emergency Arab League summit in mobilizing Arab opposition to the invasion, and it agreed to send a military force to Saudi Arabia. In mid-September, it announced it would increase its deployment to 20,000 troops and would dispatch as many troops as Saudi Arabia requested. If Saddam Hussein had come out of the confrontation over Kuwait perceived the victor, Asad's position, both regionally and internally, would have been seriously undermined—after all, he had aligned himself with the United States, Israel's main backer, and with the conservative rulers of the Arabian Peninsula against an Arab leader whose anti-imperialism and anti-Zionism found wide support within Syria. But Asad calculated that Saddam Hussein would lose in the confrontation. He quickly saw that the crisis presented an extraordinary opportunity to assist in the downfall of his archnemesis and, at the same time, earn the gratitude of the oil-producing states of the Arabian Peninsula, who could richly reward Syria financially for its support. Asad also knew that Syria's position would be welcomed by the United States, which might then be more amenable to using its influence to secure the return of the Golan Heights. Asad had much to gain diplomatically from the realignment within the region that the Iraqi invasion triggered. Most important, the crisis provided him with an opportunity to confirm Syria's move back to center stage within the region and to strengthen Syria's ties with Egypt and Saudi Arabia, two key powers, at a time when its superpower backer was disengaging from the Middle East and openly opposing its strategy of achieving strategic parity with Israel. In a world where the Iraqi leader was not much loved, Asad's anti-Saddam Hussein credentials looked impeccable (even if, to many, the human rights records of the two Ba'thi leaders looked equally dismal). At a time when the Iraqi leader was demonstrating, yet again, his exceptional talent for recklessly frittering away Iraq's considerable assets, the Syrian leader was once more demonstrating his remarkable talent for exploiting Syria's limited resources.

IRAN

Although the main goal of Asad's regional policies from the mid-1970s onward was to bring Lebanon, Jordan, and the Palestinians into Syria's orbit to counter Israeli hegemony, the regime also created alliances further afield. One of Asad's most controversial and boldest foreign policy decisions was to align Syria with Iran after the overthrow of the shah in 1979 and to back it in its war with Arab Iraq. The decision placed Syria outside the Arab mainstream and exposed the regime to bitter criticism within Syria and throughout the Arab world. To many Arabs, the alliance blatantly contradicted the Ba'th's pan-Arab ideology and brought to the surface lingering doubts about Asad's commitment to the Arab cause.

Asad has always been a geostrategist first and a Ba'thist second. He believed that Syria's friendship with Iran served, rather than hurt, Arab interests, although other Arabs, understandably, derided this argument. When the shah was overthrown, Asad quickly recognized that the regional balance of power had shifted dramatically. Iran, under the shah, had established close links with Israel, providing it with most of its oil and maintaining diplomatic ties despite intense criticism within the Islamic world. Israel's regional policies were based on cultivating friendly relations with the peripheral non-Arab states of Iran, Turkey, and Ethiopia to mitigate its extreme isolation and to counter the hostility of its immediate neighbors. In addition, the United States considered its close friendship with the shah one of the pillars of its Middle East policy because of Iran's strategic location immediately to the south of the Soviet Union and to the north of the oil-rich Persian Gulf. In the 1970s, Washington encouraged the shah's ambitions to build Iran into a major regional power and supplied it with massive quantities of arms to police the gulf. Asad detested the shah's subservience to the United States almost as much as he opposed Iran's dealings with Israel. He saw the fall of the Pahlavi dynasty as a severe blow both to Israel and to its superpower backer's regional policies. The Ayatollah Ruhollah Khomeini, Iran's new leader, like Asad, was instinctively and viscerally anti-imperialist and anti-Zionist, and was potentially a valuable ally in the Arabs' struggle against Israel. Asad also seized the opportunity to court Iran as a natural counterweight to Egypt, which had effectively absented itself from the conflict with Israel. He believed that Iran, by virtue of its large population, military power, and economic base, could compensate for Egypt's loss and redress the strategic balance more effectively than any other Middle Eastern country.

Asad's alliance with Iran had other important benefits. First, it bolstered his influence with Lebanon's Shiites, who had emerged as one of that country's most powerful communities in the late 1970s and were useful proxies in Asad's attempts to fashion a Lebanon in which Syria's interests were safeguarded.[29] Some observers suspected that Asad was trying to create a Shiite axis that ran from Lebanon, through Syria, to Iran. However, the suggestion that Asad felt solidarity with Iran purely because of his Shiite or Alawi origins is unconvincing—sectarian kinship seems to be the least likely explanation for the friendship. Nevertheless, the alliance was constructed at a time when the Asad regime was under severe attack domestically. The collapse of the shah's regime inspired fundamentalists within Syria and encouraged them to believe they could drive Asad from power. The Muslim Brotherhood, which spearheaded the opposition, attempted to mobilize the Sunni majority against the ruling Alawi minority, inveighing against the Ba'th's secularism and corruption. Asad, with good reason, was concerned that he might be overthrown by the same religious fervor that had unseated the shah. He feared that the new rulers in Tehran might encourage an Islamic revolution in Syria, the most avowedly secular of Arab countries. Always the strategic thinker, he may also have calculated that Syria was a particularly inviting target for Iranian subversion because of its location: A fundamentalist regime in Syria would give Iran access to the Shiites in Lebanon and might improve Iran's chances of defeating Iraq. By promoting friendly relations with Iran, and by helping it to accomplish its strategic goals vis-à-vis Lebanon and Iraq, Asad did not simply hope to discourage Tehran from backing the fundamentalists who sought to overthrow him. He also hoped that his association with Khomeini would bolster his regime's Islamic credentials and undermine and discredit the Muslim Brotherhood opposition. Mustafa Tlas, the minister of defense, indicated during an interview in 1985 that Syria's friendship with Iran was partly designed to ensure it did not become an adversary: "We have no interest in creating enemies of 40 million Persians. One enemy— Israel—is enough."[30] Asad's strategy worked: His secular, repressive, and corrupt regime won the backing of the fundamentalist Islamic rulers in Tehran, who denounced the Muslim Brotherhood opposition as "gangs carrying out the Camp David conspiracy against Syria in collusion with Egypt, Israel, and the United States."[31] The region has seldom seen such an ideological odd couple.

Syria's alliance with Iran also greatly strengthened its position with respect to rival Ba'thi Iraq, its most threatening and irksome Arab neighbor. Asad vigorously opposed Iraq's invasion of Iran in September 1980 as "the wrong war against the wrong enemy at the wrong time,"[32] believing that it would exhaust and divide the Arabs and divert their attention from the main battlefield—Palestine. The alliance with Iran also had economic benefits. As previously noted, after Syria closed Iraqi pipelines to the Mediterranean, Iran provided it with free and preferentially priced oil. As a result of several economic cooperation and trade agreements, Iran became one of Syria's largest markets and provided it with its main source of tourists—in 1984 some 160,000 Iranians visited Syria (posters of Khomeini were prominently displayed in most of Damascus's hotels). Syria exploited the relationship to the hilt, accumulating huge debts to Iran that it probably never intended to repay.

Nonetheless, Syria paid a heavy price for backing Iran in the war, finding itself politically isolated and reviled within the region. Financial assistance from Saudi Arabia and Kuwait declined sharply, both because of anger over Syria's position and because Iraq soaked up the region's surplus petrodollars. Syria answered its Arab critics, particularly those in the gulf, by asserting that its alliance gave it leverage with Khomeini, which it would use to ensure that Iran did not widen the conflict. Syria also claimed that it was acting as a mediator between Iran and the Arabs. However, few of the Gulf sheikdoms fully accepted Syria's claim to be their interlocutor and protector in Tehran.

From Iran's perspective, the alliance with Syria offered many benefits. First, Syria provided additional military pressure against Iraq by maintaining an atmosphere of hostility, by backing opposition groups like the Kurds, and by supplying Soviet weapons. Second, Syria engaged in economic warfare against Iraq by shutting its border and closing its pipelines. Third, Syria prevented a hostile all-Arab union, blocking the convening of an Arab summit conference against Iran in May 1982, for example. If Asad needed the friendship of a fundamentalist Islamic regime, Khomeini also valued the support of at least one Arab country. Fourth, friendship with Syria facilitated Iran's efforts to secure a presence in Lebanon and widen its influence there. The Asad regime still allows Iran access to the Bekaa Valley, where Revolutionary Guards and the Shiite Hizbullah organization have strongholds. Finally, the alliance enabled Iran to maintain another channel for communicating with the Soviet Union.[33]

In a region where alliances are often flimsy and ephemeral, the Syrian-Iranian axis has shown striking durability and flexibility, particularly in view of the dissimilarities between the two regimes. Nevertheless, the relationship has experienced many strains. Although Syria supported Iran in the war, it did not want to see a fundamentalist Islamic regime in Baghdad, which was one of Tehran's goals. Similarly, Syrian and Iranian objectives in Lebanon are not congruent: Asad views the Shiites as useful allies, but he has no desire to see an Islamic republic established in Lebanon, and has supported Amal against its Iranian-backed rival, Hizbullah. Frequent fighting between these two Shiite organizations has been a major source of tension between Damascus and Tehran. The end of the Iran-Iraq War on terms that were more favorable to Iraq than to Iran, and events in the Eastern bloc, also affected Syria's assessment of the utility of its relationship with Iran. The reestablishment of diplomatic relations between Syria and Egypt in December 1989 signified a major shift in the Asad regime's regional policies that threatened the alliance with Iran. The Iranian regime initially opposed the normalization of Syrian-Egyptian relations, which placed Syria in the "moderate, conciliatory" camp and increased Iran's isolation in the region.[34] One of its main fears was that Egypt would join Jordan, Saudi Arabia, and Libya in pressing for a reconciliation between Syria and Iraq. However, Syria played a major role in mediating an end to the quarrel between Iran and Egypt. Ironically, reconciliation between Tehran and Baghdad came more easily than between Damascus and Baghdad. After the Iraqi invasion of Kuwait, Saddam Hussein, hoping to neutralize Iran, free up some troops, and break the international trade embargo against his country, withdrew all Iraqi forces from Iran and announced that Iraq would respect the 1975 Algiers Agreement that placed the Shatt al-Arab boundary with Iran in midstream. It was a measure of Asad's concern that Iran would allow goods to flow across its long border with Iraq that in September 1990 he visited Tehran for the first time since the 1979 revolution, hoping to persuade President Hashemi Rafsanjani to repay a favor and help Syria, as it had once assisted Iran, by blocking its border with Iraq. Despite disagreements over the deployment of U.S. forces in the gulf, the visit reinvigorated the Syrian-Iranian alliance.

4

SYRIA AND ISRAEL

The conflict with Israel is the central concern of Syrian foreign policy. Syria's inability to accept an Israel created at the expense of its own political dreams generated a powerful irredentist sentiment in the country and translated into a revisionist foreign policy, particularly during the radical Ba'thi regime of Salah Jadid. Yet, through hard experience, Syria, under Hafiz al-Asad, has come to terms with Israel's reality. The search for an "honorable peace" has been the central driving force of actual Syrian policy since shortly after Asad came to power, and he has mobilized all Syria's military and diplomatic resources to attain that objective. The record gives no reason to believe that Syria will settle for anything less.

THE ROOTS OF THE SYRIAN-ISRAELI CONFLICT

Syria's conflict with Israel originated in the dismemberment of historic Syria after World War I and in the subsequent creation of Israel in what had been Palestine. These events frustrated nationalist aspirations for the creation of an Arab state in historic Syria and came at the expense of Syria's Palestinian cousins, who were deprived of their homeland. Syrian nationalist sentiment was inflamed by the struggle over Palestine, particularly during the Palestinian rebellion of 1936. In the first Arab-Israeli war of 1948, a volunteer Syrian army was raised to fight in Palestine before the small regular army was committed. Syrians universally viewed the creation of Israel as a national disaster and refused to accept its legitimacy. They perceived the new Jewish state as an imperialist-created colonial settler state unjustly implanted in the heart of the Arab world, as well as a security threat and an obstacle to Arab unity. The conflict, while originating in the claims of two peoples to the same land, was transformed into a rivalry between two states embodying contrary national ideologies and interests.

After the 1948 war, a simmering border conflict kept tensions between the two states alive for years. At the close of the war, Syria still occupied three small territorial salients in an area that had been awarded to Israel under the original UN partition plan. Israel saw these areas as crucial to its exclusive control of Lake Tiberias and insisted that the Syrians withdraw. To avert further conflict, a UN mediator proposed that Syrian forces be evacuated and that the disputed areas be demilitarized under the supervision of the UN Mixed Armistice Commission. However, because the sovereignty of these areas was left undetermined, they became a constant source of contention. Israel eventually decided to act unilaterally, establishing paramilitary agricultural kibbutzim in several parts of the demilitarized zone. When this drew Syrian fire, Israeli forces launched retaliatory raids. Tension also arose when Syria sought fishing rights in the Sea of Galilee. The escalating dispute climaxed in December 1955, when 50 Syrian troops were killed in an Israeli assault; there were also Israeli raids in 1960, 1962, and 1964. By the mid-1960s, Israel controlled most of the disputed areas.[1] A related dispute in the border area arose over Israeli plans to tap waters from the Jordan River for irrigation. In 1961, the Arabs approved a plan to divert the Jordan's headwaters to thwart Israel's ambitious National Carrier Project. After Syria began work on the diversion scheme, the Israeli air force attacked Syrian earthmoving equipment. When Syria responded with artillery fire and guerrilla raids, Israel retaliated with more air strikes.

These escalating clashes were a major part of the dynamic that led to the 1967 war. In addition, heavy Syrian losses in most of the engagements inflamed nationalist feeling and helped to radicalize Syrian politics to the Ba'th's advantage.[2] Syria harbored intense grievances over the loss of the demilitarized zones and was determined to prevail on the headwaters issue. The escalating border conflict dovetailed with the radical Ba'thi regime's decision after 1966 to go on the offensive against Israel. But Syria's shelling of Jewish settlements provoked strong anger in Israel, ultimately providing its government with the justification it needed to seize and retain the Golan Heights.

Under radical Ba'thist rule (1966–1970), Syria launched a challenge to Israel, its backers, and the region's state system. This challenge centered on Palestine, the heart of the Arab cause: "Palestine is the fundamental starting point for defining the party's policies," declared the Ba'th party's 1965 Eighth National Congress. Israel, as Ba'thi leaders saw it, was the last bastion of imperialism in the heart of the Arab nation and the principal obstacle to its nationalist aspirations. Arab leaders, including Nasser, made verbal threats, but they failed to act. Meanwhile, Israel became stronger. Increased access to the Jordan River's water would allow Israel to absorb new immigrants, and Israel would soon have nuclear weapons. It was incumbent upon Arab revolutionaries to act against Israel before its creation became irreversible. Inspired by the examples of Algeria and Vietnam, and by Maoist theory, the Ba'thi radicals argued that, while Israel might be militarily superior, the Arabs could prevail in a protracted "war of popular liberation" in which the numerically superior Arab masses, the Arab armies, and Arab oil would be fully mobilized. Syria began to train, arm, and support Palestinian fedayeen in a guerrilla campaign against Israel. The Ba'thi radicals also sought to stimulate revolution in the conservative pro-Western Arab states so that the Arab masses would be politically mobilized and the oil weapon enlisted in the struggle.[3] Finally, they sought to draw the major Arab power, Egypt, into a confrontation with Israel, or, failing that, to wrest the leadership of the Arab nationalist movement from Nasser, whose support they demanded for the Palestinian resistance and for their plan to divert the headwaters of the Jordan.

Although Nasser deflected these pressures, he agreed to a Cairo-Damascus defense pact, through which he hoped to restrain Syria. Syria's call for a war of popular liberation was largely rhetorical, and, at most, represented a very long-range vision, for the Arab armies were no match for Israel, and the mobilization of the Arab masses a mere dream. Nevertheless, the Syrian-sponsored guerrilla activity against Israel was enough to precipitate a crisis. This included a massive April 1967

Israeli air strike, in which a hundred Syrians were killed and six Syrian planes shot down, one over Damascus. Tanks were concentrated on the Syrian border, and Chief of Staff Yitzhak Rabin threatened, over Israeli radio, to "march on Damascus to overthrow the Syrian government . . . [in order to] discourage the plans for a people's war."[4] Nasser, as the leader of Arab nationalism, could not stand by as an Arab state was threatened. In an attempt to deter an Israeli attack, he ordered the withdrawal of the UN buffer force from the Sinai and deployed Egyptian troops there. To shore up his prestige within the Arab world, he also closed the Strait of Tiran to Israeli shipping. These actions set off the crisis in which Israel launched the 1967 war.

Growing Syrian militancy coincided with the rise of hardliners in Israel. Prime Minister Levi Eshkol did not want war, but at the decisive moment those who wanted a showdown, including Moshe Dayan, who became defense minister during the crisis, pushed him into it. These hard-liners had no doubts about the Israeli army's ability to defeat the Arab forces. They believed that Egypt's provocations had to be punished and saw the crisis as an opportunity to smash Nasser and Arab nationalism and annihilate Arab military power before it could become a real danger. They also were looking to expand—some to acquire more secure borders, others to incorporate areas not under Israeli control into Eretz Israel. Yet others would see the lands taken in the war as bargaining chips to force Arab acceptance of Israel.[5]

At the outbreak of the war, Syria had a 75,000-man army equipped with 450 tanks and 140 combat aircraft, but, unlike the Israeli Defense Force (IDF), it lacked offensive capabilities. Syrian forces therefore remained in defensive positions. Nevertheless, Israel did not spare them. The decision to assault the Golan Heights was taken, without Eskhol's consent, by the military, which was under pressure from Yigal Allon, Gen. David Elizar, and others who were determined to end the Syrian menace to the Israeli settlements and "deny [the Syrians] the game of false peace, while they carry on a permanent guerrilla war."[6] Israel's assault on the Golan Heights followed

Syria's acceptance of the UN cease-fire resolution, and the IDF's seizure of Mount Hermon came after Israel had itself accepted the resolution, acts that left a permanent impression on Gen. Hafiz al-Asad, who was then Syria's defense minister. During the fighting, the Syrian army—decimated by political purges after 1963, and severely weakened by sectarianism and the attempt to create an all-Ba'thi "ideological army"—collapsed. Israel seized the Golan Heights, and attacked Qunaytirah. Some 35,000 Syrians fled the Golan during the fighting and were not permitted to return; in the next six months, 95,000 more inhabitants fled or were driven off the plateau.

The war was a watershed in Syrian-Israeli relations, locking the two countries into permanent hostility. In Israel, the decisive victory fostered a heady overconfidence. Before long, Jewish settlements were being established in the occupied territories with full government approval. While Israel initially told the United States it would return the Golan Heights as part of a peace agreement, by 1968 it had reversed this stance and began building settlements on the plateau.[7] In Syria, the war at first fostered a rigidity born of frustration and despair. Although their provocative policies helped bring on the defeat, the Ba'thi radicals were determined to maintain their militant course, continue their sponsorship of the Palestinian fedayeen, and make Syria a firm obstacle to any political settlement in which the Arabs would have to accept Israel. UN Resolution 242—the land for peace solution—was rejected as a plot to isolate Syria from the Soviet Union and the other Arab states, especially Egypt, and to consolidate the Zionist occupation of Palestine. But the loss of Syrian territory in the war had fatally compromised the radicals' legitimacy, rendering them vulnerable to challenge by the "realist" faction in the regime led by Hafiz al-Asad.

Asad argued that Syria could not sustain an interminable and ineffective guerrilla war for the liberation of Palestine and that the Syrian army was unprepared to repulse the Israeli retaliation such a war would engender. Recovery of the occupied lands had to be given priority; the Ba'th, having lost the Golan Heights, had a special responsibility to get them back.

Toward this end, the shattered Syrian army had to be rebuilt in preparation for a limited conventional war. This required a détente with the Arab oil states, who alone could finance such a military buildup, and alliances with those Arab states whose armies could contribute to the battle. The divisive pursuit of revolution inside and outside Syria had to be subordinated to Arab unity in the struggle with Israel. The radicals countered that without pan-Arab revolution Arab resources could not be effectively mobilized and that deferring the liberation of Palestine meant its abandonment. The struggle between the two sides came to a head over the proper response to King Hussein's repression of the fedayeen in 1970. The radicals, in spite of threats from Israel and the United States, and in the belief that to do nothing for the cause was worse than to suffer defeat, sent forces to Jordan to save the fedayeen and, if possible, overthrow the monarchy. Asad, deterred by the threats, refused to commit air support. When the radicals tried to dismiss him, he deposed them in a coup and brought his own realist faction to power.

Syrian policy toward Israel was at the heart of the cleavage between Asad and his radical rivals, and Asad's victory marked a crucial turning point in this policy. The radical Ba'thists were thorough rejectionists: Any settlement with Israel would legitimize the Zionist seizure of Arab Palestine. Asad and his faction also rejected the legitimacy of Israel, but, for them, the 1967 defeat forced the realization that Syria could do little to reverse the establishment of the Zionist state. This marked the end of Syria's messianic revolutionary activism and the beginning of a realpolitik of limited goals.

ASAD AND THE OCTOBER WAR

Asad lost no time putting his stamp on Syria's foreign policy. At the Eleventh National Congress of the Ba'th Party in 1971, a major scaling-down of Syria's objectives vis-à-vis Israel was approved: The new aim was the mobilization of all resources for "the liberation of the occupied territories." The demand for the "liberation of Palestine" was replaced in Syrian political discourse by the more ambiguous—and in practice far less comprehensive—demand for "Palestinian rights." From this flowed a series of alterations in strategy.

The main thrust of the revised strategy was preparation for a conventional war to retake the Golan Heights. Most military analysts at the time discounted the Arabs' ability to challenge Israel, which, after 1967, appeared to possess overwhelming military superiority. But Asad believed the 1967 disaster resulted from Israel's ability to launch a surprise attack and from a woeful lack of preparation and coordination among the Arab forces; therefore, a purposeful military strategy could reverse the 1967 outcome. Moreover, as Yair Evron points out, political grievances and intangible factors—such as the Arabs' need to redeem the humiliation of 1967 and the sense that negotiation could not succeed—created a climate in which the risks of war were preferable to the burdens and political risks of inaction.[8]

To acquire the necessary arms, Asad maintained Syria's close alliance with the Soviet Union. By 1972, Soviet arms, though still inferior to those of Israel, were flowing into Syria in quantities that would make a military challenge possible. Asad also repudiated the radicals' "cold war" with the Arab oil states, forging new alliances with them that won him subsidies for his military buildup. Equally important, he struck a strategic alliance with Anwar al-Sadat's Egypt, militarily the most powerful of the Arab states, whose participation was essential to the multifront war that alone could succeed against Israel. As previously noted, Asad also tried to create an effective eastern front with Iraq and Jordan and, in fact, Iraqi forces would bolster the Syrian front when war came. The Palestinian resistance retained a reduced place in Asad's strategy. The Ba'thi-controlled al-Saiqa was expanded, and Syria continued to permit, even sponsor, guerrilla raids from Syrian bases, which occasionally escalated into military clashes with Israel. Politically, it was important for Asad to continue Syria's patronage of the Palestinian cause and the guerrilla operations contesting Israel's tightening grip on the Golan Heights. But the fedayeen were now regarded as auxiliary forces subordinated to Syria's overall strategy rather than the cutting edge of liberation, so their operations were strictly controlled.

Asad initially continued to reject UN Resolution 242, in part from a reluctance to acknowledge the legitimacy of a state imposed on the Arabs, in part because the resolution made no mention of Palestinian rights, and in part because of continued rejectionist sentiment in the army and party ranks. Moreover, according to Israel's interpretation, the resolution did not require it to withdraw from all occupied territories, and the Israelis spoke of a "territorial compromise," which Syria interpreted as a determination to keep the Golan Heights. Asad put little faith in diplomacy unbacked by military might: Syria would be able to recover the lost territories only through the threat of—or resort to—armed conflict. Asad's view, that Israel and its U.S. backer were—in the absence of a demonstrated Arab military challenge—unprepared for a settlement, was reinforced by their failure to respond to Egypt's pre-1973 attempts to reach a peaceful settlement. In any case, only a war of liberation could reverse the lopsided Israeli victory of 1967, restore Arab dignity, and establish the power balance necessary to Arab security. Unlike Sadat, who, unbeknown to Asad, merely planned to cross the Suez Canal to unblock the stalemate, Asad expected Egypt and Syria to recover a lot of territory militarily. There is some evidence that he expected to seize the Golan Heights within 48 hours of initiating hostilities and, in anticipation of this, had asked the Soviet Union to be prepared to impose a cease-fire before Israel could recover them.

Asad recognized, however, that diplomacy, if combined with military power and reinforced by Arab solidarity, was an indispensable tool in the struggle with Israel. Through its application, Syria could win international support, reversing its isolation, which had previously allowed Israel to attack with impunity. Furthermore, world opinion had to be satisfied that the Arabs had exhausted all peaceful options before resorting to war. For these reasons, Asad did not object to Sadat's exploration of diplomatic solutions in the years before the 1973 war, and, in March 1972, Syria itself "conditionally" accepted UN Resolution 242 (provided it guaranteed total Israeli withdrawal from occupied Arab territories and Palestinian rights). On the eve of war, Syria again told the UN secretary general it did not object to a 242-based settlement. Moreover, like Egypt, Syria went to war in 1973 anticipating that, should its military effort fall short, the balance of power would nevertheless be shifted enough to upset the status quo and force a political settlement incorporating minimum Arab demands. Even if the Golan Heights were recovered, negotiations over the West Bank and the conditions of peace would be necessary. Syrian decision-makers must have known that such negotiations would end in the recognition of Israel's security needs and of its right to exist. In abandoning the total rejectionism of the radical Ba'thists, Asad had, in any event, already signaled Syria's acquiescence in a negotiated settlement with Israel.

The October War was nothing like the previous one. Asad had presided over a major rebuilding of Syria's shattered army, which was much larger, more professional, and better trained, led, and equipped this time. The war was meticulously planned, and the soldiers' fighting spirit was high. With a 5-to-1 advantage in tanks (800 to 170) and superior manpower (35,000 to 2,500) in the arena of battle (the Golan), and with surprise on their side, Syrian forces initially broke through formidable Israeli fortifications, overran three-quarters of the Golan plateau, and almost reached the escarpment overlooking northern Israel. Commandos seized Israel's Mount Hermon outposts. Israel was able to mobilize, however, and through its control of the air, and the superior performance of its tank forces, slow the Syrian advance. Although the Syrian soldiers fought well, their senior officers had little field experience, flair for battle, or tactical competence. Poor coordination of the Arab forces also contributed to the failure of the offensive. Sadat's decision to refrain from further action after establishing a foothold across the Suez Canal allowed Israel to concentrate its forces against Syria.[9] This generated great distrust of Egypt in Damascus and helped to split the wartime alliance after the fighting stopped. Once the Israeli armed forces went on the offensive, they encountered a stubborn dug-in defense, leaving them with little room for the maneuvering at which they excelled. The Israelis nevertheless drove the

Syrians back to, and beyond, the 1967 lines, where they encountered Syria's second line of defense. In the end, the Syrian forces ceded a salient beyond the 1967 lines, thus bringing Israeli forces closer to Damascus.

For Israel, one of the war's lessons was that the blitzkrieg strategy it had employed so decisively in 1967 would no longer work against massed Arab armies that did not panic under attack and whose firepower favored them in defense. Israeli air superiority had been partially neutralized by surface-to-air missiles; Israel would subsequently put great effort into finding ways to counter the Arab missile systems. It also became evident that military victories in the future would only be purchased with heavy losses in men and equipment. Israel could no longer count on being able to defeat one Arab army before facing another. This new awareness of its vulnerability in a multifront war stimulated efforts to negotiate a separate peace with Egypt when hostilities ended.

For its part, Syria concluded it needed missiles or aircraft capable of reaching the enemy's rear in order to deter Israel from escalating a limited war, such as a battle for the Golan Heights, into an attack on the Syrian heartland. Although Syria's air defense umbrella had partially nullified Israeli air superiority, the Syrian air force, with its inferior aircraft and pilots, could neither defend Syrian airspace from damaging deep-penetration raids against strategic economic targets nor deter Israel with deep-offensive capabilities of its own.[10]

FROM THE OCTOBER WAR TO CAMP DAVID: SYRIA EXPLORES THE PEACE PROCESS

The October War demonstrated that the Arabs could fight, and it shattered their "fear barrier." But it also showed that even a two-front, well-prepared, surprise assault could not drive Israel out of the occupied territories, and it underlined the continuing Arab-Israeli military gap. The outcome of the war clearly fell short of Asad's expectations. As a result, he was more inclined to rely on diplomacy to achieve his ends, particularly since the war had shifted the political balance toward the Arabs. Israel had, for the first time, been seriously challenged militarily. Its belief in security through military superiority was shaken: It had taken more than two weeks for it to get the upper hand over the Syrian forces, during which time it had sustained significant casualties. Only large deliveries of advanced U.S. weapons enabled it to turn back the Arab advances. The Arab ability to initiate war, together with the oil embargo, showed the potential costs to the West of failure to accommodate Arab interests. The recovery of lost Arab dignity and the recognition of Arab interests and power by the West generated both unprecedented Arab cohesion and a new readiness for peace. Syria believed that, under these conditions, a satisfactory comprehensive settlement might be rapidly achieved if the Arabs stuck together, maintained the threat of renewed war and oil embargo, refrained from making separate deals, and refused to settle for less than a return to the 1967 lines. Hence, Syria embarked on an attempt, which would last until Camp David, to reach a political settlement with Israel. It formally accepted UN Resolution 338 regarding the cease-fire (which embraced UN Resolution 242), interpreting these resolutions to mean an end to the state of war, Israeli evacuation from all occupied territories, and the recognition of Palestinian rights. This cost Syria the support of rejectionist Iraq, whose troops were withdrawn from the front in protest. Syria supported the resolutions of the postwar Algiers Summit, boycotted by rejectionist Libya and Iraq, which set aside the "three no's" of the 1967 Khartoum Summit: no peace, no recognition, and no negotiations with Israel. In accepting the resolutions, Syria, for the first time explicitly accepted Israel's right to exist within secure borders. But actions speak louder than words, and an important indication that Syria had already abandoned any ambitions regarding Israel proper was the fact that its war plans had embraced only the retaking of the Golan Heights. Its advancing tanks had stopped, rather than descend toward the Jordan River and the old Syrian-Palestinian boundary.[11]

Damascus's hopes for an overall postwar settlement were quickly dashed, however. Asad wanted to proceed patiently, husbanding Arab leverage, but Sadat, impatient and impulsive, refused to be bound by a common strategy. Sadat was prepared to accept separate, partial deals, beginning with the first military disengagement on the Egyptian front. Asad was so alarmed at Sadat's readiness for separate dealing that he pressured him into promising that disengagement lines would have to be agreed upon for both fronts before the opening of the proposed post-war conference in Geneva. When Sadat went back on his pledge, Asad decided to stay away from Geneva, calculating, mistakenly, that Egypt would not dare go alone. Asad would later argue that "had we gone, the Egyptian and Syrian delegations would have appeared to be at odds instead of facing the Israeli delegation together." [12] Moreover, for Asad, entering into talks with Israel prior to disengagement meant making an important and politically risky concession without having acquired any gains from the war. He therefore adopted a wait-and-see attitude toward the disengagement negotiations. In the aftermath of the Egyptian-Israeli disengagement, Saudi Arabia lifted the oil embargo on condition that Secretary of State Kissinger negotiate a disengagement agreement between Syria and Israel.

Syria's leaders appear to have been divided over Kissinger's step-by-step "shuttle diplomacy." A hawkish faction reputedly rejected both direct negotiations and partial agreements with Israel under U.S. auspices, believing that the shift in the balance of power toward the Arabs permitted Syria to hold out for a comprehensive settlement on its own terms. To yield to U.S.–sponsored settlements would put an end to the Arab revolution. Others, who also believed that Syrian leverage was at a maximum in the aftermath of the war but were less sanguine about the future, argued that negotiations were necessary in order to have something to show for going to war.

As Sadat proceeded unilaterally, and the Syrians' fears of being left out mounted, Asad accepted the necessity of negotiating with Israel and began to rely on Kissinger to broker a satisfactory disengagement on the Syrian front. During these negotiations, Asad aimed to force the Israelis back as far as possible on the Golan Heights without permitting the disengagement agreement to become a substitute for an overall settlement. His minimum requirement was to acquire territory beyond the 1967 lines, which would be comparable to Sadat's gains. He bargained tenaciously, using Israeli prisoners of war for leverage and conducting a low-level war of attrition on the Golan Heights and Mount Hermon, which forced Israel to maintain a costly mobilization and threatened, in the event the conflict were to escalate, to drag Egypt back into war. Kissinger, in order to show the Arabs that reliance on the United States would pay dividends, pressured Israel to make concessions to Syria comparable to those it had made in the Sinai.

In the end, Asad had to settle for a partial Israeli withdrawal, recovering only the territory lost during the October War and a sliver of what was lost in 1967, in return for the placement of a UN observer force between the Syrian and Israeli lines. The rollback of Israeli forces, which were uncomfortably close to Damascus, was a security gain. Moreover, the fact that Syria did not have to negotiate directly with the Israelis was a plus for Asad, and there was the hope, as Kissinger promised, that the Israeli pullback would set a precedent for further withdrawal. But the agreement had costs and risks for Syria. It reduced the military pressure on Israel. The UN presence and the creation of limitation of forces zones would make any future war to retake the Golan Heights even more difficult. Asad also tacitly accepted an end to guerrilla operations on the Golan. Syria feared that defusing the wartime crisis might reduce pressure for an overall settlement. The agreement also risked legitimizing step-by-step diplomacy, an approach that weakened the hand of those, particularly the Syrians and the PLO, to whom the Israelis were least likely to make concessions. The agreement was a psychological watershed for Syria, decisively weaning it from its earlier strategy of rejectionism. Accepting an agreement that implied certain Israeli rights on the Golan was, as Kissinger acknowledged, "an agonizing concession, deeply wrenching for any Syrian leader." Syria's leaders had been forced to decide whether to begin the journey to a negotiated peace, and they had opted to do so: Asad admitted to Kissinger that, despite 26 years of hatred and emotional rejection of Israel, a rational statesman had to acknowledge that "a just peace is in the interests of our people."[13]

For roughly four years, from the Golan disengagement to Egypt's acceptance of the Camp David Accords, Syria was an active party in the U.S.–brokered peace process. Asad made it clear to Kissinger from the outset that Syria would cede no territory. A settlement, he insisted, had to be comprehensive, and that meant it had to include a solution of the Palestinian problem. Syria took every opportunity to stress the need to satisfy the legitimate rights of the Palestinians. At the Rabat Summit in 1974, it was in the forefront of the drive to designate the PLO as the sole legitimate representative of the Palestinian people, thus rejecting Jordan's right to bargain for Palestinians in the occupied territories. Whatever definition of Palestinian rights was acceptable to the PLO was, Asad declared, acceptable to Syria. When he was asked whether this included the destruction of Israel, he replied that PLO claims would not exceed their rights as defined by various UN resolutions, which did not call for the dismantling of Israel.[14] In fact, the mainstream PLO was moving toward acceptance of a two-state solution. As interpreted by Syria, Palestinian rights meant a Palestinian state on the West Bank and Gaza and the right of refugees from Israel proper to "repatriation or compensation."

At the outset, the Syrians conceived of a settlement under UN auspices, rather than a state-to-state peace treaty. Demilitarized zones and peacekeeping forces were acceptable, provided they were on both sides of the Israeli-Syrian border. Such a settlement would have buried the Syrian-Israeli military conflict. But the end of belligerency would have entailed neither diplomatic nor trade relations, which Syria considered the right of sovereign states to pursue as they wished. This fell far short of the "full peace" and direct negotiations demanded by Israel. By 1975, however, Asad was prepared to go further in making his readiness for peace explicit, a move that was not without political risk, and which opened him to attacks from rejectionists, particularly from his bitter rivals in Iraq. For the first time, he conceded that "when everything is settled it will have to be formalized with a formal peace treaty."[15] In January 1976, Syria, Egypt, and Jordan backed a UN Security Council resolution calling for a rollback to the 1967 borders in return for "appropriate arrangements to guarantee the sovereignty, territorial integrity and political independence of all states in the area and their right to live in peace within secure recognized borders."[16] This resolution echoed the substance of the Fahd and Fez plans, which were promulgated in 1981 and 1982, respectively, and were taken at the time to represent a major concession formalizing the Arabs' acceptance of Israel's right to exist.

At the same time that Syria was defining its position on peace, however, the Twelfth National Congress of the Ba'th party in 1975 added a new element of uncertainty regarding Syria's intentions. The conference declared that Syria would stand against "turning the Palestinian cause into a case of removing the consequences of the aggression of 1967" and spoke of the recovery of the West Bank as a "step . . . toward liberating all the Palestinian lands."[17] On the face of it, this pointed to a strategy in which, once the 1967 territories were recovered, the struggle against Israel would resume. At the time, some Syrian leaders explained that ending the belligerency did not mean that Syria recognized Israel's right to Palestine. The political struggle over the rights of Palestinians to return to and enjoy equal citizenship in Israel would continue. As they saw it, this would ultimately efface Israel's character as an exclusively Jewish state and alien bridgehead in the Arab world. According to Syrian officials queried in 1989, the 1975 resolutions were largely an attempt to placate persisting rejectionist sentiment in the Ba'th party's ranks, to warn Sadat that he could not ignore the Palestinian issue, and to reiterate the party's position that Palestinians outside Israel and the occupied territories should enjoy the right of return or compensation, as provided for under UN Resolution 194 (1948). Perceptions of Syria's intentions were also shaped by its occasionally militant rhetoric, such as the declaration that Palestine was part of southern Syria. Such pronouncements were for domestic consumption, however, and had little bearing on policy.

Israel's position in the decade following the 1967 war was that it was willing to negotiate a territorial compromise but not a full withdrawal from the occupied territories. Immediately after the war, Israel indicated that a return of the Golan Heights was contingent on their demilitarization and an absolute guarantee of access to the waters of the Jordan. But the Golan was soon thereafter included among the areas that, for security reasons, Israel must keep. Although the October War was a "psychological earthquake" for Israel and led a few to question reliance on military power for security, it renewed fears for Israel's security among the leadership and reinforced their determination that the Arabs' appetite would not be whetted by Israeli concessions. Several bloody Palestinian terrorist raids in Israel in the years after the 1973 war only heightened Israeli insecurity and rigidity.

After 1973, Labor party leaders continued to insist that Israel's pre-1967 borders were not defensible. They envisioned a partition of the West Bank with Jordan in which Israel would retain control of much of its resources and maintain military outposts along the Jordan River. Jerusalem, which was now in Israeli hands, was non-negotiable. The establishment of a Palestinian state, certain to become a base of operations against Israel, would never be permitted.[18] They denied the Palestinian right of repatriation or compensation for lands lost in 1948. Israel's leaders were convinced that Syria would never be ready for peace so long as Asad and the Ba'th party were in power. Prime Minister Golda Meir tenaciously resisted making any concessions during the first disengagement negotiations on the grounds that "none of our neighbors—certainly not Syria—is prepared to negotiate real peace." She argued that the Syrians had forfeited their right to the Golan Heights by shelling Israeli settlements from them and by losing them in war; if war had no costs for Syria, it would be encouraged to resort to it again. A peace treaty could easily be repudiated, especially if, in the unstable Arab world, a more militant regime were to come to power.[19] While many Israelis began to acknowledge Egypt's readiness for a settlement, Syria was viewed as remaining committed to the dreams of Arab nationalism and the Palestinian cause. It was still seen as the most hostile of Israel's neighbors and, once the peace with Egypt was achieved, the most dangerous. Israel justified the retention of the Golan Heights on the grounds that the Syrian border was close to the Israeli heartland

and the enemy so implacable. The establishment of settlements on the Golan Heights, and the control this afforded over the headwaters of the Jordan, reinforced the Israeli stake there. In 1977, Yitzhak Rabin explicitly told the U.S. government that Israel would not give up the Golan Heights.[20] Yet, occasionally, Israeli leaders assured the United States that territorial compromise was possible. Menachem Begin stated in 1977 that "Israel will remain in the Golan Heights but in the framework of a peace treaty we will be ready to withdraw our forces from their present line to a [new] line that will be . . . a permanent boundary."[21] In return for partial withdrawal, Israel expected a "full peace"— not merely a symbolic treaty that could be abrogated at any time, but one involving open borders and full trade and diplomatic relations.

Given the wide gap between the Syrian and Israeli positions, Israel tried, in the post-disengagement period, to avoid negotiating with Syria and the PLO and pursued a separate peace settlement with Sadat. Asad, in contrast, sought an international conference in which a united Arab delegation would settle for nothing less than total Israeli withdrawal from the occupied territories, thus preventing further unilateral deals on the Egyptian side. Within this context, the Soviet Union would balance U.S. influence, and Palestinian grievances would be addressed. Asad tried to create an Arab consensus against separate deals at the 1974 Rabat Summit. He also tried to forge a joint Syrian-PLO commitment that the two would make peace together or not at all, and he worked to stiffen Jordan's stance against separate negotiations. But he was unable to stop Sadat from negotiating a second separate agreement on the Sinai. This agreement, Sinai II, which largely removed Egypt from the military equation and was accompanied by a huge delivery of U.S. arms to Israel, greatly relieved pressure on Israel to deal with Syria. By 1976, both the United States and Israel believed Syria had lost much of its leverage. The idea of a second disengagement on the Syrian front was dropped, since Damascus was uninterested in the merely cosmetic gains that could be achieved under these conditions. In any case, Syria insisted on linkage between the Golan Heights and the West Bank. In allowing Israel to concentrate its forces on the Syrian front, Sinai II greatly increased the threat to Syria's security.

The Carter administration, however, recommitted the United States to a comprehensive settlement and briefly held out hope for an all-party international conference and U.S. support for a Palestinian homeland. In early discussions with President Carter, Asad edged closer to acceding to the Israeli demand for a full peace settlement, albeit one achieved in stages. The first step in this direction would be to formally end belligerency and then institute confidence-building measures. Among these would be the creation of demilitarized zones and the economic reconstruction of disputed areas, notably the Golan Heights, "to give the people confidence that the situation is good and permanent."[22] Diplomatic, and even economic, relations could be established once the necessary "psychological composure" had been achieved. Asad hinted that Syria would not object to the confederation of a Palestinian entity on the West Bank with Jordan. Interim arrangements in the occupied territories, such as autonomy and staged Israeli withdrawals, were possible, provided the final outcome was guaranteed. Moreover, the Arab delegation at Geneva could speak for the PLO. But one way or the other, the Palestinians had to be represented, so they could not say peace had been negotiated over their heads. In the summer of 1977, Syria reaffirmed to Washington that it would sign a peace treaty with Israel as part of an overall settlement.[23]

At the same time, what Yair Evron called a Syrian-Israeli "deterrence dialogue" had emerged out of Syria's intervention in Lebanon in 1976. Although Israel initially warned Syria against intervening, once it became apparent that Asad was trying to discipline the PLO and the Lebanese radicals, it saw the advantage of letting Syria get bogged down in a conflict with its former allies. Furthermore, Israel did not wish to jeopardize the emerging separate peace settlement with Egypt by engaging in another war.[24] Washington brokered an exchange of messages, as Syria sought to maximize the scope of its intervention and Israel tried to minimize it. An unwritten agreement emerged over the "red lines" Israel expected Syria to observe in return for tolerating its intervention. Syria could not deploy troops south of

Sidon. Nor could it deploy missiles or aircraft that would enable it to challenge Israel's control of the air or its ability to hit Palestinian targets in Lebanon. The intervention produced a brief convergence of aims between Israel and Syria, both of which supported the Lebanese Christian forces against the PLO. For a brief period in 1976, Israeli and Syrian naval vessels blockaded different sectors of the Lebanese coast to prevent arms shipments to the Palestinians. Of more long-term importance, the episode suggested that the two sides shared a stake in stability in Lebanon; in accepting Israel's red lines, Syria tacitly acknowledged Israel's legitimate security needs.[25] Israel's caution in dealing with the intervention probably convinced Asad that Israel was not looking for opportunities to attack Syria. The episode also demonstrated that the two states could bargain rationally and respect one another's interests.

But the negotiations over President Carter's projected peace conference revealed major procedural, as well as substantive, differences between the parties. Asad, afraid that the Egyptians would make another separate deal, and realizing that in one-on-one negotiations with Israel each of the separate Arab entities was the weaker party, wanted a united Arab delegation in which the Palestinians would be represented. This would have given Syria a veto over Egyptian initiatives and a say in the solution of the Palestinian question. Moreover, Asad wanted to engage as many other parties with an interest in peace as possible—the United Nations, the superpowers—and accord them roles as brokers and guarantors. If there were to be separate bilateral negotiations, then the participants, including the superpowers, would have to ratify them in a plenary session. Israel in contrast, insisted on separate bilateral negotiations, refused to negotiate with the PLO, and wished to minimize the influence of third parties.

Under domestic political pressure, Carter agreed to Israel's conditions. While there was to be a committee to negotiate the issue of the West Bank, Syria and the PLO would not be represented. Moshe Dayan reportedly acknowledged that Israel's aim was to exclude Syria from the negotiations and reach a separate peace agreement with Egypt: If one wheel were removed, he explained, the car could not run again. The U.S.–Israeli agreement, and Syria's reluctance to join negotiations on these terms, seemed to stalemate the peace process, although Secretary of State Cyrus Vance reported signs of flexibility in the Syrian position—for example, Asad had conceded that the Arab states could speak for the PLO.[26] As Carter retreated from the prospect of pressuring Israel to be more flexible, and the procedural stalemate continued, Sadat became convinced that Israel could not be brought into a comprehensive settlement. But, having been led to believe Israel might concede the Sinai to break the Arab front and relieve pressures for a comprehensive settlement, Sadat embarked on his trip to Jerusalem. This brought the Syrian-Egyptian coalition to a final break. Asad refused to join Sadat in conducting further negotiations, having lost all confidence that the Egyptian leader could be held to a common position. Sadat had dissipated Arab bargaining power by showing himself ready for peace at any cost and by overtly recognizing Israel and its annexation of Jerusalem without receiving anything in return. Sadat claimed his trip had broken the "psychological barrier to peace"; Asad retorted that he had broken the back of Arab perseverance.[27] As Egypt and Israel made peace, ostensibly defusing the Middle East conflict, pressures on Israel to participate in a wider settlement dissipated, and the incentive to deal with Syria or the Palestinians disappeared.

Egypt's abandonment of Syria and the Arab world was accompanied by a gradual policy transformation in Syria. Renewing the war for the occupied territories without Egypt was out of the question. Unlike the rejectionists, Asad still wished to achieve a comprehensive settlement through some combination of military and diplomatic pressures. But, having been burned by his dependence on Egypt, he set out to acquire for Syria the enhanced military and political leverage it would need to present a credible hand in any peace negotiations. Asad had to find a substitute for the Egyptian alliance and assert his leadership in the Arab arena in order to rally the Arabs behind his strategy. As early as 1975, he had begun to try to forge a new Arab concert with Lebanon, Jordan, and the PLO under Syrian leadership. Such an alliance would bolster Syria's military front and deter any of the parties from striking separate deals with Israel. By establishing Syria as the leader of a power bloc in the Arab East (Mashreq), Asad hoped to demonstrate to Washington that Syrian conditions would have to be satisfied if the peace process was to be carried further. He also aimed to increase Syria's prestige and power to such an extent that it would replace Egypt as the state with the recognized right to define the norms of Arab state behavior in the conflict with Israel. Asad had some success in the late 1970s in imposing Syrian leadership on his partners and in making Syria a serious political force in the Arab East. Jordan rejected Camp David. Syria's intervention in Lebanon made it the arbiter of the country for a period, and its "strategic alliance" with the PLO began to develop. Ultimately, however, the Syrian embrace generated its own counterpressures, and Lebanon and the PLO, in particular, became the rocks on which Asad's vessel would eventually founder.

The failure of diplomacy, made manifest by the separate peace treaty Egypt signed with Israel in 1979, led to a further shift in Syrian strategy. Convinced that negotiations would be fruitless until Syria and the rest of the Arab world achieved military and political parity with Israel, Asad adopted what might be called a policy of tactical rejectionism, largely eschewing further negotiations and seeking to obstruct U.S. initiatives pursued on Israel's terms. Renewed priority was given to a military buildup, which required a closer alliance with the Soviet Union. As previously noted, Syria also tried to block the legitimation of the "Camp David process" in the Arab world, to reconstruct the "eastern front," and to claim the support to which it felt entitled as the only remaining frontline Arab state. But before long Syrian policy was in disarray. The eastern front collapsed, in good part because of the Iran-Iraq War, while King Hussein pursued peace initiatives over the West Bank in disregard of Syrian wishes. As the threat of Iranian expansionism assumed a much higher priority than the Arab-Israeli dispute in Saudi Arabia and the gulf states, Syria's alliance with Iran alienated its main financial backers. By 1980, Asad's rejection of the U.S.– sponsored peace process and rivalries with other Arab states had left Syria isolated in both the Arab and the international arenas, utterly lacking in the diplomatic leverage that could only flow from leadership of a wider Arab bloc, and ever more likely to be left to its own devices in case of attack.

TOWARD WAR IN LEBANON

Simultaneously, a major change was taking place in Israeli policy. The rise to power of the Likud under Menachem Begin ushered in a much more activist and, in the Syrian view, expansionist phase of Israeli conduct. The Likud government's central goals were to undertake a creeping annexation of the West Bank and Gaza and to maintain an assertive policy against those Arab enemies, especially the PLO and Syria, which might challenge this.[28] Although it would take them some time to win over the whole government, the hawks began to consider the desirability of a new military confrontation with Syria which, isolated after Camp David and the collapse of the eastern front, was especially vulnerable.[29]

The main arena of Syrian-Israeli confrontation was Lebanon, and the immediate catalyst of conflict was the Palestinian presence there. For a long time, Israel had been content to prevent Lebanon from becoming a "confrontation state." However, once the PLO turned it into a front, Israel sought to deter and preempt Palestinian guerrilla operations through massive retaliation in which Palestinian camps and the population of southern Lebanon were made to suffer for guerrilla actions. Israel hoped to turn the Lebanese against the Palestinians, and, indeed, its raids helped set off the civil war and the collapse of the Lebanese state.[30] In 1976, Syria intervened and temporarily pacified the country. As peace prospects loomed early in the Carter administration, Asad sought to freeze southern Lebanon as a front in the Arab-Israeli conflict: Under the Syrian-sponsored Shtaura Agreement of July 1977, Palestinian forces were to withdraw from the border region. Syria began to collect heavy weapons from the PLO, but the peace plan was obstructed by Israel's refusal to allow a Syrian-backed Lebanese army to secure the southern Lebanese border. A political vacuum developed, which was soon filled by the PLO and Israel's Lebanese proxy, the Christian militia of Saad Haddad. Attacks by Haddad's forces on the Palestinians made it impossible for Syria to pursue their disarmament and, after Sadat's trip to Jerusalem dashed Syria's hopes for peace, it found reason to renew support for the Palestinians' operations.[31] Israel had tolerated Syria's intervention in Lebanon so long as it was directed at the PLO, but once Syria's presence turned permanent, its old alignment with the PLO was restored, and Syrian policy hardened against negotiations, Israel perceived that Asad again wanted to turn Lebanon into a confrontation state.

Under Begin, Israel initiated a more activist policy in Lebanon. A Palestinian raid on Israel sparked the Litani Operation—a massive invasion of southern Lebanon in 1978 aimed at driving the PLO from the area. Israel consolidated Haddad's forces in a buffer zone in the south, driving Lebanese Shiites out and funneling Maronite militiamen in. The Haddad zone served to keep the PLO at bay and southern Lebanon open for a possible Israeli offensive to outflank Syrian forces on the Golan Heights. Asad remained passive during the invasion, declaring that Syria would not be drawn into a war on Israel's terms. This hurt Syria's political prestige and its relations with the PLO, which were just beginning to recover in the wake of Sadat's trip to Jerusalem.

Nevertheless, during 1979 and 1980 a Syrian-PLO alliance solidified out of common opposition to Camp David and fear of Israel. Syria supported Palestinian efforts to restore a presence in southern Lebanon, and although it also took pains to keep the fighting from escalating, it seemed to believe controlled conflict in the south could be useful to demonstrate the futility of negotiating a peace agreement that bypassed Syria. Begin adopted a policy of continuous harassment of the PLO entailing massive air strikes and commando raids deep into Lebanon and even behind Syrian lines. Syria viewed these raids as a humiliating threat to its championship of Arab steadfastness against Camp David and, wishing to show solidarity with the PLO and to deter further Israeli escalation, began to send combat aircraft over Lebanon. Although the Syrians initially refrained from confronting Israeli warplanes, Israel believed Syria was violating the informal red line governing its forces in Lebanon. Israel shot down many

Syrian aircraft in an extended series of dogfights but, according to Evron, finally de-escalated by making its air raids somewhat more selective.[32]

Begin also initiated a closer alliance with the Maronites. The intellectual roots of the Israeli-Maronite alliance go back to Israel's founding, when Israeli strategists viewed the Christians as anti-Arab and anti-Muslim, hence potential adherents to an Israel-led alliance of minorities against Arab nationalism. Lebanon was the "weakest link in the chain of the Arab League." David Ben-Gurion floated a proposal to destabilize Lebanon, foster a Maronite mini-state, and incorporate the area up to the Litani, which he considered part of Palestine, and, therefore, legitimately Israeli.[33] No attempt was ever made to carry out this dream, however, until the early 1980s, when practical conditions were ripe and a risk-taking leadership was in place. The Lebanese Forces leader, Beshir Gemayel, tried to reestablish Maronite dominance and drive the Syrians out of Lebanon. To that end, in 1978 he abandoned the Maronite policy of balance between Syria and Israel and began to seek Israeli intervention against the military pressure Syria was bringing to bear on him. Begin, seeing Gemayel as a strong pro-Israeli leader who could impose his will on Lebanon, committed himself to protecting the Maronites against the Syrians. Israeli warnings played a role in deterring Syrian efforts to bring the Maronites to heel and emboldened the Lebanese Forces to continue their challenge to Syria. In essence, Israel foiled Syria's attempt to put Lebanon back together under a Pax Syriana.

Begin's policy culminated in the so-called Zahlah missile crisis. In 1981, the Lebanese Forces began to extend their control toward the Syrian-held Bekaa Valley, building a road to Zahlah, infiltrating the city, and ambushing Syrian troops. This was a bid to cut Syria off from Beirut and from central and southern Lebanon. To succeed, it had to provoke a Syrian reaction sufficient to trigger Israeli intervention against the Syrians. It almost did so. When Syria shelled Zahlah, pushed the Maronites back, took strategic Mount Sennin, and seemed to threaten the Maronite heartland, Begin warned of air intervention. In a counter-warning to Israel, Syria deployed surface-to-air missile (SAM)

launchers without missiles. After Israel shot down Syrian heli-
copters, Syria deployed the missiles. Begin, who saw the missiles
as a challenge to the credibility of his guarantee to the Maronites,
announced that their deployment violated the red-line agreement and threatened to destroy them.[34] The United States intervened to defuse the crisis. The missiles stayed in Lebanon,
although Asad promised not to use them against Israeli recon-
naissance flights. Syria had turned back Gemayel's threat to its
hegemony over Lebanon. It had also used the crisis to demonstrate to the United States that the Israeli-Egyptian peace treaty,
which excluded Syria, could not guarantee peace in the region.
In the eyes of some Israelis, Asad had appeared willing to play a
game of brinkmanship, risking war. This was interpreted as a
sign of his confidence following Syria's recent military buildup,
which Israel increasingly considered dangerous. Yitzhak Rabin,
however, accused Begin of having been the one to violate the red
lines by escalating his commitment to the Lebanese Forces. Begin
justified his action as aimed at "saving" the Maronites from total
collapse and preventing a Syrian takeover of all of Lebanon.[35]
For Begin, Syria's apparent victory in the showdown was unacceptable. As if to show his contempt for Syria, he soon thereafter
annexed the Golan Heights—an act Asad interpreted as having
slammed the door on any possibility of a negotiated settlement.

At the same time, Begin suffered another setback. Although
the Haddad and UN buffer zones had been established in southern Lebanon, the PLO still possessed rockets capable of hitting
northern Israeli settlements. Since the PLO had embarked on a
"peace offensive," and guerrilla activity against Israel was subsid-
ing, the rockets may have chiefly been a deterrent erected in
defense of the virtual mini-state the Palestinians were construct-
ing between Tyre and Sidon. When the PLO responded to Israeli
air raids by firing their rockets at Israeli settlements, Begin,
unable to silence them through the use of air power, accepted a
U.S.–mediated cease-fire. Syria, wishing to head off an Israeli
invasion, lent its weight to the pacification efforts.[36] The PLO's
ability to threaten Israel was profoundly irksome to Begin.
Moreover, Arafat's peace diplomacy threatened to give the PLO
greater international credibility. The unsatisfactory outcome of

the confrontations over the PLO and the Zahlah missiles were part of the immediate motivation behind Israel's invasion of Lebanon in 1982.

This invasion was the brainchild of a group of hawks, including Begin, Defense Minister Ariel Sharon, Chief of Staff Rafael Eitan, and Foreign Minister Yitzhak Shamir, who dominated the Israeli government. The most ambitious among them, Sharon, encouraged by growing Arab fragmentation, Syria's post–Camp David vulnerability, and the Reagan administration's sympathy for an activist policy against Soviet allies, promoted a view of Israel as a regional superpower that was capable of reshaping the area into a "new order" if it used its military power boldly.[37] First, Israel would strike at the PLO in Lebanon. Israel's declared aim was to eliminate the PLO threat to northern Israel by pushing the guerrillas back 40 kilometers from the border. But the PLO, seeking to avoid confrontation, had kept the border quiet. The real aim of the Israeli operation was, in fact, to destroy the PLO, which, Israel knew, would otherwise return to southern Lebanon. The hawks believed that so long as the PLO remained a force, Israel might one day be pressured into making concessions to the Palestinians. Destroying the PLO militarily could break Palestinian resistance to the incorporation of the West Bank and allow a new, more cooperative Palestinian leadership, ready to accept Begin's very limited "autonomy" plan, to emerge in the occupied territories. Israel's second strategic goal was to establish a friendly Maronite state in Lebanon that would sign a peace treaty with Israel, thereby extending Camp David and creating a Cairo-Jerusalem-Beirut axis that would further isolate Syria, the main opponent of Camp David, and put an end to Asad's long-standing ambition to establish hegemony in "Greater Syria."[38]

None of this could be accomplished without forcing a Syrian withdrawal from Lebanon. The conditions for this seemed to be right: Syria's role in Lebanon had been weakened by Maronite opposition, fighting among its own allies, and the decline of support in the Arab world for its "peacekeeping" presence. Upcoming presidential elections in Lebanon rendered the political situation fluid. Syria would try to install its candidate, but Israel now had its own candidate in Beshir Gemayel. While Begin

evidently hoped the threatened Syrian forces would quickly retreat, Sharon believed the achievement of Israeli aims would
require the destruction of the Syrian forces in Lebanon.[39] Chief
of Staff Eitan believed that, with Syria isolated, this was the time
to smash its army: Breaking the only major Arab fighting force
on Israel's border would win ten years of peace. Despite their
defensive purpose, Syria's introduction of SAMs was adduced as
evidence of its aggressive intent toward Israel. Syria's military
buildup also loomed large in Israeli thinking. For some, therefore, the invasion took on the character of a preemptive war
against Syria.[40] A few hard-liners, including Sharon, appear to
have seen the possibility of achieving even greater gains in the
invasion. Israeli ascendancy might permit the expulsion of West
Bank Palestinians to Jordan, precipitating the fall of the monarchy and justifying Israeli intervention there.[41] There was also a
possibility that the Syrian regime might collapse, bringing on a
Lebanon-like sectarian breakup into readily subordinated Alawi,
Druze, and Sunni mini-states. Israel would be unchallenged in
the Middle East.[42]

Asad sought to avoid war, hoping the Israeli invasion would
be limited, similar to the Litani Operation; indeed, Israel at first
assured the Syrians it would not attack them. Syrian forces even
held their fire when fired on and never unleashed their SAMs
against the Israeli aircraft swarming over Lebanon.[43] Begin presented Asad with an ultimatum: Remove the SAMs and pull back
the Palestinians under his protection in eastern Lebanon to 40
kilometers from the border. However, even as U.S. envoy Philip
Habib was delivering the Israeli ultimatum to Asad, Syrian
forces came under attack.

Israel's forces in Lebanon—some 76,000 men and 1,250
tanks—were three times as large as Syria's. Once fighting started, Asad tried to evade Israeli efforts to encircle his Bekaa forces
and cut them off from Beirut and the road to Syria, which would
have allowed Israel to destroy them or force them out of
Lebanon. Israel rapidly destroyed Syria's air defense system and
inflicted dramatic losses on its air force. Yet, although they were
outnumbered and deprived of air cover, Syrian ground forces
were often effective and stubborn in combat. Their resistance,

particularly in an ambush of Israeli forces at Sultan Yakoub, and Israeli logistical logjams stalled the Israeli drive toward the Damascus-Beirut highway and prevented the encirclement of Syrian forces. A U.S.–imposed cease-fire on June 11 left Syrian forces entrenched in the northern Bekaa Valley. Syria established new defensive positions and refused to be pushed out of the country, thus denying Israel its strategic objective. But the cease-fire was politically costly because Asad appeared to be leaving the Palestinians to their fate. Although Syrian units continued to defend Beirut, where the cease-fire did not hold, the Israelis expelled the PLO from most of Lebanon while Syria looked on ineffectually. Militarily, Syria had taken a beating: The Syrian army suffered serious losses and was pushed from strategic sectors of Lebanon, including Beirut. Damascus came within range of Israeli guns that had moved into the southern Bekaa Valley on Syria's western flank. The Israeli victory, which underlined Arab military impotence, appeared in Damascus to strengthen "capitulationist" opinion in the Arab world.[44] But Asad refused to knuckle under.

In the wake of the war, Israel aimed to reap the political rewards of victory by installing a friendly regime in Beirut prepared to make peace on Israel's terms. The first serious setback to this plan was Beshir Gemayel's assassination—allegedly by Syrian intelligence operatives—depriving Israel of the strongman who it had hoped would demand the evacuation of Syrian forces and sign a peace treaty. His murder set off the massacre of Palestinians at Shatila and Sabra, which led to the resignations of generals Sharon and Eitan, undermined the Israeli government's domestic authority, and lost it its mandate to carry on in Lebanon. Beshir's replacement, Amin Gemayel, valued Lebanon's connections to its Syrian and Arab hinterland above the Israeli alliance, but Israel would not withdraw without political concessions, which were contained in the U.S.–brokered Lebanese-Israeli accord of May 17, 1983.

This accord was, as an Israeli official put it, a separate peace treaty "in all but name."[45] It opened Lebanon to Israeli influence, diplomats, and products. It expanded and legitimized the role of Haddad, Israel's client, in the south. While Israel acquired rights to maintain surveillance posts and conduct patrols and overflights in Lebanon and was accorded a role in Lebanese security decisions, Lebanon's Arab treaties were superseded and Arab forces were to be excluded from Lebanese soil. In Syria's view, Lebanon's Arab character was thereby gravely compromised. Israel's withdrawal was made contingent on Syria's, putting Syria's role on an equal footing with Israel's. Asad considered the accord to be a pale copy of Camp David that would have legitimized Egypt's separate peace settlement and advanced a "peace process" that excluded Syria. Indeed, the Reagan Plan of September 1982 had made no mention of Syria and invited Jordan to negotiate a separate deal for the West Bank. As the *New York Times* commented, the accord would come "close to ending in a Greater Israel."[46] The *Times* anticipated that a pro–U.S. coalition of Egypt, Saudi Arabia, Jordan, and Lebanon would acquiesce in the destruction of the PLO and Israel's absorption of the West Bank and the Golan Heights and use its financial strength to make Syria acquiesce as well. Not surprisingly, Asad perceived a U.S.–Israeli combination seeking to encircle and isolate him. The United States and Israel believed a militarily weakened and isolated Syria had no choice but to accept the accord and withdraw from Lebanon or face continued Israeli occupation of the country, with the attendant security threats to Syria itself.[47] But Asad, determined that Israel would reap no political advantage from the invasion, chose to defy Israel's overwhelming military power and, in a short time, brought about a remarkable turnabout in the balance of forces.

Since Israel's withdrawal from Lebanon had been made contingent on Syria's, Asad had been unwittingly given a veto over the agreement. Emboldened by Soviet aid in the rebuilding of his army and the emplacement of a sophisticated air defense network, he refused to withdraw. Despite Israeli threats to launch a preemptive strike against Syria's new SAMs, the growing Soviet role in Syria circumscribed Israeli options. At the same time, Asad mobilized Lebanese resistance to the Israeli presence. Interestingly, a high Syrian official had explicitly signaled Syria's strategy in advance of the Israeli invasion:

> If the Israeli intervention takes the form of strikes against Pales-
> tinian positions in Lebanon, Syria's intervention will remain lim-
> ited . . . but if it is a matter of occupation Syria will certainly give
> the Palestinians and the Lebanese patriotic forces all the means
> necessary for . . . turning the occupier's life into an unbearable hell
> [leading to] the attrition of the occupying forces.[48]

Taking advantage of the growing Muslim resentment of Israeli and Maronite domination, Syria struck alliances with the Lebanese Shiite and Druze militias, channeled Palestinians evacuated from Beirut back into Lebanon, and backed their guerrilla activities against Israeli forces. After May 17, Asad succeeded in creating a coalition of Lebanese politi cians, militias, and nationalist parties opposed to the accord, the National Salvation Front, which was aimed against both the occupiers and the Gemayel government.

A year after the invasion, Asad concluded that Israel had lost the will to use military power against him. Wearied by casualties, disillusioned by the unreliability of the Gemayel regime, and aware of the risks of a renewed drive against a Syrian army reinforced by Soviet arms and backing, Israel began to withdraw from Lebanon. Buttressed by Syria, Muslim militias successfully contested the Gemayel government's attempt to consolidate power over the country. Throughout the staged Israeli withdrawal, the Gemayel government failed to fill the power vacuums the Israelis left in their wake. Thus, when Israel withdrew from the Shuf, the Druzes drove out the Maronite forces. As Israel gradually extricated itself, Washington tried, without success, to forge a new Lebanese army to enforce Gemayel's authority. But U.S. intervention on Gemayel's behalf could not deter Syria and its allies from contesting his power. The bombing, in October 1983, of the U.S. Marine barracks in Beirut and the downing of two American fighters by the Syrians in December demonstrated the costs of involvement. Once Gemayel's army crumbled before the Muslim militias in West Beirut, Washington decided to cut its losses. The weakened Gemayel government was forced, in February 1984, to annul the accord with Israel, and the United States pulled out the Marines the following month. By 1985, the Israelis, harassed by Syrian-backed guerrillas, completed their withdrawal from Lebanon except for the "security zone" in the south, ending the immediate military threat to Syria. Thus, through a combination of the shrewd use of proxies, steadfastness under attack, an enhanced military capability on the ground, and Soviet backing, Asad snatched victory from the jaws of defeat. The limits of Israel's military power were exposed: It could win on the battlefield and still fail to shape political events to its liking. Syria had too much invested in Lebanon to give up easily. Begin had "ignored the geopolitical reality that Lebanon is vital to Syria's security but not Israel's."[49] Syria's prestige in the Arab world was enhanced by its willingness to stand up to Israel and the United States. This made it more difficult for Arab governments to defy Syria in dealing with these powers and diluted the "capitulationist" climate prevalent after the Israeli invasion of Lebanon. Asad could feel satisfied that he had reinforced the lesson that no stability in the area was possible at the expense of Syrian interests.

Even after Israel's withdrawal, Lebanon remained a flashpoint. There was a small replay of the Zahlah missile crisis in late 1985, when Syria showed its displeasure with Israel's air activity over Lebanon by preparing SAM sites and launching interceptor aircraft within its own borders near Lebanon. Israel responded by shooting down two MIGs, apparently over Syrian territory. Syria, declaring that it would no longer tolerate "turning Lebanon into a Zionist air space," moved SAMs into Lebanon. Again, the United States intervened, the missiles were withdrawn, and a new understanding was reached over Lebanon's air space. In 1987, a hang glider attack on Israel by a pro-Syrian Palestinian group, which was possibly initiated to derail Israel's attempts to draw Jordan into a separate autonomy arrangement on the West Bank, could well have set off another confrontation between Israel and Syria. The hardening of Israeli public opinion that such incidents provoke shows how easily southern Lebanon can be used to derail a peace process that is unacceptable to any major party to the Arab-Israeli conflict. The reactions to such incidents also suggest how easily another major confrontation could result from miscalculation and inadvertent escalation in this volatile environment. Lebanon remained the most dangerous flashpoint in the Arab-Israeli conflict. It is there that

Israel and Syria rubbed against one another and where Palestinian, Maronite, and Shiite radicalism came together. Throughout the late 1980s, the U.S. embassy in Damascus was preoccupied with defusing the explosive situations that developed as a result of Israeli overflights and terrorist operations in Lebanon.

THE 1980S: "TACTICAL REJECTIONISM" CONSOLIDATED

Beginning with the failure of the peace process of the mid-1970s to accommodate Syria, and during the Begin years, in particular, a new, "darker" view of Israel emerged in Syria.[50] Asad believed that while he had tried to wean the Syrian people from the expectation that all of Palestine could be liberated, the Israeli leadership had encouraged expansionist sentiment in Israel. Indeed, the Syrian interpretation of Israeli history stressed an inexorable and continuous expansionism in which military conquest was followed by colonization. In Asad's view, there was ample evidence in Israel's political pronouncements and its behavior to suggest that its ambitions had not yet been fulfilled. In his meetings with visitors to Damascus, Asad frequently referred to the Likud's commitment to Eretz Israel and its supposed dream of an empire from the Nile to the Euphrates. Shamir's declaration that the wave of immigration from the Soviet Union required a "large" Israel confirmed and reinforced Asad's view of Israel as expansionist. Syrians, who remember the way the French exploited communal differences in order to rule the Levant, also fear that Israel wishes to establish sectarian mini-states in the region in order to dominate and weaken the Arabs. Whether such fears are warranted is irrelevant: They are genuinely and deeply felt. But it was the war in Lebanon that created the greatest fears of Israeli ambitions: It showed that "Syria could no longer be confident that an Israel-initiated war could be avoided by Syria's adherence to the limits defined by Israel itself."[51]

If Syrian views seem alarmist, many Israelis have an image of Syria and the Arabs that is equally apocalyptic. When Saddam Hussein threatened, in 1990, to burn Israel, many Israelis feared that he expressed the wishes of all Arabs, including Asad. It is a common view that the Arabs' "boundless and unremitting hatred" of Israel makes any territorial concessions infinitely dangerous. Distrust of Syria (and the Palestinians) is widespread among ordinary Israelis. According to one worst-case scenario, radical Palestinians would seize control of any Palestinian state established on the West Bank and invite Syria to absorb it into a Greater Syria. The Palestinians, with Syrian backing, would then attempt to capture Jerusalem and split Israel in half. With its huge army, its arsenal of chemical weapons, and Soviet backing, Syria was poised to attack: It could occupy Jordan, and absent Israeli control of the Golan Heights, an invasion through Galilee and northern Jordan could not be stopped. Egypt would join the Arab conquest.[52] Quite apart from the exaggeration of Syrian aims, there is no mention in this scenario of Israel's nuclear deterrent or of what the U.S. response to such an attack might be. Nor is there any recognition of Israel's consistently demonstrated military superiority or of the historic unwillingness of the Soviet Union to back any Arab military designs beyond the recovery of the occupied territories.

In this climate of zero-sum perceptions, Asad's tactical rejectionism hardened into a seemingly unbending rigidity during the 1980s. Negotiations were impossible with such men as Begin and Shamir, who announced in advance that they would never withdraw from the occupied territories. Likud's public commitment that "Western Eretz Israel will never be divided again"[53] (meaning that the West Bank would not be returned to Arab rule), Israel's refusal to talk with the PLO, and its annexation of the Golan Heights led Damascus to believe there was no hope of a settlement. Even the Labor party believed that Israel should hold on to the Golan Heights, and many moderate Israelis shrank from the prospect of having to make concessions on more than one front, which negotiating a comprehensive settlement would entail. Moreover, after Camp David, and especially during the Reagan administration, Asad lost hope that the United States could be trusted to broker a comprehensive peace settlement.

Asad insisted that until Israel was serious about wanting peace, the United States stopped pursuing separate partial deals, and the Arabs had a credible bargaining hand, peace negotiations could only divide and weaken the Arabs, lead to the ceding of Arab rights, and result in a strengthened Israel positioned to dominate the Arab world. Moreover, a real peace could not, he believed, be built on rewarding Israel for its expansionism. A long-term, continuous, determined struggle was the only way to defeat Israel's ambitions. Unlike Arafat, who saw time running out, Asad seemed to think time was on the Arabs' side: Modernization could only enhance their strength, while the burdens of occupation would weaken Israel. The battle need not immediately take a military form. Indeed, Asad insisted that Syria would choose the time and place for any such encounter and would resist being drawn into a war when the balance of power was unfavorable. In the meantime, Arabs had to stop deluding themselves that Washington would deliver Israel; it was time for them to begin to confront the Israelis themselves.[54]

Until conditions were right for a confrontation, Asad was determined to head off partial deals that excluded Syria and conceded Palestinian rights. Specifically, any attempt by Jordan or the PLO to negotiate a Begin-style autonomy plan for the West Bank or an Israeli-Jordanian condominium over the region had to be blocked. This is why he rejected the 1981 Fahd Plan. Even though it had called for a peace settlement along lines long advocated by Syria, because it implied recognition of Israel at a time when Israel was unprepared to make concessions, it was unacceptable. Moreover, because the Saudis had failed to consult Syria beforehand, acceptance of the plan would only encourage separate dealing by Jordan or the PLO. Syria used every means at its disposal, including initiating terrorist attacks, carrying out military maneuvers on Jordan's border, and encouraging a Palestinian rebellion against the PLO leadership, to derail various initiatives in which Arafat would have empowered King Hussein to negotiate over the West Bank. Ironically, Asad's main allies in scuttling such initiatives were Likud leaders who opposed any territorial compromise on the West Bank.

Asad was just as opposed to an interim or partial settlement between Israel and Syria that would leave the Palestinian issue unsettled as he was to other partial deals. While some Israelis toyed with the notion of such a partial settlement, and Palestinians feared that the Syrians might agree, Asad has consistently insisted on linking the two fronts. He showed little interest in a "second disengagement" on the Golan Heights. Some believed that his 1976 intervention in Lebanon was designed to deliver the Palestinians into any settlement that would allow him to recover the Golan, but even after PLO forces were defeated he made no attempt to force the PLO into a deal for less than a Palestinian state. Indeed, Asad passed up a chance to "deliver" the Palestinians, if that was his intention, when he insisted on a role for the PLO in the proposed 1977 international conference. Over the years, Asad has generally voiced more concern for overall pan-Arab interests in the struggle with Israel than for the recovery of the Golan Heights. From a pan-Arab point of view, the loss of Palestine was the major disaster. The Golan, forfeited in a battle over Palestine, was of secondary concern. As Asad put it:

> Had Syria thought of its own interests only . . . it would have . . . achieved a unilateral solution. . . . For its long-term interest, Israel favors the abandonment of the Golan and the conclusion of a separate deal with Syria. If Syria had been regionally oriented, it would have proceeded from its regional [i.e. state] interests. But it did not and will not do this. . . . The Golan was originally occupied in a battle waged for Palestine.[55]

To some degree, Asad is locked into this interpretation because no other one would be politically acceptable. If he were to enter into a separate settlement to recover the Golan Heights, he would forfeit the nationalist legitimacy and the claim on Arab support that Syria's position with Israel has given it.

This is not to say the Golan is unimportant to Syria. On the contrary, there is no chance Asad will settle for less than its return. He argues that Israel's demand for secure borders at the expense of Syrian sovereignty over the Golan is both outdated (in an age of missiles) and unbalanced: "It is strange to insist on secure borders on other people's territory. Why should secure borders be 50 kilometers from Damascus and 350 kilometers from Tel Aviv?"[56] Furthermore, since Asad bears a lot of the responsibility for the Golan's loss, he simply cannot afford to settle without it. If he has shown little interest in a diplomatic settlement over the Golan Heights, it is because he believes the most he can expect to recover, given Israel's present stance, would be a part of the plateau. Partition is hardly an attractive outcome, since the Golan's main value is partly security related— Syria wants to remove the Israeli threat to Damascus—and partly symbolic—the Ba'thi regime needs to recover the honor it lost in 1967 and deny Israel the fruits of conquest. Only the return of the entire territory would achieve these ends.

If a Palestinian or Jordanian deal with Israel for a territorial compromise over the West Bank were in the cards, Asad would be faced with some complicated dilemmas. One would be whether to give priority to the Golan and abandon his champion-ship of Palestinian rights, a decision that would certainly make compromise with Israel easier. Although Asad's commitment to the Palestinian cause, as the touchstone of Arab nationalism, is deep-rooted, if most Palestinians themselves (and not just an Arafat-led rump PLO) were willing to accept half a loaf and only continued Syrian demands for something more blocked real prospects for the return of the Golan, Asad would be hard put to continue demanding the whole loaf. After the 1988 Arab League Summit in Algiers, a Syrian official said that if the PLO decided to make peace with Israel, it would have to bear the responsibility: Syria would "no longer carry the banner" for the Palestinian cause, and would be "free in any future negotiations to concentrate on its narrow national interest in regaining the Golan Heights."[57] If, on the other hand, Israel seemed to rule out such a return, Asad would have every incentive, and proba-bly the means, to obstruct a separate deal over the West Bank.

Asad's opposition to the Bush administration's attempt to foster a dialogue between Israel and the Palestinians and to promote elections on the West Bank under the Shamir/Baker Plan was foreseeable, although his criticism was remarkably muted. Not only had Washington excluded Syria from the proc-ess, but separate Palestinian negotiations with Israel were, in his view, likely to lead to the forfeiting of Palestinian rights to self-determination. As he saw it, the Israelis would try to use the proposed elections on the West Bank to dampen the *intifadah* and, by ruling out PLO participation in the elections, produce an alternative leadership that would concede Palestinian rights. The most the Palestinians could expect to gain from the process, in Syria's view, would be a Camp David–style "autonomy" under Israeli control. The Shamir/Baker Plan for the West Bank, Syria noted, conceded even less to the Palestinians than the Camp David Accords, which Israel had reneged upon. Arafat unilaterally conceded everything Israel and the United States demanded—notably recognition of Israel—in hopes of winning U.S. recognition and worldwide backing, but he got nothing in return. The episode only exposed Israel's unwillingness to make any concessions involving Arab rights. Given the PLO's concessions, the lessening of Soviet hostility toward Israel, and the *intifadah*, Israel should have been ready to negotiate, observed a Syrian diplomat in 1989, but, in fact, it had only become more rigid. Syrians were too proud to concede their rights, Asad declared, simply to win world opinion.

Asad was convinced the PLO alone lacked the leverage to wrest the West Bank and Gaza from Israel and that Arafat could not settle for less without splitting the PLO and giving Syria the chance to sponsor an alternative Palestinian leadership. Expecting the process to fail, and suspecting that Shamir would sabotage his own plan if it looked like it had any chance of success, Asad felt no pressing need to try to scuttle the process. In any event, he preferred that Israel, not Syria, be blamed for its failure. He also calculated that the costs of trying to impede a process that had wide Arab, Palestinian, and international backing might be too high. Furthermore, there was an outside chance that the negotiations might develop into a real peace process in which Syria would want to be included. Syrian policy, as Asad put it, was to "wait and see."[58]

Asad's disputes with Arafat during the 1980s provided new insights into the Syrian notion of Palestinian rights. Syria insisted that Arafat alone, despite his backing by the Palestine National Council, did not represent Palestinian opinion, and that radical Palestinian factions opposed to him may have been more representative of Palestinian aspirations. Furthermore, it was Syria's position that Palestinians from the occupied territories could not bargain away the rights of other Palestinians. Because Palestine was once part of Syria, Damascus insisted it had a legitimate say in defining Palestinian rights. Thus Syria made it clear that it would not automatically accept the PLO's definition of Palestinian rights.

The cleavage between Syria and the PLO has been a major obstacle in the peace process. Asad's belief that Arafat could not be held to a common bargaining position was a major factor in his determination to avoid negotiations with Israel in the 1980s. In an effort to show that Arafat could not deliver the whole Palestinian community into a separate peace, he sponsored guerrilla attacks by more militant Palestinian factions on Israel from southern Lebanon and through Jordan; this, of course, only hardened Israeli determination to make no concessions to either Syria or the PLO. Despite a decade of conflict, Asad failed to impose his strategy on the PLO. Therefore, a reconciliation between the two parties is necessary if they are to forge a credible joint bargaining position in the peace process.

THE PURSUIT OF MILITARY PARITY

Between 1978 and 1988, Syria engaged in an enormous military buildup, which gave it a formidable military machine for a country of its size and turned it into a major regional power. This buildup was almost exclusively a product of the renewed struggle with Israel that had been set in motion by the exhaustion of the peace process. After Egypt signed a peace treaty with Israel and Iraq launched a war against Iran, the military balance tilted sharply against Syria. Asad, with Soviet help, set out to give Syria "strategic parity" with Israel.

This was not easily achieved. By the late 1970s, however, Syria's military force of 230,000 men, 2,500 tanks, and 500 airplanes was larger and better equipped than it had been in 1973. And although Syria added only one division during this period, increasing the number from five to six, its infantry divisions were now all mechanized. However, the number of Israeli armored divisions also grew, from seven in 1973 to eleven in 1982.[59] In addition, Syria's Soviet-equipped forces were a technological step behind Israel's, which were equipped with electronically advanced U.S. weaponry. Israel also acquired electronic countermeasures to neutralize Syrian air defenses. At the time of the invasion of Lebanon in 1982, the Israeli army was superior to Syria's in leadership, organization, and training and retained a quantitative superiority in overall manpower.

The 1982 war, in encouraging the idea that Israel could be matched and in exposing Syria's vulnerabilities, gave further impetus to Syria's buildup. On the one hand, Syria's ground forces had "proved their mettle in an uneven battle."[60] According to an Israeli military historian, the qualitative gap between the Israeli and Syrian troops "took a nosedive" in this war compared to previous wars.[61] Even with a significant technological and numerical advantage, Israel could not inflict a quick and decisive defeat. On the other hand, Syria could not cope with Israeli high-performance aircraft, Airborne Warning and Control (AWAC), and electronic warfare capabilities. Its army clearly lacked the capacity to defend both the Golan and Lebanese fronts simultaneously. The war also showed Syria that it could not avoid an Israeli attack just by refraining from provocation. Finally, U.S. intervention in Lebanon after the war posed new threats to Syrian security.

Syria's accelerated buildup resulted in an extraordinary expansion of its armed forces after 1982. By 1989, the Syrian military possessed over 4,000 tanks, including advanced T-72s and T-74s, the best in the Soviet inventory. It had over 2,000 artillery pieces, more than 500 combat planes, including 200 high-performance aircraft (MIG-23 interceptors and MIG-27 ground attack aircraft), and 102 missile batteries. Twenty-two missile boats, several submarines, and a coastal missile defense system buttressed the navy. Three new divisions were formed, and by 1989 Syria had two army corps comprising a total of nine mechanized or armored divisions, each with its own artillery and air defense. Syria's standing military enlisted 585,000 men by 1986, with 300,000 regular forces and the rest active reserves. By 1989, the standing army had been reduced to 404,000, but there were almost 300,000 soldiers in the reserves. Syria's large reserve force suggested it was approaching the total mobilization achieved by Israel. By the end of the 1980s, Syria had closed the

TABLE 1.   THE SYRIAN-ISRAELI MILITARY BALANCE, 1988–1989

	Israel	*Syria*
Manpower	645,000	676,000
active	141,000	404,000
reserves	504,000	272,000
Tanks	3,850	4,050
Artillery	1,361	2,150
Armored Personal Carriers	8,100	3,800
Combat Aircraft	635	500 +

Sources: The International Institute for Strategic Studies, *The Military Balance, 1988–1989* (London) and Shlomo Gazit, *The Middle East Military Balance, 1988–1989* (Boulder, Colorado: Westview Press, 1989).[63]

gap with Israel in quantitative terms (Table 1), but Israel clearly retained its qualitative superiority.[62]

Syria has addressed some, but not all, of its qualitative weaknesses. Most important, a new Soviet-supplied long-range air umbrella is in place. Short-range SAMs, long-range high-altitude SAM-5s, radar, electronic jammers, and an advanced command-and-control system are integrated into an air defense system that is comparable to the one used in the Soviet Union's home defense. This network, which is dense and effective on the military fronts, would cost the Israelis much greater losses than they suffered in 1982 if they were to decide to destroy it. But there are gaps in the defense of other areas of the country. Moreover, the reliability of the system has been cast in doubt by the United States' ability to counter SAM-5s in Libya in its strike against Muammar el-Qaddafi in 1986 and by ineffectively countered Israeli overflights. Israel remains far superior in sophisticated electronic warfare capabilities and has access to the United States' very best weaponry. Soviet-supplied equipment (especially its electronic components) is generally inferior to the Western equivalents supplied to Israel.[64] Without doubt, Syria closely observed the performance of the U.S., British, and French high-technology air forces in the war against Iraq to get a better idea of what its Soviet-equipped forces might be confronted with in a future air war with Israel. Its conclusions cannot have been heartening.

Syria is also trying to assemble a deterrent force. With its 200–250 missiles and strike aircraft, it is capable of hitting Israel itself. In addition to its older Scud missiles, it has acquired highly accurate SS-21s and improved Scuds. Syria also has chemical warheads. Israeli experts estimate that if all Syrian missiles were chemically armed they could inflict 2,000 deaths and 10,000 injuries.[65] How far this constitutes a deterrent is unclear. In a time of high tension, the Syrian missiles could invite a preemptive strike, although their dispersal makes it hard for Israel to destroy them all before Syria could launch a counterstrike. But because the destructive capacity of Israel's nuclear weapons is many times that of Syria's chemical arsenal, Israel may calculate that Syria would not risk responding to a preemptive attack.

The Syrian-Israeli military gap is most marked in respect to the human element. Syrian generalship remains a big question mark. Syria also remains far behind in command-and-control capabilities. Although they are quite competent in conducting simpler operations, such as concentrating firepower, the ability of Syrian commanders to coordinate rapid, large-scale mobile operations is limited by the army's level of training and equipment. There have been gradual improvements in the technical and tactical capabilities of the Syrian soldier. However, even though the army's professionalism has increased, it remains afflicted with politicization, sectarian tensions, and corruption, ills that are bound to reduce the efficiency, cohesion, motivation, and combat performance of its men. The officer corps cannot match Israel's in tactical flexibility and initiative. Although the more basic Soviet equipment is rugged and easily maintained, the army suffers from chronic maintenance and service problems and is having difficulty absorbing its most advanced equipment. Reportedly, the most advanced aircraft are not regularly operational.[66]

By the late 1980s, the Syrian military buildup leveled off: The large deliveries of arms and equipment had been completed, the exceptional threat of the early 1980s had passed, economic constraints were tightening, and the Soviet Union was indicating its unwillingness to continue backing Syria's arms race with Israel. Syria's military capability seemed unlikely to suffer a precipitous decline, since Moscow was reducing, not abandoning, its commitments, and Syria continued to take delivery of new arms that qualitatively upgraded its forces. But there were fewer deliveries on less desirable terms than in the mid-1980s. As a result, Syria may fall further behind Israel, since the latter will not stand still, and its military is likely to develop its high-technology dimensions in ways Syria will find impossible to match.

To what extent, if at all, has Syria achieved military parity with Israel? In its most limited sense, parity signifies a defensive deterrent. But its implications go beyond this. Syria believes successful diplomacy cannot be conducted from weakness. Therefore, a relative power balance is an essential condition of negotiations. In its most ambitious dimension, parity amounts to a credible threat to make war, or at least the ability to keep tensions high, in the absence of a peace settlement. In a wider sense, Syria has defined parity so as to include economic strength, technological advancement, and the availability of human resources, as well as a system of Arab alliances and a favorable international context.

Defensively at least, the Syrian army has become a formidable force. Given the current balance of forces, an Israeli attack on Syria would likely be very costly. Since 1973, the Syrian army has a record of tenacity that has consistently denied Israel a knockout blow. On the Golan Heights, the ratio between force size and the area to be defended permits concentrated Syrian deployment in depth and allows the most effective use of the weapons Syria excels in, such as artillery and anti-tank weapons. Israeli troops on the offensive here would run into heavily fortified defenses, forcing Israel to choose between a costly war of attrition and risky escalation. Syria is more vulnerable to an Israeli strike through the Bekaa Valley. But a blitzkrieg war resulting in an early Israeli victory, low casualties, and a limited period of mobilization appears to be a thing of the past. Indeed, a basic element of Syria's deterrence strategy is maintaining the capacity to inflict greater casualties than Israel can politically withstand when the country's very survival is not at stake. Until recently, Syria also appeared to enjoy a Soviet pledge, understood by the Israelis, to come to its aid if attacked on its home territory.[67]

A basic strategic issue is whether Syria possesses a credible means to break the current stalemate with Israel. In practice, the question is whether it has the ability to launch a limited initiative on the Golan Heights without the expectation of total defeat. If Syria could make some territorial gains, wage a war of attrition confined to the Golan, and prevent a quick Israeli victory, the negative political effect of casualties and the high costs of mobilization could put Israel in a disadvantageous position. The ensuing crisis might invite superpower or international intervention. Such an initiative would require an army large enough to contain an Israeli counteroffensive and a deterrent (air defenses and a missile or chemical warfare capability) against Israeli escalation.

In theory at least, Syria may have such a capability. Since the ratio of forces stationed permanently on the Golan is to Syria's advantage, and because Syria can launch an attack without sizable preliminary movements, a surprise attack might, as in 1973, result in the seizure of at least part of the Golan before the rest of Israel's forces could be mobilized.[68] But once Israel was fully mobilized, Syria would find itself at a sharp disadvantage. Syria would also have to calculate whether it could prevent Israel from widening the war beyond the Golan theater. Moreover, many of the conditions that facilitated Syria's limited success on the Golan is 1973 are less in evidence in the 1990s. Lebanon would almost certainly be part of the theater of operations, forcing Syria to spread its defenses more widely. The Arab war coalition, which fell apart after 1973, has not been reconstructed, and Iraqi support, which would probably be essential, is unlikely today. The Soviets could not be expected to support an offensive on the Golan (and might actually be able to veto one). And Syria can have little faith in superpower action to rein in Israel. At the same time, after the U.S.–led war to push Iraq out of Kuwait, Syria can have no illusions about how Washington would respond if Israel's security were really threatened. If Syria were to attack Israel now, it would run a serious risk of losing even more territory and of once again suffering heavy damage to its infrastructure as a result of strategic bombing, just as it did in 1973.

Therefore, in reality, Syria does not appear to possess sufficient offensive capability to make a decision to go to war rational or likely. Syrian planning appears to be geared primarily to absorbing an Israeli attack and then counterattacking on the Golan. When some Syrian leaders began to claim that Syria had achieved strategic parity, the ever-cautious Asad reminded them that parity involved not just tanks but economic and social capabilities as well. Although a Syrian offensive is highly unlikely, the possibility cannot be completely ruled out. Decisions to go to war are rarely based only on a calculus of the balance of power, but are also shaped by frustrations. If, at some point, Damascus believed that diplomatic avenues were totally exhausted, it might consider war preferable to unending stalemate. Moreover, assessments of the balance of forces are matters of judgment. On the eve of the 1973 war, the Central Intelligence Agency held that an attack on Israel would be "suicidal" for Syria. Asad obviously thought differently.[69]

If Syria were able to reconstruct an Arab war coalition similar to the one that launched the 1973 war, the strategic balance might be more favorable to the Arabs and, therefore, the threat of a Syrian strike much more credible. Although in every previous Arab-Israeli war to date Israel actually deployed more men than the combined Arab armies, the ratios could be quite different if a new Arab alliance were to emerge. George Ball calculated that by 1986, Syria, Jordan, and Iraq alone would have been able to mobilize 1.27 million men to Israel's 700,000.[70] Moreover, if an Arab coalition including Egypt were reconstructed, Israel would be forced to fight on more than one front. To be sure, there are powerful obstacles to the realization of this scenario, but in an area as volatile as the Middle East, where a single assassin's bullet or a coup d'état can change the political environment and military equation overnight, the possibility cannot be disregarded. Israeli war planners have to prepare for the worst case. Even if an Arab war coalition could not be forged in advance, under the right political conditions other states might join in a war of attrition started by Syria. Israel clearly understands the strategic importance of preventing the emergence of an Arab war coalition, as indicated by its public declaration that any movement of Iraqi forces into Syria or Jordan, or any violation by Egypt of the Sinai demilitarization agreement, could constitute grounds for war. An Israeli preemptive strike in the face of such an Arab threat is one way in which a general war could be set off.

Syria's drive for parity has bolstered its military standing: One calculation of the elements of power (including population, GNP, and military order of battle) shows a decreasing gap between Syria and Israel from 1970 to 1984.[71] But the effort to match Israel has been costly and contributed to the economic stagnation that afflicted the country in the 1980s. By the early 1990s, the economic (and political) realities limiting Syria's ability to compete militarily with Israel were generating new incentives to find a peaceful way to resolve the conflict.

NEW DANGERS, NEW OPPORTUNITIES

There were signs at the beginning of 1990 of an alteration in Asad's strategy, if not in his goals, which opened up new diplomatic avenues. Asad realized that the prospects for a military solution were melting away with the decline of Soviet power. Unable to mount a credible threat of war, no longer able to play the Palestinian card, challenged by General Aoun and by Iraq in Lebanon, its Iranian alliance frayed, and unable to depend on strong Soviet political backing, Syria was at a new low point. Asad also realized that the policy of tactical rejectionism could leave Syria behind any peace bandwagon should one, against all expectations, start moving.

While eschewing any major departure from his goals, Asad nonetheless began to adapt to changing realities. He toned down his opposition to negotiations and began to rebuild his links to the Arab world. Syria's rapprochement with Egypt in December 1989 was a major step along this road. Some saw the reconciliation as an attempt by Asad to draw Egypt gradually back into the Arab-Israeli strategic equation. But it is more probable that it was an acknowledgement that Egypt's peace strategy could be a viable option and that Egyptian-Syrian solidarity was essential to a strong Arab bargaining hand. Asad anticipated that, once the failure of Arafat's peace initiative and the Shamir/Baker Plan became evident, his position against separate negotiations would be vindicated and other Arab parties would again recognize Syria's centrality, both requisites for the effective pursuit of a comprehensive settlement.

The point of Asad's policy, easily missed, was to position Syria to rejoin a serious peace process if one seemed to be in the cards and Arab solidarity could be reconstructed. Despite a decade of tactical rejectionism, Syria had never abandoned the ultimate aim of attaining a political settlement. Syria was, after all, a party to the 1982 Fez Declaration, which expressed the Arab consensus on pursuing a peaceful settlement based on UN Resolution 242 and the establishment of a Palestinian state; in its aftermath, the Syrian information minister had reaffirmed Syria's willingness to sign a peace agreement if Israel withdrew to its 1967 borders. Asad also formally signed on to the Casablanca PNC resolution in which the PLO stated it would accept Israel in return for a Palestinian state. In the late 1980s, Asad indicated to a number of U.S. delegations his readiness to make peace with Israel under the right circumstances.[72] To be sure, if Syria were to participate in a peace settlement in which the Fez conditions were not met, the regime would be deprived of its role as the champion of Arab grievances, which is a crucial source of its legitimacy. If the only possible settlement is one that legitimizes Israel's conquests and confirms its dominance, Asad is likely to see his historical role as the last keeper of the Arab cause against the capitulationism of the other Arab leaders. But Syria basically carries the banner of a just peace, not rejectionism, and a settlement based on UN Resolution 242 would garner Asad credit for having led the Arabs to an honorable peace that restored their dignity.

Asad's conditions for a settlement remained largely unchanged at the beginning of 1990. Israel's withdrawal to the 1967 lines was essential. Syria would not enter open-ended discussions that held out little prospect of success. Rather, a proper "legal framework" had to be agreed upon: Israel had to demonstrate that it really wanted peace by accepting as a basis for negotiations UN Resolution 242 and other resolutions dealing with the Palestinian right of return or compensation. Asad would not negotiate unless he believed that the Israelis were serious about trading land for peace or that the international situation was such that they could be forced to do so. If he is cautious in this respect, it is because the political costs of failure are high: It could delegitimize his regime and, in showing that his strategy had reached a dead end, fuel opposition, particularly from Islamic fundamentalists. Because Asad believes it is a matter of honor to carry out the terms of agreements, he is all the more cautious in making such commitments. To those who advocate that he enter into unconditional negotiations or make a gesture like Sadat's trip to Jerusalem in order to overcome the psychological barriers that block progress in reaching a settlement, he responds that Israel's concession to Egypt resulted from its interest in splitting the Arabs and that no such interest exists on the other fronts.

Asad believed that negotiations must take place within the framework of an international conference with PLO and Soviet participation. While he did not exclude bilateral negotiations on purely bilateral matters under the umbrella of such a conference, he maintained that "comprehensive" issues had to be decided by the Arab side collectively. Because he now had some cause to fear the imposition of a U.S.–Soviet deal at his expense, he, like the Israelis, did not want a conference that would simply legitimize a peace dictated by the superpowers. But since Israel resisted all concessions, Asad believed Washington had to be prepared to play an active and even-handed role if such a conference were to succeed. Asad also wanted superpower and UN guarantees that Israel would comply with its agreements, particularly since any settlement was likely to be a phased one. Open and ironclad guarantees, not toothless or private assurances, were essential. A phased settlement would be acceptable so long as Syrian sovereignty over the Golan Heights was acknowledged. In return for a just settlement, a full peace was possible. Friendship could not be imposed, but as confidence built and Palestinian rights were acknowledged, the normalization of relations could be expected to follow. These conditions were almost identical to the world consensus, but far, indeed, from what Israel was prepared to accept.

The precipitous rise of war fever in the Middle East during the first half of 1990 showed how quickly the political climate can change in this volatile area. The decline of the Soviet Union, the influx of Soviet Jews into Israel, the growing fear among Palestinians that they would be expelled from the West Bank, the exchange of threats between Israel and Iraq over the use of weapons of mass destruction, the breakoff of the U.S.–PLO dialogue, and the rise of the hard-line Shamir government in Israel revived fears of war and Israeli expansionism in Syria and the Arab world. Asad, in several apocalyptic speeches, reflected the new mood. He warned that the "new international order" threatened to "unleash wild beasts" against the Arab world. Israel would find new opportunities for expansion while the Arabs were paralyzed by confusion and rivalry. But while Israel could inflict disaster on the Arabs, the Arabs could retaliate and, having more "human depth," prevail: "What is coming is not a limited danger but a danger of destiny."[73]

There were indications, too, that Arab leaders were awakening to the need for Arab solidarity in the face of common dangers and that the failure of bilateralism vindicated Asad in his insistence on a strong Arab stance as the key to a settlement. While remaining at odds with the Syrian leader, Saddam Hussein of Iraq echoed his belief that Israel would only negotiate when the Arabs had military credibility. Syria supported Iraq in its war of rhetoric with Israel. The PLO, which considered the "dialogue" with Israel to have been aborted, reverted to pushing for an international conference. Asad declared that Arafat would be welcome in Damascus. Washington's allies moved closer to the Syrian position too. Jordan's growing fear of Israel was leading it to seek protection under the umbrella of Arab solidarity. Egypt warned the Israelis that it would not stand idle if Israel attacked Iraq (this was prior to the Iraqi invasion of Kuwait) and worked to bring about the Arab unity needed to play a strong hand in peace negotiations. Participants in the 1990 Baghdad Summit spoke of the need for a new Arab order to guarantee "Arab national security" and affirmed the obligations of the Arab states, including Egypt, under the Arab Defense Pact. A certain radicalization of Arab public opinion, fueled by the apparent failure of the U.S.–brokered peace process, was apparent. But Asad refused to attend the Baghdad Summit, evidence that the Syrian-Iraqi rivalry continued to poison the waters of Arab solidarity.

The Shamir government, which was formed in mid-1990 and was perhaps the most right-wing government in Israel's history, returned to power many of the same men who were responsible for the 1982 invasion of Lebanon, most notably Ariel Sharon and Rafael Eitan. The inclusion in the governing coalition of a party that openly called for the expulsion of Palestinians from the occupied territories greatly intensified Arab fears. Throughout the Arab world, Shamir's new government was seen as a war cabinet. Shamir assured the Arabs that Israel harbored no aggressive designs and called upon Asad to come to Israel to negotiate peace. He also asserted that the Middle East conflict was between the Arab states and Israel, intending thereby to exclude the PLO as a party to negotiations. Syrians took this as a bid by Shamir for a separate peace settlement at the expense of the Palestinians.[74] Although Asad used the occasion to signal to Arafat that Syria, too, could make a separate deal with Israel, he is unlikely to permit Syria's conflict with Israel to be separated from the Palestinian issue.

The Iraqi invasion of Kuwait in August 1990 gave another shake to the Middle East kaleidoscope and had major consequences for the Syrian-Israeli conflict. Israel was initially relieved of pressures to negotiate a settlement: The emerging Arab solidarity was shattered, as Iraq replaced Israel as the immediate security threat to the Arab states, and the United States was diverted from the peace process. Syria's stand against Iraq was motivated in part by Asad's strategy in the Arab-Israeli conflict: He gambled that any solution to the Iraqi occupation of Kuwait would have to be followed by a solution to the Israeli occupation of Arab lands. This is one more piece of evidence that Asad, far from being a pan-Arab revolutionary, is essentially a conservative-minded backer of the status quo state system in the Middle East. His cautious outlook and limited goals were reflected in his reaction to Saddam's invasion: It had, he declared, jeopardized Syria's security by initiating a regional war into which Israel might be drawn, and it had undermined the principle of the inadmissibility of acquiring territory by force—the very principle the Arabs cited to justify their claims to lands lost to Israel. Asad's status quo policy, together with Syria's and Israel's common fear of Iraq, could generate a perception of shared interests favorable to the peace process. Asad's unwillingness to allow Saddam Hussein to drag Syria into a wider Arab-Israeli war, even if Israel had responded to Iraqi missile strikes, should give Israel greater confidence that Syria's ambitions are limited. The apparent resurrection of the Egyptian-Syrian-Saudi axis, which pursued a peace settlement in the 1970s, may also favor the peace process. But this was a high-risk strategy for Asad: It was very unpopular at home, where Saddam Hussein was seen as a hero of Arab nationalism. In appearing to put his personal and regime interests ahead of pan-Arab concerns, Asad risked what legitimacy his regime retains.

In July 1991, Asad accepted U.S. proposals for a peace conference, making major concessions on the procedural arrangements Syria has traditionally demanded. Syria would enter into bilateral negotiations as opposed to participating in negotiations as part of a united Arab delegation; the United Nations would have a minimal role; and the full conference would convene only sporadically. U.S. assurances that it viewed the UN land-for-peace resolutions as the basis for a settlement and rejected the Israeli annexation of the Golan Heights gave Syria reason to hope that if bilateral negotiations deadlocked, the full conference would be reconvened and the United States would play a role in pushing Israel toward an acceptable position.

Asad has invested so much political capital in his rapprochement with the United States and the revival of the peace process that further risks seemed preferable to the costs of failure. His procedural rigidity was always rooted in his fear of separate deals being struck in bilateral negotiations; he may have calculated that he now has less reason to fear exclusion from negotiations and a separate peace settlement by Jordan and the PLO, given Syria's greater standing and the diminished stature of these parties as a result of the Persian Gulf War. Asad does not want Syria to be blamed for any failure of the peace process and painted as a regional bully that must be dealt with in the same way as Saddam Hussein's Iraq was. Rather, his move puts the ball in Israel's court. So far, Israel appears unprepared to satisfy Syria's conditions for a settlement: The Shamir government denied that UN Resolution 242 applies to the Golan Heights, assured settlers that Israel will never withdraw, and committed itself to new housing designed to double the Israeli population there. If Israel refuses to budge in its attitude toward Syria, Asad is likely to retreat from his position of moderation, and this unprecedented opportunity to settle the Arab-Israeli conflict will end, once more, at a dangerous impasse.

5

SYRIA AND THE SUPERPOWERS

Although the Syrian-Israeli conflict has been confined for the most part to the immediate region, Hafiz al-Asad has never lost sight of the broader global context within which the dispute is embedded. He recognizes the necessity of mobilizing all available resources within the regional environment in support of his goals, but he also knows that Syria cannot fight Israel or, equally important, make peace with it, without superpower involvement. For most of his rule, Asad has expertly exploited Cold War tensions to Syria's advantage, relying on Soviet military, economic, and diplomatic assistance to enable him to build his country into a major regional power. Without that backing, Syria could not have supported so large a military machine and could not have sustained its ambitious regional policies. But the world has entered a period of tumultuous and dramatic change, the many consequences of which are not yet fully apparent. What is clear is that many of Asad's inveterate assumptions about a relatively stable bipolar world in which he could manipulate superpower rivalries to Syria's benefit no longer hold true.

Since the mid-1980s, Soviet policy toward the Middle East has undergone a major shift, the many effects of which have been magnified by the Soviet Union's sharply declining global power and growing preoccupation with its own severe internal problems. Perhaps no country stands to be so affected by this shift as Syria. At the same time that circumstances within the Soviet Union have forced it to disengage from the Middle East, Moscow has sought to cooperate constructively with the West in resolving the region's disputes. In effect, the Middle East has ceased to be a zone of confrontation in which the superpowers compete in a zero-sum game and their clients and proxies can exploit Cold War tensions. The crisis brought on by Iraq's invasion of Kuwait in August 1990 underlined how the end of the Cold War has radically and dramatically transformed super-

149

power relations in the Middle East: Not only was the Soviet Union powerless to oppose the deployment of U.S. forces in the Persian Gulf, it actively supported U.S. objectives and cooperated with the UN Security Council in trying to end the Iraqi occupation. It is possible that this first post–Cold War crisis will be a historic turning point, out of which may be fashioned a framework for the resolution of other regional disputes. The Helsinki Summit between presidents Bush and Gorbachev in September 1990 showed that the United States was at least beginning to recognize the benefits of including the Soviet Union in future efforts to resolve the Arab-Israeli dispute.

At the same time, U.S.–Syrian relations have improved, despite Washington's entirely appropriate concerns about the Asad regime's human rights record. The two governments have worked closely on the issue of Lebanon and have a common, if not completely identical, interest in the overthrow of Saddam Hussein. Secretary of State James Baker's visit to Damascus in September 1990, and the meeting between presidents Bush and Asad in Geneva in November 1990, underlined the importance that both Washington and Damascus attach to developing a closer relationship. In sum, by early 1991 the global climate had, in many respects, never been better for a joint superpower effort to solve the conflict.

THE SOVIET UNION AND SYRIA

Origins of the Soviet-Syrian Relationship

Historically, Soviet policy toward the Middle East has been shaped more by geostrategic considerations than by ideological ones. Because of the the Middle East's proximity, the Soviet Union has traditionally considered the region to be a key element in its defense perimeter. Moscow's primary goal, until very recently, was to prevent intervention by a rival power in the countries along its southern flank and to nourish a friendly local environment, a formidable challenge given the numerous opportunities for Western involvement afforded by the multitude of conflicts and the existence of some two-thirds of the world's proven oil reserves within the region.[1] The Arab-Israeli conflict has, for most of the post–World War II period, provided Moscow with its main opening in the region: Soviet influence is largely based on its consistent political and military support for the Arab position. Within the Middle East, Syria has been one of the Soviet Union's principal points of access and one of its closest allies since the early 1970s (Iraq has been its other major client). This continues to be the case, despite the upheaval within the Eastern bloc and despite strong indications recently that the relationship has lost some of its value to Moscow.

The Syrian-Soviet relationship has evolved almost entirely within the context of the Arab-Israeli dispute. From Syria's perspective, the alliance is based solely on its need for military, diplomatic, and economic support. With the exception of a shared antipathy toward Western imperialism, there is no particular ideological sympathy, no natural kinship, and no tradition of cultural interaction with the Soviet Union to nourish and sustain the friendship otherwise. Syria's Communist parties have always been small and lack influence in a country where most of the population is Muslim and where capitalist instincts and entrepreneurial skills are highly developed, notwithstanding the Ba'thi regime's quasi-socialist economic policies. Nonetheless, it is largely Soviet backing that has permitted Asad to transform Syria from a weak country into a major regional power whose interests must be accommodated to some degree.

Despite the closeness of their relationship, Syria and the Soviet Union have not always agreed with one another, and Syria has demonstrated its independence on numerous occasions (a Soviet joke has it that the Asad regime accepts everything from Moscow except advice). However, because both sides needed one another, they were careful not to let differences of opinion threaten the relationship. Although the dependencies are mutual, they have seldom been symmetrical. Understandably, the Asad regime is currently much more concerned about how reliable an ally the Soviet Union is than vice versa—in sharp contrast to the 1970s, when the roles were reversed.

Prior to the mid-1950s, the Soviet Union was less interested in what happened in the Arab world than in the neighboring countries of Turkey, Iran, and Afghanistan. But it could not ignore efforts by the West to sponsor a military alliance in the region through the Baghdad Pact, which it viewed as a dangerous extension of NATO into its southern periphery. Consequently, it joined with Egypt and Syria to undermine the creation of an alliance that Arab nationalists considered a means of perpetuating Western imperialist control of the region. Syria favored a neutralist foreign policy but was driven to seek support from the Soviet Union primarily out of defensive considerations: To the north lay Turkey, a powerful NATO member and close American ally; to its east and south lay Hashemite Iraq and Jordan, which were closely aligned with Britain; to its west lay freewheeling Lebanon, a haven for antiregime Syrian exiles and where the United States intervened militarily in 1958; and, most important, to the southwest lay Israel, with which there were frequent border skirmishes. Syria first purchased arms from the Eastern bloc in 1955, which accentuated Western fears about growing Soviet influence in the region. To counter the perceived threat, the United States covertly backed antiregime elements in Syria and prodded Turkey to initiate military maneuvers along Syria's border. These threats heightened Syria's sense of vulnerability and pushed it further into the arms of the Soviet Union, which seized the opportunity to sell Damascus more weapons and to sign a major economic assistance and technical cooperation agreement with the Syrians in October 1957.

Soviet-Syrian ties blossomed after the Ba'thi revolution in 1963 and flourished after 1966, when the radical neo-Ba'th came to power. The left-wing regime of Salah Jadid moved Syria closer to the Soviet Union than ever before, and, for the first time, a strong element of ideological affinity linked the two governments, although Moscow reportedly had certain misgivings about Jadid's recklessness. Jadid fashioned an authoritarian one-party state, which advocated the region's revolutionary transformation and called for the overthrow of conservative pro-Western monarchical regimes. Syria's economy was transformed along nominally socialist lines, and an ambitious program of rapid industrialization, agrarian reform, and infrastructural development was initiated with large-scale assistance from Moscow

(Soviet help was especially important in the Euphrates dam project, oil development, and port and railway construction).

After each of Syria's major wars with Israel, Soviet involvement increased sharply. Following its stunning defeat in 1967, Syria was forced to rebuild its armed forces almost completely, a task that could only have been accomplished with massive Soviet assistance. For Moscow, the investment seemed worthwhile: The Jadid regime broke off diplomatic relations with the United States and several other Western countries after the war and offered itself as a key ally in the very heart of the Middle East.

The Asad Regime

Initially, Moscow was concerned about Asad's assumption of power in 1970 since it was known that he had misgivings about Syria's growing dependence on the Soviet Union and was reputed to be an independent-minded nationalist who always placed self-interest above ideology. Although Asad did not favor such close ties to Moscow as Jadid, he recognized that Soviet support was indispensable to achieving his goal of reclaiming the Golan Heights. He therefore moved quickly to reassure Moscow about his intentions when he visited the Soviet Union in February 1971, shortly after coming to power. As a result, the coup hardly disrupted relations at all: The volume of bilateral exchanges and economic activity with the Eastern bloc grew significantly, and several arms deals were concluded in 1971 and 1972. The Soviet Union soon came to prefer the cautious and predictable Asad to his predecessor.

The turning point in Soviet-Syrian relations occurred after Egypt expelled some 15,000 Soviet advisers and technicians in July 1972, dealing a severe blow to Moscow's plans and prestige in the region. Until then, the Soviets had clearly regarded Syria as secondary to Egypt, the pivotal state in the Arab world. Syria became the main Soviet point of entry to the region after the breach with Sadat. One of Moscow's objectives in building ties with Syria was to obtain port facilities for its naval squadron in the Mediterranean. Another was to make Syria a showcase, so as to demonstrate the benefits of Moscow's backing to other third world states and restore the Soviet Union's image in the Middle East, which had been tarnished by the break with Cairo.

The October War and Its Aftermath

Despite the Soviet Union's growing influence, it was never able to dissuade Syria from pursuing any course of action that it deemed to be in its national interest. From the beginning of his rule, Asad was determined to regain the Golan Heights. To this end, he began devising secret war plans with Egypt early in 1971. After the failure of the Nixon-Brezhnev summit conference in June 1973 to devise a plan to break the deadlock in the region, Asad gave up all hope that the occupied territories could be recovered by peaceful means. The Soviet Union was not in favor of war, which it feared would hinder détente and possibly lead to a confrontation with the United States in the region. However, to retain its influence with Egypt and Syria, it had to be responsive to their requests for weapons. Once the war began, Moscow tried to contain the fighting and end the hostilities, but it could not sit back and see its allies suffer another defeat. Consequently, it airlifted massive quantities of arms to the region and instructed Soviet personnel to offer advice and support. After Israel recaptured the Golan Heights and began advancing across the prewar cease-fire line toward Damascus, Moscow placed several airborne divisions on full alert and informed Washington that it would defend the Syrian capital.

The war ended the stalemate and set negotiations between the Arabs and Israelis in motion. The Soviet Union favored the convening of an international conference to be chaired by both superpowers under the aegis of the United Nations to hammer out a comprehensive settlement. However, Soviet pressure on Syria to participate in the planned Geneva Conference—in which Moscow hoped to play a major role—was to no avail, and in December 1973 Asad announced that he would not attend. One of the Soviet Union's chief concerns was that it would be excluded from the peace process and that Syria would follow Egypt's lead and participate in U.S.–sponsored negotiations. It did not oppose the U.S.–mediated Israeli-Egyptian and Israeli-Syrian disengagement agreements—signed in January 1974 and May 1974, respectively—which defused the risk of military confrontation in the region and which it hoped might eventually lead to a comprehensive settlement. But the disengagement agreements confirmed that the United States was better positioned to act as a peace broker, and the prospect that it might achieve a Pax Americana in the region was disquieting to Moscow. Reconvening the Geneva Conference and building a multilateral peace process was the most obvious way to forestall this possibility and ensure that the Soviet Union would have a role to play.

Moscow's desire to internationalize the peace process—that is to say, to secure a role for itself—heightened as Egypt moved out of its orbit and Asad expressed a desire to improve Syria's ties with the United States. After Syria signed the disengagement agreement with Israel, President Richard M. Nixon visited Damascus, and diplomatic relations, which had been severed in 1967, were restored in June 1974. But the honeymoon did not last long: Asad soon recognized that Washington was investing its energy in brokering another separate Egyptian-Israeli agreement. Asad's opposition to separate deals, which split Arab ranks, further soured his relations with Sadat and created a convergence between Syrian and Soviet interests. During a visit to Moscow in September 1974, Asad came around to the Soviet position favoring the reconvening of the Geneva Conference.

The U.S.–mediated second Egyptian-Israeli disengagement agreement of September 1975, which Damascus and Moscow both opposed, led to a sharp deterioration in U.S.–Syrian relations. At the same time, the agreement once again suggested that the United States alone could persuade Israel to make concessions. In March 1976, Egypt formally abrogated its 1971 Treaty of Friendship and Cooperation with the Soviet Union, ending two decades of close ties. Syria's assessment that the Egyptian-Israeli deal left it exposed and weakened the Arab position pushed Damascus even closer to Moscow, which now saw Syria as pivotal to its Middle East policy. In October 1975, Asad once again visited the Soviet capital, where his request for more arms was favorably received.

The Lebanese Civil War

The mutual dependence between Syria and the Soviet Union, which grew as Egypt pursued a separate peace settlement with Israel under U.S. auspices, did not preclude the rise of serious differences between them. Syria's intervention in Lebanon, in particular, created tension. Initially, the Asad regime's attempts to defuse the worsening situation in Lebanon in 1975 met with Moscow's approval, since Syria had aligned itself with the PLO and the leftists. Damascus and Moscow shared the view that the strife in Lebanon was the result of a U.S.–supported Zionist plot to divide the Arabs and provide cover for a separate Egyptian-Israeli deal. But when Syria intervened militarily in June 1976, it did so to prevent the PLO-Muslim leftist alliance from defeating the Christian rightists. The ensuing confrontation between its allies placed the Soviet Union in an awkward position, and, in July, Leonid I. Brezhnev sent a letter to Asad that strongly criticized the intervention and threatened sanctions if Syria did not withdraw. The Soviet Union also temporarily stopped arms deliveries. Asad ignored the reprimand, but at the same time he was careful to avoid an open break. Gradually, the Soviet Union, recognizing that it could not push the Syrian regime to act against what it perceived to be its vital interests, came to accept Syria's role in Lebanon.

The Impact of Camp David

Jimmy Carter's assumption of the presidency in 1977 revived hopes that the Geneva Conference would be reconvened and that the Soviet Union would be permitted to take on a more important role in resolving the Arab-Israeli dispute. A joint U.S.–Soviet statement issued by Secretary of State Cyrus Vance and Foreign Minister Andrei A. Gromyko in October 1977 clearly expressed a change in attitude on the part of Washington regarding Soviet involvement, but this proved unsustainable in the face of opposition from Israel and the U.S. Jewish community. In any event, Syria's hopes collapsed with Sadat's trip to Jerusalem in 1977, which accentuated its sense of isolation. Asad concluded that Syria would have to confront Israel on its own, but this required a massive arms buildup, which could only be achieved with Soviet assistance. As a result, Syria's reliance on the Soviet Union increased significantly. Moscow, in turn, viewed Sadat's trip and its aftermath as an opportunity to exploit Arab rage and win Arab support, primarily through the Front for Steadfastness and Confrontation, which was formed at summits in Tripoli in December 1977 and in Algiers in February 1978.

The Soviet Union had wanted to formalize its relations with Syria since the early 1970s, but Asad, ever mindful of his nationalist credentials, was loath to sign a treaty that might compromise Syria's independence. However, as the balance of power in the Syrian-Soviet relationship shifted in Moscow's favor in the late 1970s—when the Asad regime found itself facing Israel alone, in conflict with Egypt, Iraq, Jordan, and the PLO, bogged down in Lebanon, and severely shaken by widespread internal opposition—his reluctance dissipated. Asad pressed for closer ties during his visit to Moscow in October 1979, at which time the Soviets forgave $500 million of Syria's debt and the two countries concluded their largest arms deal to date. Subsequently, Syria received approximately 1,400 tanks (including advanced T-72s), 200 combat aircraft (including MIG-25s), 2,000 armored vehicles, and 1,700 artillery pieces. One measure of how far Syria had strayed from its anti-imperialist path, and how dependent it had become on Moscow's goodwill, was its failure, along with a very small number of other countries, to criticize the Soviet invasion of Afghanistan in December 1979.

The Treaty of Friendship and Cooperation

In light of the two countries' close relations at the time, the twenty-year Treaty of Friendship and Cooperation that Syria and the Soviet Union signed in October 1980 almost seemed a formality. However, they interpreted the treaty somewhat differently: Syria considered it to be a commitment by the Soviet Union to guarantee its security, which would enable it to pursue its regional policies more boldly, whereas the Soviet Union saw the treaty as a vehicle for crisis management and downplayed its bilateral aspects.[2] The treaty was put to the test twice within the following six months. In November 1980, Syria threatened to invade Jordan to destroy Muslim Brotherhood sanctuaries. Moscow, fearing that hostilities would provoke Israeli intervention and another war it did not want, worked hard to contain the crisis. The missile crisis in Lebanon in April 1981 again brought Syria and Israel close to a war the Soviet Union did not want.

When the United States and Israel signed a Memorandum of Strategic Understanding in November 1981, Syria sought to upgrade its relations with the Soviet Union as a counterbalance. But the Soviets did not want a strategic alliance and were reluctant to sign a defense pact with a country that seemed to flirt so readily with military confrontation.[3] One of Syria's greatest frustrations was that, notwithstanding its treaty with the Soviet Union, its relationship with its superpower patron was not the equal of its adversary's relationship with the United States. Certainly Moscow was not as generous financially as Washington. From Damascus's perspective, the United States had given Israel carte blanche and demonstrated extreme reluctance to criticize its ally or even to apply minimal pressure on it. The United States also appeared willing to deliver unlimited quantities of the most advanced weapons in its arsenal to Israel and always seemed to comply with Israel's requests—in comparison, the Soviet Union must, at times, have seemed niggardly and uncooperative.

The Lebanese War

When Israel invaded Lebanon in 1982 and confronted Syria, the Soviet Union provided the Asad regime with military and political support but was "extraordinarily passive"[4] as Israel trounced the Syrians: Within a matter of days, Syria lost 85 MIG fighters, 350 tanks, and 19 SAM batteries. Far from removing Syria from the military equation, however, Israel's invasion of Lebanon forced the Asad regime to embark on an unprecedented military buildup and drove it even further into the arms of the Soviet Union, which was deeply concerned that the failure of its weapons might tarnish its reputation and afraid that Washington might use its military presence in Lebanon as a springboard to expand its influence in the region.

Between June 1982 and April 1983, the Soviet Union delivered some 800 T-72 tanks, 160 fighter aircraft (including advanced MIG-23s and MIG-27s), SAM-5s, SAM-6s, SAM-9s, and SSC-1 and SS-21 missiles, as well as trucks, armored personnel carriers, guns, and rocket launchers.[5] Yuri Andropov, who succeeded Brezhnev as general secretary of the Communist party in November 1982, opened a new era in Soviet-Syrian ties, favoring closer military cooperation with Syria than any of his predecessors and agreeing to provide it with weapons that had never before been made available to a third world country. The SS-21, a new generation surface-to-surface missile that was far more accurate and effective than Syria's existing Scud missiles, had only been placed in service in the Soviet Union in 1982. The SSC-1, a long-range antiship missile, greatly improved Syria's coastal defenses. What attracted most attention, however, was the deployment of sophisticated long-range, high-altitude SAM-5s, which had never before been shipped outside of the Soviet Union. The SAM-5s constituted the backbone of an elaborate, integrated Soviet-built air defense system that also included other types of missiles, advanced radar, and electronic jamming devices. However, the technological sophistication of much of the new equipment required an expanded Soviet presence, both to operate the new systems and to train Syrians in their use. Between 1982 and 1984, the number of Soviet advisers in Syria increased from 2,500 to over 5,000. In return for supplying Syria with these advanced weapons, particularly the SAM-5s, the Soviet Union demanded greater control over their use. The massive arms buildup between 1982 and 1984 therefore changed the relationship between the two countries. Because the air defense system and long-range missile batteries depended on Soviet personnel, Syria "could no longer consider starting hostilities as it had done in 1973."[6] Syria was a more formidable military adversary and better defended than ever before, but the Asad regime had lost some of its freedom of action. Nonetheless, the massive infusion of arms, in conjunction with Soviet hints that it might come to Syria's aid if Israel attacked, boosted Asad's confidence and helped Syria to recover from its defeat in Lebanon and regain its stature as a major regional power. The regime felt strong enough to block the 1982 Reagan peace plan and undermine the 1983 Israeli-Lebanese Accord.

Syria's subsequent efforts to reestablish its influence in Lebanon were expressed in policies that made the Soviet Union nervous, however. Guerrilla attacks on Israeli forces in Lebanon from Syrian-controlled areas threatened to provoke another military conflagration. The Soviet Union was also very concerned about the possibility of a confrontation between Syria or its Lebanese and Palestinian proxies and the West, particularly the United States, which was becoming increasingly involved in backing President Amin Gemayel. While Moscow did not want to see an expanded U.S. presence in the region, neither did it want a showdown between the United States and Syria. The Soviet Union was therefore greatly relieved when the Multinational Force was withdrawn and the Israeli-Lebanese Accord was abrogated in early 1984.

Another source of tension between the Soviet Union and Syria was the latter's stormy relationship with the PLO, especially after the 1982 war, when Asad sponsored a rebellion of dissident Palestinians against Arafat. The Syrian-PLO and intra-PLO disputes posed a major dilemma for the Soviet Union, since both Syria and the PLO were important allies. It tried to maintain good relations with both Asad and Arafat while urging reconciliation and PLO unity. The Asad regime paid no attention. For years, differences between Syria and the PLO remained a source of friction between Damascus and Moscow.

When Yuri Andropov died in February 1984, Syria lost a good friend who had promoted close military cooperation and who had been exceptionally generous with arms deliveries, in both qualitative and quantitative terms. Konstantin Chernenko, his successor, was not as sympathetic or responsive and tried to broaden the Soviet Union's interests in the Middle East. Indeed, the Soviet Union made a number of moves in the region that were disquieting to Syria and underlined Moscow's determination not to invest all of its energies in its relationship with the Asad regime. In July 1984, it issued a peace plan that supported confederation between Jordan, which it was actively courting, and a Palestinian state. In the same month, it restored full diplomatic relations with Egypt, which Syria was still ostracizing because of its separate peace treaty with Israel. In September, the Soviet and Israeli foreign ministers met at the United Nations in New York, and the following month the Iraqi foreign minister visited Moscow. In October, Gromyko met Arafat in Berlin (this was the first meeting between the Palestinian leader and a high-ranking Soviet official in two years). When Asad visited Moscow that month, the Soviets tried to persuade him to reconcile with Jordan, Egypt, and the PLO. However, the changes that occurred during Chernenko's brief tenure were insignificant in comparison with those initiated by Mikhail S. Gorbachev, who became general secretary of the Soviet Communist party in March 1985.[7]

The Gorbachev Era

The Soviet Union has long advocated a peaceful solution to the Arab-Israeli dispute and has consistently and frequently counseled Syria and all other parties in the region to use maximum restraint in their dealings with one another. But Gorbachev has stated his preference for a negotiated settlement with more forcefulness and conviction than any of his predecessors and has urged Syria to seek a political solution to the conflict. The Soviet Union did not even oppose Yitzhak Shamir's plan for Palestinian elections (perhaps because it was sure the plan would fail). Under Gorbachev's leadership, the Soviet Union has sought cooperation rather than confrontation with the United States and has presented itself as a force for moderation in the Middle East in order to play a more influential role in the region. As part of this strategy, it has significantly broadened its diplomatic contacts with conservative Arab states, particularly Egypt, Jordan, Saudi Arabia, Kuwait, Bahrain, the United Arab Emirates, and Oman. To Asad's consternation, Gorbachev has also opened a dialogue and promoted bilateral contacts with Israel. These significant shifts in Soviet Middle East policy have seriously shaken the foundations of Syria's strategic paradigm and compelled it to reassess its own regional policies.

Eduard A. Shevardnadze, then the Soviet foreign minister, made the most comprehensive and explicit statement of Soviet policy with regard to the Middle East conflict in February 1989, during a trip to Syria, Jordan, Egypt, Iraq, and Iran. The fact that Shevardnadze delivered his important address in Egypt, from which the Soviets had been expelled in 1972, and not in Syria, its closest ally, underlined Moscow's desire to broaden its Middle Eastern reach beyond Syria. Shevardnadze suggested that the superpowers abandon their policy of trying to exclude one another from the region "in favor of constructive coopera-tion for the sake of peace and tranquility." He conceded that the Soviet Union had no magic formula for resolving the dispute and did not offer universal remedies. Nevertheless, his speech was a striking reminder of the constructive role the Soviet Union could play in bringing peace to the region. No recent U.S. administra-tion has stated its vision for the region with such clarity, frank-ness, and breadth.

Shevardnadze observed that the conflict, when stripped of "distorted ideas and hypertrophied emotions," was about "what should be done to ensure that two peoples can live in one com-mon historical homeland." A peaceful resolution required Pal-estinian self-determination, the return of Arab territory seized in 1967, and guarantees of Israel's right to a "secure existence within recognized borders." No party could achieve its goals through force, the use of which would inevitably lead to increas-ingly bloody and destructive wars. Noting pointedly that the Middle East is a "museum of lost civilizations," Shevardnadze warned that without a comprehensive and peaceful solution to the dispute, Israel and its neighbors could follow the same pre-dictable path of nuclear escalation as the superpowers, with the result that "future archaeologists will find yet another layer of buried civilization in the Near East." Something could be learned from the Soviet Union's experience, he said, about the conse-quences of "dogmatic approaches and the over-ideologization of inter-state relations." The world was changing rapidly, but in the Middle East "many think as before, that everything can be solved with the help of arms." Indeed, the global disarmament process could come to a standstill because of the arms race in the Middle East, where military expenditures totaled $59 billion in 1987. During the last decade the region had spent $600 billion on the military (a good deal of it in the Soviet Union). Only NATO and the Warsaw Pact had spent more, but in both of these alliances, Shevardnadze noted, "an understanding of the danger of being armed to the teeth is taking root," whereas "in the Near East . . . the false idea that is today being rejected everywhere still predominates: the more arms, the more reliable the security." With 25,000 tanks, 4,000 combat aircraft, and 7 million people under arms, the Middle East's military might far exceeded its real global economic and demographic weight. The states of the region could not "set themselves against universal human interests" or impede global disarmament. Accordingly, the search for a solution to the region's problems had to be internationalized. The Soviet foreign minister, listing the regional conflicts where there had been progress toward a settlement or where there had been efforts to begin or to keep alive a dialogue—in Afghanistan, the Persian Gulf, southern Africa, Cambodia, Central America, the Western Sahara, the Korean Peninsula, and Cyprus—asked provocatively: "Will the Near East really lag behind the times and drop out of the general tendency of world politics?"

According to Shevardnadze, the Soviet position was that the Middle East dispute, like all regional conflicts, could only be resolved through the balancing of interests. The parties to the Middle East conflict could find much that was instructive in the experience of others. Regional conflicts elsewhere suggested three useful principles for resolving the Middle East problem. First, a dialogue had to be arranged and assisted by intermediaries, which could be the United Nations, groups of countries, or individual states. Second, the withdrawal of forces by a state involved in a conflict had to be accompanied by political treaty obligations safeguarding its interests. Finally, agreements had to be backed up by superpower guarantees and monitored by the United Nations. Shevardnadze noted that there had never been such wide international agreement that the Arab-Israeli conflict had to be settled by peaceful means and observed that the UN

General Assembly, the permanent members of the UN Security Council, the European Community, and the Arab states all favored the convening of an international conference—only Israel opposed this. The Soviet Union believed it was possible "to compile a package of obligations and verification measures that [could] satisfy the most exacting requirements and create the necessary conviction that security is safeguarded" for all parties. Mutual on-site inspections, international verification mechanisms, explicit commitments by all parties not to encourage terrorism or subversion against one another either directly or indirectly, and the creation of nuclear and chemical weapon-free zones and demilitarized or reduced-force zones could all help to alleviate security concerns. The present situation could not continue—there was no alternative to reconciliation and a peaceful settlement.

Because the Arab-Israeli conflict is exceptionally complex and intractable and involves so many parties, Shevardnadze continued, "its solution must be all-embracing, based on a multilateral dialogue and on negotiations at several levels simultaneously." For this reason, it was the Soviet Union's firm conviction that a settlement should be approached "through collective international efforts." The form and content of an international conference, and the question of who should participate, remained to be discussed, preferably through "flexible and multichannel mechanisms." Shevardnadze proposed that preparations for such a conference be conducted through informal discussions among the five permanent members of the UN Security Council and through bilateral and multilateral dialogue among all interested parties, either directly or through intermediaries. The main task at this stage was to create an instrument for a settlement, not to elaborate its parameters. The Soviet foreign minister also called on the UN secretary general to appoint a special representative on the Near East, who would be involved in preparing the conference. Shevardnadze insisted Israel had nothing to fear from such a conference: Its security, far from being diminished, would be enhanced as the security of the other states in the region increased. Although the idea of an international conference was not highly regarded within Israel, the Soviet Union believed such a forum offered "the chance of a historic compromise between the Arabs and the Israelis." Furthermore, if Israel agreed to participate in an international conference and to enter into a dialogue with the PLO, the Soviet Union would restore full diplomatic relations with it.[8]

Soviet Opposition to Syria's Strategic Parity Policy

In theory, the Soviet Union and Syria see eye-to-eye on the desirability of convening an international conference under the auspices of the UN Security Council. They also claim to hold similar positions on a wide range of other regional issues. Nevertheless, Syria has felt the effects of the Soviet Union's internal transformation and global policy shifts under Gorbachev perhaps more acutely than any other state in the region, simply because it is Moscow's principal ally there and depends so heavily on the Soviet Union for its credibility as a major regional power. In the past four years, the Soviet Union has made it clear to Syria that there are limits to its backing and that it opposes the Asad regime's central strategic doctrine. During a visit by Asad to Moscow in April 1987, Gorbachev indicated that he would not support Syria's quest for strategic parity with Israel and openly urged Asad to seek a political solution to the conflict, remarking pointedly that "the reliance on military force in settling the Arab-Israeli conflict has completely lost its credibility."[9] Syria has consistently argued that no durable and just peace can be achieved between the Arabs and Israelis so long as the former negotiate from a position of military weakness or inferiority. Since the Asad regime's goal of achieving military parity with Israel has depended wholly on the Soviet Union, Gorbachev's public admonition was extremely significant and could not have been welcome.

The Soviets warned Syria that efforts to achieve parity will not succeed: Israel would strike preemptively long before Syria attained its goal and, with its firm U.S. support, would come out ahead in any arms race. On the other hand, the Soviets indicated their willingness to assist Syria in modernizing its armed forces to achieve a credible defensive capability. According to this doc-

trine of "reasonable defensive sufficiency," the Soviets will provide Syria with the means to deter Israel from attacking, but they
will not support any Syrian attempt to launch a war. Thus,
Moscow has not supplied Syria with certain types of offensive
weapons (the advanced surface-to-surface SS-23 missile, for example). It has also been unwilling to provide arms in the quantities Syria wants and has insisted on stiffer payment terms. But
there is little danger that it will cut off deliveries altogether—
Syria will continue to be one of its principal clients for arms and
to receive some of the most sophisticated weapons in the Soviet
arsenal. Between 1982 and 1989, the Soviet Union delivered $14
billion of military equipment to Syria. However, shipments have
steadily declined since the massive buildup following the 1982
war. The Soviet Union asserts that this decline, and the withdrawal of Soviet military advisers and technicians, is primarily
attributable to the end of a delivery cycle and the completion of
contracts.

The Soviet Union's recent willingness to discuss its differences with Syria in public has also been disconcerting to the Asad
regime, whose credibility as a major military power in the region
rests in part on the perception that it has Moscow's firm backing.
On September 18, 1989, Alexsandr Zotov, the Soviet ambassador to Syria, stated during a news conference that Syria's
requests for military aid for the next five years were being "scru-
tinized critically" and that "if there are any changes, they will be
in favor of reductions" because "the Syrian government's ability
to pay is not unlimited." He added, pointedly, that hitherto Syria
had paid for its weapons "maybe not to the full extent." [10] Clearly,
Moscow was serving notice that there were limits to its generosity
and that it expected to be paid for the arms it delivered. Syria
reportedly owes its patron $15 billion, a debt that cannot be
ignored given the magnitude of the Soviet Union's current economic problems.

Zotov confirmed during an interview in November 1989
that Moscow was encouraging Syria to give up its goal of military
parity with Israel. Once Syria attained reasonable defensive sufficiency, it would have "the capability to inflict unacceptable
losses" on an attacker and make Israel "think twice" about going

to war.[11] But he reiterated that the Soviet Union had to take into consideration Syria's ability to pay for sophisticated weapons. This was hardly the sort of remark Asad wanted to hear. Two days after Zotov's interview appeared in the Washington *Post,* he held a news conference in Damascus, during which he accused the Western press of trying to disturb good relations between Syria and the Soviet Union by distorting facts and by deliberately highlighting certain points of his interview and ignoring others. The Soviet Union, he affirmed, fully intended to fulfill its commitments to Syria by providing it with the means to guarantee its security—Syria had a right to obtain the weapons it needed in order not to be in a weak position in talks with Israel. Zotov also denied reports that Moscow was asking Syria to repay its debts in hard currency.[12] Nevertheless, the Soviet ambassador's comments in the *Post* were surely intentional and must have been troubling to the Syrian government.

The Immigration Issue

The Asad regime is also concerned about the improvement in Soviet-Israeli relations under Gorbachev, which is an essential component of Moscow's efforts to play a more influential role in the region and to present itself as a peacemaker. Although the Soviet-Israeli rapprochement began before Gorbachev came to office, efforts to rebuild the relationship have expanded considerably during his tenure. During Asad's visit to Moscow in April 1987, Gorbachev remarked that the absence of diplomatic relations between the Soviet Union and Israel was "abnormal." Numerous direct high-level contacts have occurred between the two countries since February 1989, when Shevardnadze met Moshe Arens, the Israeli foreign minister, in Cairo. These culminated in a meeting between Gorbachev and the Israeli ministers of finance and science in Moscow in September 1990, the first meeting between a Soviet leader and Israeli cabinet members since relations were severed in 1967. In December 1990, the United States helped to arrange a meeting between Shevardnadze and Prime Minister Shamir in Washington. Although Moscow has said it will not restore full diplomatic relations until

Israel participates in an international peace conference and begins talking to the PLO, it agreed to reestablish consular ties on September 30, 1990. It has also demonstrated its desire for warmer ties by permitting direct flights between Moscow and Tel Aviv as of October 1990 and, particularly, by allowing a huge exodus of Soviet Jews to Israel.

One consequence of the Soviet Union's political liberalization under Gorbachev has been the easing of emigration restrictions for Soviet citizens. Since the desire to emigrate has been especially strong among Jews, who face rising anti-Semitism and seek greater economic opportunities abroad, this opening of doors has had a direct impact on the Middle East, especially since September 1989, when the Bush administration, citing humanitarian, financial, political, and bureaucratic concerns, imposed an annual ceiling of 50,000 on the number of Soviet refugees it would admit to the United States. Barring any changes in Soviet emigration or U.S. immigration policies, over the next decade hundreds of thousands of Jews who might have entered the United States will be diverted to Israel. Only 2,300 Soviet Jews immigrated to Israel in 1988 and some 13,000 did so in 1989, but approximately 200,000 arrived in 1990, and as many as 800,000 are expected in the next two years. The demographic and political implications of this wave of immigration cannot be understated: It is possible that Israel's Jewish population will increase by 25 percent. Prime Minister Shamir fed Arab fears when he remarked that a "big Israel" would be necessary to accommodate these immigrants. The Arab world grew alarmed that Palestinians would be expelled from the occupied territories to make way for Soviet Jews. Arabs also feared that colonization of the West Bank by Soviet Jews would preclude the territory's eventual return to Arab control as part of a peace settlement.

For Syria, the issue caused particular anguish and embarrassment. Here was its principal backer opening its doors wide so that its citizens could freely emigrate to Israel, which had expelled the Palestinians and refused to allow them to return. Here was its friend and protector supplying its foremost adversary with the demographic means to alter the cultural and political landscape of the occupied territories forever. In Syria's eyes, the

Soviet Union was providing Israel with the means to ensure the continued superiority of its human and technological resource base. Nevertheless, public criticism of the Soviet Union has been extremely restrained because Syria cannot afford to antagonize its patron at the moment. Much of Syria's anger was aimed, instead, at the United States, which was attacked for imposing immigration quotas and for providing financial assistance for the settlement of Soviet Jews in Israel. Indeed, the regime went out of its way to excuse the Soviet Union, which it portrayed as a victim: "The Western powers in general and the United States in particular applied intense pressure on the USSR and East European states to make them allow massive Jewish immigration to occupied Palestine under the pretext of upholding human rights. . . . The Americans and their allies closed their doors to Jewish immigrants as part of the Zionist scheme to Judaize the occupied territories and establish Greater Israel."[13] Another curious canard that found its way into the Syrian media was that "the Soviet Jews are neither Israelites nor Semites. . . . They are the remains of the Khazars . . . from the Far East."[14]

Syria communicated its concern over the changes in the Soviet Union's attitude toward Israel and sought reassurances from Moscow, particularly regarding the settlement of Soviet Jews in the occupied territories. On February 8, 1990, Ambassador Zotov issued a statement affirming the Soviet Union's strong objection to the settlement of Jewish emigrants from the Soviet Union on occupied Arab territory, which he termed "a crude violation of international law and [a] blatant defiance of the United Nations." However, Zotov also made it clear that Moscow would not terminate Jewish emigration, which was permitted under legislation that gives all Soviet citizens, regardless of race or religion, the right to enter and leave the country.[15] Two days later, the Soviet Foreign Ministry issued a statement asserting that settling immigrants in the occupied territories conflicted with international law and impeded efforts to resolve the Arab-Israeli conflict. The ministry had earlier communicated its position on this matter to the Israeli government (on January 29) and did so to Arab governments on March 12, the eve of an Arab

League Council session in Tunis. Zotov reiterated the Soviet position on April 19.

The emigration issue was one of the main topics discussed during President Asad's visit to Moscow at the end of April 1990 (and was high on the agenda during President Mubarak's visit shortly afterward). Gorbachev conceded that the problem had to be seen in the context of Arab rights, not just human rights in general, and stated that the rights of certain people should not be guaranteed at the expense of others. In response to the universal and extreme alarm within the Arab world over the immigration issue, Gorbachev, at the conclusion of his summit meeting with President Bush in June 1990, threatened to restrict Jewish emigration from the Soviet Union unless Israel gave assurances that Soviet Jews would not be settled in the occupied territories. The United States also expressed its opposition to the settlement of Soviet Jews in the occupied territories. Initially, the Likud government, which assumed power in Israel shortly after the summit, was reluctant to give such assurances to the superpowers and asserted that, although it was not its policy to settle Soviet immigrants in the territories, Israel was a free country in which Jews could live where they wished. The appointment of the hawkish Ariel Sharon, who favors greatly expanding Jewish settlement of the West Bank, as housing minister with special responsibilities for absorbing and settling Soviet Jews, aroused fears that many of the new immigrants would be steered into the occupied territories. The Shamir government is aware that the Soviet Union is reluctant to restrict emigration, which would harm relations with Washington and scuttle chances for the passage of a trade bill granting it most-favored-nation status with the United States. Nevertheless, in June 1990 it offered ambiguous assurances that Soviet Jews would not be settled in the occupied territories.

The Impact of the Upheaval in Eastern Europe

The collapse of the Communist regimes of Eastern Europe has also had far-reaching consequences for Syria. Since the mid-1950s, the Eastern European countries have been unwavering supporters of the Arab cause, providing arms, military advice, guerrilla training, diplomatic support, and economic and technical assistance. Syria, as one of Moscow's closest allies in the region, had especially close links with these regimes. In the mid-1980s, there were an estimated 1,600 to 2,000 Eastern European economic advisers in Syria, and the Asad regime's vast state security apparatus also relied heavily on assistance from several hundred Eastern bloc advisers.[16] Eastern European countries have played a major role in Syria's economic development, helping to build oil refineries, phosphate plants, and a steel rolling mill, among numerous other factories, and assisting in land reclamation and power projects. By 1984, some 200 industrial plants and other economic projects had been completed with Eastern bloc assistance, and another 50 were underway.[17] Eastern European universities and specialized training institutes educated thousands of Syrians every year. Despite these close ties, the Eastern European countries took only 12 percent of Syria's exports and provided only 9 percent of its imports in 1988.

The collapse of the Eastern European regimes will have both political and economic costs for Syria. Since 1989, Hungary, Poland, Czechoslovakia, and Bulgaria have restored the diplomatic relations they severed with Israel following the 1967 war. East Germany's apology to Israel for the Holocaust and its unification with West Germany in October 1990 signified the loss of another important ally. The creation of multiparty democracies in Eastern Europe has been accompanied by a major realignment in their foreign policies and by a strong urge to repudiate the friendships formed by the totally discredited ancien régimes. To people who are enjoying their first taste of freedom in 40 years, maintaining a close friendship with the Asad regime must seem distasteful: In many respects, it resembles the regimes they have just cast off, and they do not need to be reminded that it uncritically extolled the dubious accomplishments of the dictatorships that oppressed them. In addition, as the Eastern European countries embrace capitalism, their trade with Syria will probably decline sharply. Why should their consumers purchase inferior Syrian goods foisted upon them as a result of politically expedient barter deals when they have access to Western products?

Without a doubt, the Syrian regime's base of international support has been severely eroded over the last two years. Asad, in a key speech on March 8, 1990, commemorating the anniversary of the Ba'thi revolution, admitted as much, noting that "unfolding worldwide developments present[ed] the Arabs with new and heavy burdens" and that "Israel has become the main beneficiary among all world nations from the international changes which have taken place." He complained that "the Zionists are active everywhere" in the socialist countries. Had anyone predicted ten years ago that "Zionism . . . would attain the present position in the socialist bloc countries, we would have considered him to be unrealistic and unsound, and we would have expressed our astonishment and utter rejection of such a possibility." Wistfully, and without risk of contradiction, he lamented: "How different is the situation today from yesterday!" [18]

The State of Soviet-Syrian Relations

Syria has gone out of its way to demonstrate that its relations with the Soviet Union are on a solid footing, despite all of the recent changes in the Eastern bloc. Asad, in his March 8, 1990, speech, accused Syria's enemies of engaging in wishful thinking when they claimed that its relations with the Soviet Union had deteriorated. On the contrary, the relationship was "as firm as it has always been." A week later, Asad reiterated this point: The Soviet Union was "the firm friend of Syria and the Arab nation" and "no weakness or slackness" had occurred in their relations. The Syrians, he said, were not a people who would "sacrifice their friendship or act in an ungrateful manner" toward a country that had extended its support and had always stood by them. [19] The charge that Syria's adversaries were trying to drive a wedge between the two countries was a persistent theme in the Syrian media. Such efforts were futile: The friendship, after many tests, was "immune to sabotage." [20] After Asad's visit to Moscow that spring, a radio commentary trumpeted that Western circles which resented Syrian-Soviet ties had once again been "disappointed." Those who had "wagered on an unraveling of . . . ties have been disillusioned."[21] For their part, the Soviets characterized their relations with Syria, "a strong and reliable partner" with which there was "a high level of understanding," as "exemplary"[22] and "a model of Third World country relations."[23]

In truth, links between the Soviet Union and Syria are still close, and neither Moscow nor Damascus has shown any signs of abandoning their friendship. The Soviet Union still counts Syria as its main partner in the Middle East. Nevertheless, the relationship has changed fundamentally since Gorbachev came to power. The dissolution of the Soviet Empire in Eastern Europe, the negotiation of arms reduction agreements, the emergence of a reunified Germany, the assertion of nationalism in the Baltics and other peripheral Soviet republics, the restructuring of the Soviet economic and political systems to avert their collapse— these, and other vexing problems, preoccupy the Soviet leadership. Syria's relative importance on the Soviet agenda has inevitably slipped. Furthermore, Soviet repositioning within the Middle East has reduced Syria's maneuverability. Indeed, Asad must have contemplated the possibility that the Soviet Union may yet sacrifice Syrian interests in peace negotiations or downgrade relations in favor of greater influence with Iran, Egypt, Saudi Arabia, and even Israel.

Even so, the Soviet Union has an interest in playing a major role in any peace process, and, as things stand, Syria is still essential to that goal. Syria also provides the Soviet Union with port facilities for its Mediterranean fleet. But in this changed world, what else does Syria offer that cannot be obtained more abundantly or more easily from any number of other Middle Eastern states? Asad must have been shaken by the suddenness and apparent lack of hesitation with which the Soviet Union relinquished its interests in Eastern Europe in pursuit of other goals. If Gorbachev could let the Warsaw Pact (and possibly even the Soviet Union) disintegrate, if he could stand passively by (or, even worse, nod approvingly) as friendly Communist regimes collapsed throughout Eastern Europe, if he could contemplate the possibility of a reunited Germany within NATO, he certainly was not going to come to the Asad regime's defense. Asad knows that he can no longer count on the Soviet Union but, more seriously, so does Israel. And Asad must also realize that Gorbachev is more interested in building good relations with the United States and the West than with maintaining strong links with Syria. He has undoubtedly considered the implications of the Soviet Union siding with the United States against Saddam Hussein, an old ally, when Iraq invaded Kuwait. Would the Soviets also cut off Syria's arms supply if it tried to reclaim the Golan Heights? So long as doubts exist about how reliable a patron and protector the Soviet Union will be, the credibility of Syria's war option is considerably diminished.

Since Soviet commitments to Syria's security are clearly weaker than they were a decade ago, Asad has to be more cautious in dealing with Israel and the United States.[24] This is especially true because the Soviet Union is no longer able or willing to confront the West in Europe, the Middle East, or anywhere else. In some respects, there are no longer two superpowers: There is one great power and one middle-level one. Accordingly, the United States can now deal with the Arab-Israeli conflict on its own merits, instead of refracting it through the prism of the Cold War. This is a time of extraordinary opportunity: The United States and Israel can safely bring the Soviet Union into the peace process, confident that it will play a constructive role. In many respects, the global environment has never been so favorable for resolving the Arab-Israeli dispute as it is now. But for this to happen, Syria and the United States will first have to overcome a legacy of mutual suspicion and mistrust.

THE UNITED STATES AND SYRIA

Historically, U.S. interests in the Middle East have included the protection of Israel, support for moderate Arab allies, unimpeded access to petroleum, and the exclusion of Soviet influence. American policymakers have generally viewed the radical nationalism of Syria as a threat to these goals which had to be contained, rather than an expression of legitimate interests which should be accommodated. After the 1973 war, when the United States became actively engaged in the peace process, it came to realize that Syria was too important a participant in the Arab-Israeli conflict to ignore. Later, when it attempted to work around Syria, its Middle East diplomacy languished. For its part, Syria views the United States with ambivalence: Although the United States is the main backer of Israel, it is also the one power that can restrain Israel and broker a peace settlement. Asad clearly recognizes the importance of maintaining relations with Washington. Thus, both the United States and Syria have discovered that, whether they like it or not, the success of their policies in the region hinges, to some degree, on the other.

The Roots of U.S.–Syrian Hostility

Syria's world-view has been shaped by a profound sense of having been victimized by Western imperialism. As a result, Syria associated itself with the so-called anti-imperialist camp and looked to the Soviet Union for material support against Western and Israeli threats. To be sure, the earliest U.S.–Syrian contacts, before Washington assumed a significant role in the area, were positive: At one time, Syrians even expressed a desire that the post–World War I mandate for Syria be given to the United States. But once it showed its support for Israel, the United States quickly replaced France and Britain as Syria's main antagonist. The formative experiences of the current Syrian political elite occurred during the 1950s, against a backdrop of U.S. support for Israel and intervention in the Middle East against Syrian interests. As early as 1943, the founders of the Ba'th party protested against U.S. support for Zionist settlement in Palestine. During the Eisenhower administration, Washington viewed Middle East issues through the lens of the East-West conflict; consequently, it focused on harnessing the Arab states to the anti-Soviet Baghdad Pact and Central Treaty Organization (CENTO). Most Syrians, committed to the concept of nonalignment, perceived these schemes as imperialistic plots to maintain Western dominance at the expense of Arab nationalism. The fate of the Western alliance system turned on the struggle for influence over Syria between pro-Western Iraq and Nasserite Egypt, and on several occasions Western intelligence agencies intervened covertly, attempting to shift Syria's internal balance of power. Once Syria, with Soviet support, joined the Arab nationalist camp, the United States and Britain intervened militarily against Arab nationalists in Lebanon and Jordan, tried, under the Eisenhower Doctrine, to "quarantine" Syrian radicalism, and sponsored a CIA attempt in 1957 to subvert the National Front government in which the Ba'th party was a leading member.[25]

The Johnson Administration and the 1967 War

When the Ba'thi regime came to power in 1963, it was already hostile to the United States and the West. However, the 1967 Arab-Israeli war greatly increased the animosity between Damascus and Washington. Syria severed its diplomatic relations with the United States during the war, and not until January 1974 did the State Department open an interests section in the Syrian capital. During the crisis that led to the war, President Lyndon B. Johnson, afraid that an Israeli attack might trigger Soviet intervention, which would require a U.S. response, publicly urged Israeli restraint. But Syria believed the U.S. government was secretly encouraging Israel and had delayed a UN Security Council meeting until Israel could complete its conquest of the Golan Heights. Johnson accepted Israel's assurances that it would be willing to exchange the occupied territories for peace with the Arabs and, on this basis, strongly supported it in its victory.[26] The United States soon became Israel's main arms supplier, abandoning its policy of maintaining a local arms balance in favor of one backing Israeli military superiority.[27] Radical Ba'thi doctrine held that the United States, as the head of the world's imperialist bloc, was organically linked to Israel. From this perspective, Israel was seen as a regional surrogate for the United States, in turn for which Washington was providing the strategic depth required for Israel's survival. The Arab-Israeli conflict was part of a wider struggle between imperialists and Arab nationalists, a struggle mandated by oil and strategic location. Before the 1967 war, Syrian radicals asserted that the imperialists would use Israel to maintain their interests in the region so long as the Arabs were reluctant to launch a war of resistance. Afterward, they changed their tune: It was because the Arabs had challenged Western control of their resources that the imperialists had unleashed Israel in a bid to destroy the progressive Arab regimes and instill a sense of permanent inferiority in the Arab people.[28]

The Nixon Administration

The first direct confrontation between the Ba'thi regime and Washington came during the 1970 "Black September" crisis in Jordan. Richard Nixon came to office viewing the Arab-Israeli conflict largely in the context of the U.S.–Soviet power balance. He feared it could spark a superpower confrontation, while the State Department believed that U.S. support for Israel was radicalizing the Middle East, polarizing it between pro-Western and Soviet-backed forces and strengthening the latter.[29] Nixon saw the Palestinians and Syria's radical Ba'thi leaders, whom he regarded as Soviet surrogates and extremists, as special threats to U.S. interests. In response, the United States put forward the Rogers Plan, which was essentially based on UN Resolution 242 and called for a "full" (including normalization of relations) peace settlement from the Arabs in exchange for "substantial" Israeli withdrawal to the 1967 lines. Secretary of State William P. Rogers agreed with the Arab position that a peace settlement should not "reflect the weight of conquest." Egypt simply wanted to end the state of war. But Israel rejected the plan, and Syria, which was totally rejectionist at this time, denounced it as a ploy to split Egypt from the Arabs. Nonetheless, Egypt and Israel were eventually persuaded to accept the essence of the plan as part of the 1970 cease-fire agreement ending the war of attrition along the Suez Canal—a move widely criticized by Arab radicals as implying Egyptian acceptance of Israel. By this time, however, Washington was moving toward an alternative policy espoused by Henry Kissinger, then the national security adviser. Kissinger was not in favor of the attempt to broker a 242-based peace settlement, arguing that full withdrawal was incompatible with Israel's security. He believed that Israel was a strategic asset, and, as such, should be kept stronger than the Arabs, who would come to realize that reliance on Soviet arms could only lead to failure. Once the Arabs understood that only the United States could broker a peace settlement, Soviet influence in the area would wane. Kissinger's criticism of Rogers to Israeli ambassador Rabin, and Nixon's efforts to court Jewish voters in his 1972 reelection campaign, sent the message that Israel need not take the Rogers Plan seriously.[30]

The Jordanian crisis seemed to vindicate Kissinger's view. The crisis was precipitated by hostilities between the PLO, symbol of the revolutionary forces fostered by the Arab-Israeli conflict, and the pro-Western Jordanian monarchy. When Syrian armored forces went to the aid of the Palestinians, King Hussein called for help. Washington saw a Soviet surrogate challenging a Western-backed regime. This was yet another test of U.S. credibility. Although Syria was acting on its own agenda—the radical Ba'th's ideological commitment to the Palestinian resistance and pan-Arab revolution—and probably ignored Soviet counsels of moderation, Kissinger believed that the Soviets had failed to live up to their obligation under détente to restrain their client. The Sixth Fleet was dispatched to the area, but the United States was not well positioned to intervene and asked Israel to mobilize in its stead for a possible intervention. The combined U.S.–Israeli threat emboldened King Hussein and deterred Asad, then the Syrian minister of defense, from committing air support for Syrian armored forces, thus exposing them to losses from Jordanian air attacks. Syrian forces withdrew from Jordan, enabling it to smash the PLO forces. This, combined with the death of Nasser and Asad's ousting of the radical Ba'thists, which was a direct outcome of the crisis, seemed to check the threat of radicalization in the Arab world. Gratitude toward Israel for its help in the crisis erased Washington's irritation over its earlier rejection of the Rogers Plan.

The lesson drawn in Washington was that Israeli power, backed by U.S. arms, could be relied upon to protect U.S. interests against Soviet clients and erode Soviet influence in the area. But if Syria had not pulled back, and if Israel had intervened, the outcome could have been very different. The United States was committed to neutralizing Egypt and the Soviet Union as regional actors, but since it lacked the conventional capabilities to intervene even against Syria, this could presumably only have been accomplished through nuclear brinkmanship. Washington had acted without consulting area experts, in the absence of any communication whatsoever with Syria, and with little consideration of diplomatic options.[31] The success in Jordan bred complacency and encouraged the belief that military power alone could stabilize the area. Indeed, Kissinger aimed for what he later called a "complete frustration" of the Arabs, such that they would have to break with the Soviets and accept the existence of Israel.[32] Thus, Washington neglected Sadat's diplomatic initiatives, even after he expelled Soviet military advisers, as it had demanded. The Egyptian leader came to believe that the United States would do nothing until the Arabs showed they could fight. As he began to consider taking military action, the Soviets agreed to provide Egypt with the military aid it needed. Syria, which had announced its acceptance of UN Resolution 242 in 1972 to no avail, joined Egypt with the backing of Saudi Arabia, which had grown increasingly pessimistic about U.S. diplomacy. The result was the 1973 war, which jeopardized détente, strained the Atlantic alliance, and precipitated a serious energy crisis.[33]

Syrian leaders believed the Arabs' credible military challenge to Israel in the 1973 war and the subsequent rise of Arab oil power might lead to a divergence in Israeli and U.S. interests and give the Arabs new leverage over the United States. Although massive U.S. arms shipments during the war had allowed Israel to reverse the Syrian advances and keep its grip on the Golan Heights, Damascus hoped that Washington might still pressure Israel to withdraw from the territories it had occupied in 1967 in order to protect its own stake in the Middle East and to remove a major cause of instability in the region. At this juncture, Syria renewed diplomatic relations with the United States and accepted Kissinger's mediation in the Golan Heights disengagement negotiations.

From the outbreak of the 1973 war, Kissinger's primary goals were to enhance U.S. power in the Middle East at the expense of the Soviet Union and to protect the security of Israel.

But the war created grave dilemmas for U.S. policymakers. Israel had to be protected, but unqualified support for it would unleash an oil embargo and a storm of anti-Americanism from which the Soviets could benefit. Kissinger also understood that the war had rendered his previous policy obsolete: Israeli military might was not enough to maintain the peace and the "no war–no peace" situation had become intolerable to the Arabs. A stable Middle East in which Israel would be safe and U.S. interests protected had to be built on at least a partial peace settlement, which entailed making some concessions to Arab interests. If the United States were able to broker such a settlement, Soviet influence would be decisively rolled back. With these thoughts in mind, Kissinger favored a stalemate in the war, since this presented the best opportunity for negotiating a compromise settlement. Although the Arabs could not be allowed to win with their Soviet arms, neither did he want a total Israeli victory. Thus, the United States briefly delayed arms shipments to Israel and intervened at the war's conclusion to prevent the destruction of Egypt's Third Army in the Sinai. The United States sought to demonstrate that it was committed to Israeli security but not to an Israeli victory over the Arabs.

Kissinger's postwar strategy was to establish the United States as the only reliable mediator between the Arabs and Israel. As Israel's arms supplier and banker, the United States alone could win concessions from Israel. Kissinger also sought to defuse the international pressures the war had created for the rapid completion of a comprehensive 242-based settlement.[34] Instead of convening an international conference in which the Soviets would have a role, he would conduct bilateral diplomacy. He would avoid presenting any plan for a comprehensive peace settlement and the resolution of the Palestinian issue. Rather, he would work on peripheral issues, defusing the military threat by negotiating disengagement agreements and stretching out the settlement process, resisting any attempt to link its phases with the final outcome. Meanwhile, Kissinger led the Arabs to believe he favored a comprehensive settlement, and Nixon made private commitments to the Arab leaders to work for the implementation of UN Resolution 242. However, Kissinger refused to guarantee the outcome of negotiations and told the Israelis that the purpose of making small concessions was to avoid the big ones that a comprehensive settlement would entail. A key to his overall strategy was the building of a new position for the United States in the Arab world based on an alliance with Egypt, which seemed to be the Arab state most prepared to reach a settlement with Israel and which, Kissinger believed, the rest of the Arab world would have to follow. This meant that Sadat's needs had to be satisfied to some extent while, at the same time, he had to be detached from those who insisted on a comprehensive peace settlement that included a Palestinian state and total Israeli withdrawal from the occupied territories. If Syria could not be brought to accept less than a comprehensive settlement, Egypt would be encouraged to proceed unilaterally.

Kissinger's strategy was first evident in the Egyptian-Israeli disengagement negotiations. Allegedly, he twice vetoed Israeli concessions (offers to withdraw to the Sinai passes) on the grounds that they would whet Syria's appetite for similar concessions. Moreover, he believed Israel should be seen to budge only under intense U.S. pressure.[35] During his first meeting with Asad in December 1973, Kissinger deflected the Syrian leader's queries about why Palestinian rights were not on the agenda of the proposed international peace conference and whether the United States was in favor of a land for peace settlement. Kissinger said that he could not guarantee the outcome of negotiations, but he indicated that an Israeli withdrawal would come in several stages and that, eventually, the peace process would deal with all issues. President Nixon later told Asad that the U.S. aim was to push the Israelis back step by step on the Golan until they tumbled over into Israel.[36] But Kissinger apparently tried to discourage Nixon from giving Asad firm assurances, and after Gerald R. Ford became president, he told Syria that Nixon's commitments did not bind the new administration.[37]

Kissinger's actions cast doubt on whether he aimed to achieve the momentum that would lead to a comprehensive settlement. Nevertheless, he recognized that the partial peace settlement he wanted would get nowhere without Syria. Therefore, he invested a great deal of energy in brokering the 1974

Syrian-Israeli military disengagement on the Golan. Syria had to be given something comparable to Egypt's first military disengagement along the Suez Canal if the credibility of the United States as a mediator was to be established. Achieving a permanent end to the oil embargo depended on this. Moreover, if Sadat was seen to be too far out in front of Syria, he would be accused of pursuing a separate peace settlement and consequently isolated in the Arab world. Sadat's policy had to be given a "radical anchor." Once Syria reached an agreement with Israel, this would legitimize and give crucial momentum to the peace process desired by the moderate Arabs and seal American domination of Middle Eastern diplomacy. However, although the Israelis had understood the advantages of conciliating Sadat, Kissinger had to apply intense pressure on them to make concessions to Asad. He argued that it was in Israel's interest to protect Sadat and warned that the failure of the peace process could lead to renewed warfare, which would benefit the Soviet Union, possibly involve Egypt, and increase pressure for an imposed settlement. Eventually, Nixon turned the financial screws on Israel by asking for an accounting of all official aid and tax-free private contributions. Kissinger's diplomatic virtuosity was, of course, crucial to the successful outcome. His method was to elicit proposals from each side and then try to bridge them by explaining the consequences of failure to agree and by emphasizing the opportunities for peace. Only in the end did he present a U.S. proposal. His diplomatic creativity was crucial in circumventing obstacles. For example, at one point the negotiations threatened to collapse because Asad refused to comply with a last-minute Israeli demand that he publicly guarantee there would be no Palestinian guerrilla operations from the Golan. Kissinger got the Israelis to accept a formula under which the United States, with Asad's private commitment in hand, would inform Israel that it interpreted the accord to prohibit such raids. Asad has scrupulously held to this commitment. Kissinger's success in convincing the Syrian leadership that he was acting as a fair broker was also crucial to the success of the negotiations. For their part, once the Syrians committed themselves to Kissinger's shuttle diplomacy, they were invested in the U.S. peace process.

They urged Kissinger to play an active mediating role, rather than simply conveying the Israeli position, and made important concessions to convince the United States that Syria was not an obstacle to peace and wanted the process to be carried beyond a mere disengagement agreement. The good will that developed between Kissinger and Asad in the negotiations could have paved the way for an attempt at a comprehensive settlement.[38]

Over Asad's protests, however, Kissinger proceeded to broker a second disengagement agreement (Sinai II) on the Egyptian front. Israel openly admitted that its objective here was to detach Egypt from Syria and the Arabs. And Kissinger has acknowledged that it was his strategy to prevent the formation of a united Arab front against Israel. During the Sinai II negotiations, Israel made it clear that it was unwilling to make the same territorial concessions it had been ready to give in the immediate aftermath of the war unless Egypt agreed to a formal end to belligerency, that is, a separate peace, which would isolate Sadat politically. Kissinger warned Israel that if there was no movement on the Egyptian front, the stalemate might lead to a reconstructed Arab coalition, which would entail a renewed focus on the Palestinian problem, linkage of a settlement on the Sinai with the Golan, and demands for an international conference. With no progress being achieved, the Ford administration conducted a "reevaluation" of its Middle Eastern policy in which elders of the foreign policy establishment and regional experts advised a return to the pursuit of a comprehensive solution. But Ford and Kissinger were unwilling to pay the domestic political costs this would entail.[39] Eventually, Israel accepted an agreement which, in drastically limiting Egyptian forces in the Sinai and inserting American monitors between the two sides, amounted to a non-belligerency accord in all but name. In return, it received massive shipments of high-technology arms, which promised to give it superiority over Egypt, Syria, and Jordan combined for the next decade. To secure Israel's agreement, Kissinger also promised that the United States would not talk to the PLO until it recognized Israel, that it would coordinate its diplomacy with Israel, and that it would settle for merely cosmetic changes in a second Golan disengagement agreement. These commitments hobbled U.S. diplomacy in the region for years to come. Kissinger assumed that Israel, with its security significantly enhanced by arms deliveries and by the greatly diminished threat of a two-front war, would feel confident enough to pursue a wider peace settlement. However, some Israeli strategists saw Sinai II as an opportunity to drive another nail in the coffin of the Rogers Plan, giving Israel time to entrench itself on the Golan and the West Bank.[40] As Kissinger himself admitted, "When I ask Rabin to make concessions he says he can't because Israel is weak; so I give him more arms and he says he doesn't need to make concessions because Israel is strong."[41] The acrimony generated by Kissinger's pressure on the Israelis for concessions "exhausted Israel's tolerance for further concessions."[42]

By this time, Asad had come to believe that Washington's strategy was to keep Israel strong while dividing the Arabs, whose only hope for obtaining a comprehensive peace settlement was to maintain their solidarity and refuse to settle for less than UN Resolution 242. From Syria's perspective, Sinai II threatened its security by allowing a strengthened Israel to concentrate its forces on the northern front. At the same time, it undermined any diplomatic leverage Asad might have derived from a combined Syrian-Egyptian military threat: In signing Sinai II, Sadat had agreed not to join any Syrian attack on Israel.

Kissinger steered away from a comprehensive peace settlement for several reasons. Apparently, he believed that it was impractical, both because Israel would not accept it and because radical Arabs would use it to threaten Israel's security. Furthermore, given his overriding goal of enhancing U.S. power in the region at the expense of Soviet power, achieving a breakthrough in the peace process took priority over working toward a comprehensive outcome. A separate peace with Egypt was not only easier to attain, it would serve to neutralize the Arabs' capacity to launch a new war. Kissinger may, however, have missed a unique opportunity to broker a lasting settlement.[43] The Arabs were ready for peace and the Israelis more vulnerable than ever to U.S. pressures; as Kissinger himself told the Israelis, "If we wanted the 1967 borders we could do it with all world opinion behind us."[44] In theory, step-by-step diplomacy served to build confidence and momentum, but, in practice, by Sinai II it had led to a stalemate. Whatever Kissinger's intentions, his diplomacy clearly separated Egypt and Syria, as Asad had feared, and enhanced Israel's military superiority. By reducing pressure on Israel for concessions and by undermining Egypt's moderating influence, it lessened the already limited prospects for achieving a comprehensive peace settlement. If the objective was to prevent an Arab-initiated war, taking Egypt out of the Arab war coalition achieved this. But, ironically, in strengthening Israel, it set the stage for the later Israeli involvement in Lebanon, where Arab weakness and an imbalance of power created the conditions for war. Moreover, in certain ways the Lebanese civil war was itself precipitated by the lack of a comprehensive settlement: Since the Maronites had no hope of being relieved of the PLO presence in Lebanon by any other means, they initiated hostilities against the Palestinians, who had no choice but to defend their Lebanese base. The absence of a settlement turned Lebanon into a killing ground for rival powers and an enduring flashpoint of the Syrian-Israeli conflict.[45] On the other hand, Kissinger's diplomacy demonstrated that, if offered an alternative to war, the Arabs would accept it. The agreements Kissinger brokered, trading some land for some peace (or territory for security), were not only workable but created a modicum of trust, although, in the case of Syria, this trust was subsequently undermined by a growing suspicion of American motives.[46]

Despite Asad's disillusionment with step-by-step diplomacy, he could not afford to burn his bridges with the United States. He understood that Washington alone could restrain a more powerful Israel. U.S. mediation proved its value more than once in keeping the Syrian-Israeli rivalry in Lebanon from escalating out of control. A good part of Asad's strategy after Sinai II was aimed at demonstrating to Washington that if Syria's interests were accommodated, it could facilitate a settlement, but if they were not, no peace would be possible in the Middle East. Part of the rationale for Asad's intervention in Lebanon in 1976 may have been to show that Syria was a key to stability in the region. When the Carter administration came into office, apparently committed to achieving a comprehensive peace settlement, Asad responded positively.

The Carter Administration

The Carter administration, believing that step-by-step diplomacy was exhausted, initially committed itself to an active role in seeking a comprehensive settlement, including the return of the Golan to Syria and the establishment of a Palestinian homeland. Carter was the first U.S. president to show much sensitivity to Arab grievances. The administration was very conscious that the conflict threatened moderate Arab regimes and Western access to oil at a time of an acute energy crisis. Less interested in excluding than in enlisting the help of the Soviet Union, the administration envisioned joint sponsorship of an international peace conference. The main obstacles to a settlement were seen to be Israel's reluctance to cede land, the unwillingness of Arab leaders like Asad to consider a "full peace" with normalization of relations, and the PLO's refusal to recognize Israel. Carter agreed that Israel was entitled to a full peace settlement, but he believed no peace was possible without Israel's withdrawal to the 1967 lines. To bridge the gap between the opposing positions, Carter planned to proceed incrementally on specific issues in order to build confidence and momentum. He also intended to remain actively involved so the parties would have the confidence to take risks for peace.[47]

Carter believed that Syria was a major player in the region and had to be dealt with. In 1977, he met Asad in Geneva to explore Syrian views and later invited Syria to attend a proposed international conference.[48] But Asad, fearing Sadat's propensity for making unilateral deals, and wishing to have a say in the Palestinian question, demanded a united Arab delegation. The prospects for an international conference soon began to dim. Israel strenuously objected to a joint U.S.–Soviet declaration calling for a comprehensive settlement, consideration of Palestinian rights, and superpower guarantees. Carter then retreated on the principles on which the conference would be convened and, to gain Israel's participation, agreed to all its procedural conditions, particularly its demand for bilateral negotiations— which Syria opposed. Moshe Dayan admitted that this was a strategy to exclude Syria. Nevertheless, the United States accused Asad of obstructing the conference with his inflexibility. Carter tried to get Menachem Begin to agree that UN Resolution 242 applied to all fronts, a requisite for a comprehensive peace settlement. Begin, however, not only disagreed with this interpretation, but continued establishing Jewish settlements on the West Bank. Under these conditions, Asad saw little hope the conference could succeed because the United States refused to put forward a clear-cut formula for a solution. Secretary of State Vance thought that Asad missed the opportunity to participate in a conference at which everything could have been negotiated. Ismail Fahmy, Egypt's foreign minister, claimed that President Carter told Egypt he could not put pressure on Israel because this would be political suicide. This apparently confirmed Sadat's suspicion that it would be impossible to negotiate a comprehensive settlement and was a factor in his decision to go to Jerusalem.[49]

After Sadat broke the deadlock and scuttled the Geneva Conference by going to Jerusalem, Carter concentrated on Egyptian-Israeli negotiations. At Camp David, he did not pursue a comprehensive peace settlement, pushing instead to have Begin's autonomy plan for the West Bank made into an interim regime of transitional arrangements and placed in a framework for a future final settlement.[50] At best, an Israeli-Jordanian condominium over the West Bank might have been established. But the negotiations over Palestinian autonomy went nowhere. In the end, Egypt signed a peace treaty with Israel. Asad, who had believed Carter when he pledged to seek a comprehensive peace settlement, viewed the outcome as yet another case of the United States reneging on its promises and splitting the Arabs to Israel's advantage.[51] In fact, the agreement freed Begin to pursue a much more ambitious policy toward the Arabs, and Syria in particular.

The Reagan Administration

U.S.–Syrian relations hit a new low after Ronald Reagan came to office. Driven by anticommunist militancy, and intent on a rollback of Soviet influence in the Middle East, the Reagan administration unrealistically sought to bring Arabs and Israelis together in a new anti-Soviet security arrangement. This would focus on the defense of the Persian Gulf, which Washington eyed with some apprehension because of the Iranian revolution and the Soviet invasion of Afghanistan, and was based on the assumption that the gulf and U.S. access to oil could be insulated from the Arab-Israeli conflict. The notion of Israel as a strategic asset in the conflict with the Soviet Union was a cornerstone of administration policy. Reagan personally had little command of Middle Eastern realities but admired Israel's toughness and was deeply sympathetic to its concerns. Unwilling to antagonize Israel, the administration largely let the peace process lapse, while showing an increased willingness to use or sanction military force against supposed Soviet surrogates. The administration ignored the voices of critics with a greater understanding of the area. It was asked: "What good will it do to build an anti-Soviet strategic consensus in the Middle East without an equally vigorous effort to remove the political conflicts on which Soviet aggression feeds?"[52] The only real counterbalance to the administration's pro-Israeli sentiments was a certain fear of the repercussions among its allies in the Arab world. This, and the lack of presidential leadership, introduced a certain hesitancy and inconsistency into administration policy.

Another big change from the Kissinger and Carter eras was that Syria was no longer seen as a potential participant in the peace process. On the contrary, some within the Reagan administration, notably Secretary of State Alexander M. Haig, Jr., viewed Syria as a Soviet surrogate whose interests could be disregarded and whose punishment represented a victory over Moscow. Such thinking resulted in the 1981 Memorandum of Understanding to coordinate U.S. and Israeli policies against the Soviet Union and its local allies, including Syria and the PLO. Although the memorandum was temporarily suspended later that year to protest Begin's annexation of the Golan Heights, the United States vetoed a UN resolution condemning the annexation, early displaying an incoherence of policy that was to typify the Reagan administration.[53]

The main arena of U.S.–Syrian conflict was Lebanon. Prior to the Reagan administration, Washington had played a major role in reducing the risks of Syrian-Israeli conflict there. Kissinger brokered the original Syrian intervention, convincing Israel that Syrian pacification of the country was in its interests and communicating the Israeli objections that helped define the red lines limiting Syrian deployment. When the Syrians came too close to Israel's northern border at Nabatiyah, U.S. envoy Philip Habib negotiated a pullback. Beginning with Kissinger, U.S. negotiators tried in vain to get Israel to agree to the deployment of Syrian and later Lebanese army troops on the southern Lebanese border in order to pacify this "no man's land."[54] The Carter administration also played a stabilizing role in dampening the conflicts in southern Lebanon, often in concert with Syria. The United States and Syria jointly muted the Palestinian-Haddad conflicts of 1977. Carter acted vigorously to contain the scope of the Litani Operation, sponsoring the UN resolution calling for Israel's withdrawal and for the deployment of a UN buffer force. He even threatened to cut off arms deliveries when Begin used U.S. weapons in southern Lebanon. When the Maronites challenged Syrian forces in an effort to upset the status quo, Washington blamed them for the fighting. The United States also played the major role in dampening the 1979 conflicts and in arranging a cease-fire in the south.[55]

The Reagan administration at first continued along these lines, brokering the 1981 PLO-Israeli cease-fire and intervening to defuse the Zahlah missile crisis. Thus, it seemed to recognize that Syrian-Israeli tensions threatened regional stability and, by extension, U.S. interests. Syria, for its part, tried to use the missile crisis to start a dialogue with the new administration and to signal that stability was threatened by the stagnation of the peace process.[56] But Washington did not appear to be interested in widening the peace process. Indeed, as Habib was trying to dampen the conflict, Haig was in Israel denouncing Syria. The administration's policy was snared in a contradiction between the desire to punish Soviet surrogates and the need for their cooperation to preserve regional stability.

Arguably, U.S. policy—or lack of it—played a role in encouraging the Israeli invasion of Lebanon in 1982. Had Reagan pursued the West Bank autonomy talks, this might have created an atmosphere of negotiation and made an invasion unthinkable. Instead, when Haig visited Israel to promote an anti-Soviet Middle Eastern alliance, he labeled Syria a Soviet surrogate, denounced its role in Lebanon, and left the impression that Israel was free to adopt a more militant posture toward Damascus. Whereas the Carter administration had disapproved of Bashir Gemayel's challenges to Syria, the Reagan administration welcomed them. Begin and Sharon gave Washington plenty of warning of the invasion, although perhaps not of its scope. The administration insisted there had to be a sufficient provocation, but Haig left the Israelis with the belief they had a green light. The mildness of Reagan's official letter opposing an invasion also reinforced the impression that the United States would not stand in Israel's way.[57] Once the invasion began, Washington saw it as a strategic opportunity to destroy Soviet influence in the area, get Syria and the PLO out of the country, and broker a U.S. settlement in Lebanon. In fact, as the Soviets lost credibility, the Arabs had no choice but to turn to the United States to restrain Israel.[58]

Once the administration awakened to the negative side effects of the invasion—the threat of Soviet intervention, the dismay of pro-Western Arab regimes—it sought a truce. Habib's first efforts to arrange a cease-fire between Israel and Syria were not promising. He relayed Israel's assurances that it would not attack Syria, but even as he was in Damascus delivering Begin's pullback ultimatum, Israel struck at Syrian forces in Lebanon.[59] To get Asad's agreement to a cease-fire, Habib told him Reagan supported an Israeli withdrawal from Lebanon, and a letter from the U.S. president to Asad seemed to confirm this. Technically, the United States may have merely committed itself to try to sway Israel but, in fact, Haig persuaded Reagan to refrain from putting any pressure on Israel to withdraw. Moreover, after the cease-fire agreement was arranged, Washington failed to act against creeping Israeli advances against Syria, which violated the accord it had brokered. Asad asked Habib: "Is the word of the United States not to be trusted? What then is the meaning of any international agreement?"[60] The massacre of Palestinians at Shatila and Sabra, after the administration had guaranteed the safety of Palestinian civilians following the PLO evacuation of Beirut, brought U.S. credibility in the area to an all-time low.[61]

In the aftermath of the war, the United States set out to fashion a new Lebanon in which Syrian and Soviet power would give way to U.S. and Israeli influence. Washington took Amin Gemayel's government under its wing and set about mediating an Israeli-Lebanese accord on Israeli withdrawal. Although Syria could have scuttled such an accord by refusing to withdraw from Lebanon, Washington ignored it: "Let's leave the Syrians on the outside looking in," Reagan told Israeli foreign minister Yitzhak Shamir.[62] Secretary of State George Shultz failed to include Damascus on his itineraries until the agreement was signed, hoping to present it as a fait accompli and not wishing to give the Syrians a chance to raise objections or to seek a quid pro quo, such as inclusion of the Golan, in the Reagan Plan.[63] Syrian foreign minister Abd al-Halim Khaddam had told the United States that Syria would withdraw from Lebanon, but only if Israel did so unconditionally. In Syrian eyes, the May 17 agreement rewarded Israel for its invasion and was taken by Asad as a threat and an insult.[64] The U.S. embassy in Damascus kept Washington apprised of Asad's opposition, but this was ignored. Instead, Shultz accused Asad of bad faith and of playing the spoiler.[65] In fact, Washington expected to force the accord on Syria. With Israeli forces deployed on the Lebanese-Syrian border only 20 kilometers from Damascus, Asad's hand appeared weak; an Israeli withdrawal should reasonably have been a first priority for him. The Reagan administration apparently believed Israeli military threats and Saudi financial pressures would force Syria out of Lebanon, but neither proved to be enough leverage over a stubborn Asad. The administration then hoped to establish a Lebanese government strong enough to rally the Lebanese against the Syrian occupation. This also failed. The U.S. approach was essentially based on establishing what one official described as "Christian military dominance" and on trying to train and rebuild a reliable army under Gemayel's command.[66] But military means were insufficient to reconstruct a viable Lebanon or to force the Lebanese to support a government lacking legitimacy. The United States largely neglected the political track. Indeed, in falling in with Israeli demands for a surrogate peace and in foisting the May 17 accord on Gemayel instead of merely brokering a security agreement for southern Lebanon, the administration robbed him of the legitimacy he needed to establish credible authority. When Gemayel realized this and asked Washington to reopen the negotiations with Israel, he was rebuffed.[67]

As the effectiveness of Syrian obstruction in Lebanon became apparent, there was some debate in the U.S. foreign policy establishment over whether to accommodate Syrian interests. But the majority view was that the United States should "close ranks with Israel" and "get tough" with Syria.[68] In December 1983, U.S. aircraft and naval guns struck against the Syrian-backed militias attacking Gemayel's army units. By taking sides, the U.S.–led peacekeeping force in Lebanon was reduced, in Thomas Friedman's words, to "just another warring faction."[69] Car bombings by pro-Syrian, Iranian-backed terrorists inflicted heavy casualties at the U.S. embassy in April and at Marine headquarters in October. Congress cut off the modest economic assistance that Syria had been receiving from the United States since 1975. Washington revived the strategic cooperation agreement with Israel and urged it to stand fast in Lebanon until Syria was ready to compromise for, as Henry Kissinger warned, a unilateral Israeli withdrawal would be a "Soviet triumph over America."[70] But Israel, tired of the war, was unwilling to bail the Americans out. When Syrian forces shot down two attacking U.S. airplanes, the spiral of escalation seemed to bring the two countries to the brink of war. A divided U.S. government was sapped of the will to pursue the conflict, however. Shultz, convinced that Syria had to be taught a lesson for its obstructionism and support of terrorism, urged military action, but Secretary of Defense Caspar W. Weinberger opposed it.[71] It was unclear to many

Americans what the United States' interests in Lebanon were and why it had become so entangled there. When the U.S.–trained Lebanese army collapsed, U.S. forces were withdrawn. The United States was easily outlasted by Syria and its surrogates, whose stake in Lebanon far outweighed its own. It was unwilling to commit ground forces to combat, and naval and air bombardment proved too crude an instrument to settle the Lebanese imbroglio. Defined in the Reagan administration's own terms, the withdrawal was a defeat: A Soviet-backed regime had triumphed over a U.S.–sponsored "peace plan" for the first time since the 1973 war. The episode seemed to show that the United States could not untangle the Middle Eastern morass alone and that attempts to exclude the Soviet Union were likely to be counterproductive.[72] The failure of U.S. military power in Lebanon also appeared to make Asad's point that Syria could not be ignored.

Throughout much of this period, Syria and the United States were involved in a test of wills over the Reagan Plan, which Asad, and many other observers, interpreted as an effort to isolate and encircle Syria.[73] The plan, in part meant to appease moderate Arab opinion in the wake of the Israeli invasion, attempted to revive Camp David and, in essence, invited King Hussein to negotiate for the West Bank. The negotiations over the Israeli-Lebanese accord and subsequent Arafat-Hussein talks on how to take up the Reagan Plan looked in Damascus like a U.S. effort to roll back Syria's influence over its neighbors and isolate it by encouraging Israel to negotiate peace treaties with all Arab parties except Syria. It strains credibility to believe, as U.S. officials claimed, that the issue of the Golan was unintentionally omitted from the Reagan Plan. Rather, Washington believed that the defeat of Syria and the PLO, and the ensuing decline of Soviet influence, offered it a unique opportunity to override Syrian and radical Palestinian objections to a U.S.–defined peace settlement. Syria was also left out to minimize Israeli objections to the plan. Some diplomats believed the United States missed an opportunity by not including Syria, which, by the fall of 1982, was at a low point in its fortunes and might possibly have been more flexible than previously. Indeed, at this time, Syria, having rejected the 1981 Fahd Plan, bowed to the Arab consensus and accepted the similar Fez Declaration.[74] But accommodating Syria ran counter to the administration's strategic view that the purpose of the Lebanon enterprise was to destroy Soviet influence and punish Soviet surrogates.

As it turned out, the Reagan Plan was stillborn. Begin, who believed the defeat of Syria and the PLO created opportunities for the annexation of the West Bank, instantly and sharply rejected it. Moreover, Washington's inability to get Israel out of Lebanon or to discontinue its settlement of the West Bank gave King Hussein little encouragement to take risks. If the United States could not prevail on Israel over such lesser matters, how could it secure an Israeli withdrawal from the West Bank? Syrian pressure on the PLO probably also helped scuttle the Arafat-Hussein talks regarding the plan. Thereafter, the Reagan administration pursued it halfheartedly.[75] In the end, the administration's policy, both in its diplomatic and its military dimensions, proved largely ineffective. Asad professed to believe that "the United States does not have an independent policy in the Middle East; it implements the policy that is decided by Israel."[76] He was pleased at the prestige Syria had reaped in standing up to U.S. and Israeli designs.

Washington also came into conflict with Syria over its reputed sponsorship of terrorism. There was, indeed, a new wave of terrorism in the wake of the Israeli invasion of Lebanon, and the Reagan administration identified Syria as a prime target in its antiterrorist crusade. Asad, for his part, insisted on distinguishing between terrorism and the struggle for national liberation: He extolled guerrilla warfare against the Israelis in Lebanon and Palestinian operations against military targets in Israel, but he condemned attacks on civilians, hijackings, and hostage-taking. Nevertheless, terrorism, even by his own definition, was an instrument in his inventory. Even if Syria did not have a direct hand in the bombings of the U.S. embassy and Marine headquarters, these actions served Syrian goals. The Asad regime clearly backed Shiite resistance to the U.S. and Israeli presence in Lebanon. Syrian intelligence also sponsored assassinations and bombings against opponents outside the Middle East. In his post-1973 drive against Arafat, Asad had struck up alliances with some of the most violent Palestinian factions, notably Ahmad Jibril's PFLP-General Command. The Abu Nidal group carried out assassinations of Jordanian officials on behalf of Syria's effort to abort the Arafat-Hussein accord over the West Bank. Once "turned on" these groups could not easily be turned off: Post-invasion Lebanon, anarchic and seething with grievances, became a permanent breeding ground of radical Shiite and Palestinian factions that were not necessarily under Syrian control and were behind terrorist attacks in Europe and hostage-taking in Lebanon. Although he disapproved of these acts and was aware that they were being used to discredit Syria, Asad was reluctant to move against allies important to his larger strategy unless, in so doing, he could extract concessions or gain political credit from the West. Syria did play a major role in ending the 1985 TWA hijacking to make the point to Washington that, with its cooperation, progress could be achieved in the Middle East; Asad's only reward, however, was a telephone call from Reagan, which he deemed insulting.

The United States was not passive in the face of terrorist activities, bombing Libya and sending strong warnings to Syria. Asad often pointed out that Syria was itself also a frequent victim of terrorism: The day after the United States attacked Libya, terrorist bombs detonated inside Syria, killing 144 people.[77] It was in this highly charged atmosphere that the Hindawi affair, the attempt to place a bomb on an Israeli airliner, took place. Although Syria asserted that Israel was using Hindawi to discredit the Asad regime, it seems certain that Syrian intelligence was behind the attempt, perhaps in revenge for Israel's forcing down of an airliner carrying Syrian officials. If Asad did order this operation, it was out of character. Asad is a cautious man with an astute sense of timing and tactics, and a military showdown with Israel during a period of heightened tensions, when Syria was isolated internationally, was the last thing he wanted. Following the incident, the United States and several European countries imposed economic sanctions on Syria and withdrew their ambassadors. To Asad, it appeared that Washington was preparing global opinion before taking military action against

Syria. It was just at this time, however, that Syria fortuitously uncovered and, through the Lebanese press, exposed the U.S. and Israeli arms deals with Iran, which Reagan had frequently depicted as a "terrorist state." The Reagan administration was soon paralyzed and distracted by the resulting Iran-contra scandal. Syria did, however, suffer from the loss of valued economic relations with Western Europe.

Syria subsequently reassessed its policy. The intelligence official directly responsible for the Hindawi affair was demoted and moved to a nonintelligence post. After the United States presented the Syrians with evidence that Abu Nidal was behind the hijacking of a Pan American flight, his group was expelled from the country. This cleared the way for the U.S. ambassador to return to Damascus. Asad promised that if convincing evidence were presented showing that Ahmad Jibril was behind the 1988 bombing of Pan American flight 103, Syria would also move against him. This would be politically costly, for Jibril's group is one of Syria's more credible allies against Arafat, and it is the Palestinian faction historically closest to Syria, although Jibril, anticipating a break with Syria, has sought Iranian patronage as well. As yet, the U.S. embassy has provided no concrete evidence with which to test Syria's commitment. Syrian foreign minister Farouk al-Sharaa has admitted that Syria's surveillance of certain groups operating from its territory has been lax and claims that it has tightened controls over them. But Washington remains unsatisfied that Syria has turned its back on terrorism. Syria is still on the official "terrorist list" and hence remains ineligible for U.S. aid.

The Bush Administration

U.S.–Syrian relations have improved under the administration of George Bush. Both Bush and Asad instructed their diplomats to initiate a dialogue to find out if there was any common ground between the two countries. U.S. ambassador Edward Djerejian played an important role in restoring a certain amount of trust between Damascus and Washington. Toward the end of the Reagan administration, Washington had already reverted to its traditional policy of promoting stability in Lebanon. This dove-tailed with Syrian efforts, and the United States and Syria worked together to find an acceptable presidential candidate at the end of Amin Gemayel's term. Although this effort failed, the Bush administration shared Syria's support for the Taif Accord on settling the Lebanese civil war and opposed General Aoun's attempt to oust Syria from the country. The United States played a major role in the international legitimation of the pro-Syrian Hrawi government.

Nevertheless, Damascus and Washington remained at odds over the Middle Eastern peace process. The Bush administration was committed in principle to a 242-type settlement and urged Israel to lay aside the unrealistic dream of Greater Israel. In substance, however, the administration's policy initially departed little from that of its predecessor. The United States continued to provide Israel with significant amounts of aid and to stand behind it in the United Nations. It also rejected an international conference as impractical, given Israeli opposition, and held that a bilateral Palestinian-Israeli dialogue to build trust and pave the way for West Bank elections was the best alternative. The United States assured Syria that it was merely concentrating on the Israeli-Palestinian problem first and that it understood that eventually Syria had to be included in any Middle Eastern peace settlement, but it showed little practical interest in drawing Syria into the process. Prior to the Persian Gulf crisis, the United States also continued to exclude Soviet participation in its peace diplomacy, which Damascus considered essential if negotiations were to advance. Syria, for its part, calculated that the Shamir/Baker Plan would fail and clung to the belief that negotiations had to proceed on all fronts. Despite its opposition to the plan, Syria did not obstruct U.S., Egyptian, and Palestinian efforts to get talks off the ground. When efforts to start an Israeli-Palestinian dialogue failed, as Damascus had predicted, U.S.–Israeli relations soured, and the peace process collapsed altogether. Direct communication between Bush and Shamir, who reportedly have a poor personal rapport, virtually ceased. The fragile dialogue between the United States and the PLO, begun in December 1988, was also broken off after Arafat refused to condemn a terrorist attack on Israel to Washington's satisfaction. Syria was not disappointed by this latest failure of U.S. peace diplomacy, however, since it was confident that this would simply advance the day when an international conference would be convened.

The new cordiality in U.S.–Syrian relations, and Syria's détente with Egypt, were signs that Asad was rethinking the strategy of tactical rejectionism. The withdrawal of the Soviet Union from superpower rivalry in the Middle East appeared to render this strategy unviable and left no check on Israeli power projection. Syria shared the sentiment of the wider Arab world, voiced at the 1990 Baghdad Summit, that the United States was ultimately responsible for Israeli expansionism. But, anticipating that the United States was destined to emerge in the post–Cold War era as the sole superpower, Syria recognized the importance of improving relations. If Kissinger believed that there could be no war in the Middle East without Egypt and no peace without Syria, Asad believed that Syria could not wage a war without the Soviet Union and could not achieve peace without the United States. At the same time, Damascus hoped that the end of the Cold War might allow Washington to view the Arab-Israeli conflict in terms other than as a struggle between U.S. and Soviet client-states. It even hoped that Israel's role as a U.S. strategic asset might wane with the end of the East-West conflict.

Syria's participation in the U.S.–led coalition in the Persian Gulf crisis may, in part, have represented a strategic decision that, given the collapse of Soviet power, Syria can no longer seek its goals in opposition to the United States and must give a U.S.–sponsored peace initiative another try. Asad hoped to use the crisis to demonstrate that Syria could behave responsibly and was central to Middle Eastern stability. Above all, he hoped its resolution would generate momentum that would impel the Arab-Israeli peace process. Asad gambled that the United States would not be able to consolidate a new security order in the gulf without also addressing Israel's continued occupation of Arab territory. He will have lost his gamble if Washington only uses the crisis to smash Iraqi power, weaken the Arabs, and entrench itself in the gulf while continuing its traditional pro-Israeli policies.

By early 1991, U.S.–Syrian relations had greatly improved, although the Asad regime's human rights record will ensure that Washington keeps a certain distance. After a long period in which high-level Washington seemed to ignore Syria, Secretary of State Baker visited Damascus, and President Bush began making frequent telephone calls to Asad. The support of Syria, a state with strong Arab nationalist credentials, provided the U.S. military presence in Saudi Arabia with crucial legitimizing cover. Syria also worked to keep Iran in the anti-Iraq coalition. This not only obligated Washington but, in demonstrating Syria's commitment to the regional status quo, may have made it a more credible participant, so far as the United States is concerned, in a revived Arab-Israeli peace process. Syria reaped immediate rewards for its newly improved relations with the United States and for its stance in the Persian Gulf, including an apparent green light for military action against General Aoun in Lebanon and the restoration of ties with and economic aid from Western Europe. Asad's meeting with President Bush in Geneva in November 1990—his first with a U.S. president in thirteen years—seemed to crown his campaign to win U.S. acknowledgment of Syria as a key power in the Middle East on which the region's stability partly depends. Whether this will translate into a new respect for Syrian interests remains to be seen. But, significantly, early in 1991 Washington made Syria a focal point of its efforts to revive Arab-Israeli peace talks following the gulf war.

6

SYRIA AND THE PEACE PROCESS: OPTIONS FOR THE UNITED STATES

So long as the Arab-Israeli conflict remains unresolved, the Middle East will not enjoy real stability, and the dispute will continue to divert the region's energies from other pressing problems. Moreover, existential fears and deeply felt grievances will continue to fuel a profligate arms race that has already made the Middle East the world's most heavily militarized, and perhaps most dangerous, region. It would be imprudent to assume that the status quo, in which another war seems unlikely, can be maintained indefinitely. Without an equitable settlement in which the legitimate interests of all parties are addressed, the possibility of military confrontation will grow. The next war—which would be the sixth since Israel's birth—would almost certainly be more destructive than any of the previous ones because of the proliferation of atomic, biological, and chemical weapons in the region. The United States, therefore, cannot afford to let the peace process die, despite formidable obstacles in the way of a diplomatic solution to the conflict.

In mid-July 1991, prospects for a comprehensive settlement improved greatly as a result of Syria's decision to accept U.S. proposals for convening a regional peace conference under the auspices of the United States and the Soviet Union. While several issues still had to be resolved before a conference could be convened, Syria's agreement to come to the negotiating table with Israel and its willingness to make important concessions concerning the role of the United Nations in any peace talks opened up an extraordinary opportunity to conclude a comprehensive peace agreement. Secretary of State Baker characterized Syria's acceptance of U.S. proposals for a peace conference as "a very important decision" and "an extraordinarily important and positive step." Whatever the final outcome of the peace initiative that the United States launched following the Persian Gulf War,

Syria has confirmed its importance to the outcome of the peace process.

SYRIA AND ISRAEL

Given its pivotal geographical location and disproportionate political influence and military power within the immediate region, Syria is well positioned to advance, as well as to obstruct, the peace process. As the last active frontline state and the self-described beating heart of Arabism, its imprimatur on a peace accord would give a settlement legitimacy. Syria has consistently opposed any further separate peace agreements since Camp David. It successfully blocked the Lebanese-Israeli peace treaty in 1983 and would make every effort to keep Jordan from making a similar deal. Amman, whose participation in the peace process may be a key to resolving the Palestinian problem, will be reluctant to reach an agreement with Israel without Syria's approval. Syria, given the incentive, could also tether rejectionist Palestinians who might otherwise try to sabotage a peace settlement that falls short of their maximalist demands. As the quiet on the Golan front since 1974 shows, Syria's commitment to pacific borders would go a long way toward guaranteeing the peace.

The Asad regime, by accepting UN Security Council Resolution 338 in 1973, acknowledged that Israel is an integral part of the Middle East's state system. Their crushing defeat in 1967 forced the Syrians to confront the fact that they could not reverse the establishment of the Zionist state in Palestine. Asad's view of Israel is significantly more accommodating than that of the radical Ba'thists he deposed in 1970, notwithstanding his reputation as a rejectionist—which comes with his opposition to partial, separate peace agreements and his unwillingness to enter into negotiations under what he sees as unfavorable terms. Asad's assumption of power marked the end of the Ba'th's messianic revolutionary activism and the beginning of a period of realpolitik in which Syrian goals were more limited. The call for the "liberation of Palestine" gradually gave way in Syrian political discourse to a more ambiguous and less comprehensive demand for "Palestinian rights" and for the return of territories occupied in 1967. Thus, after the 1973 war, Asad opposed Iraqi rejectionism in favor of diplomacy. For approximately four years, from the signing of the Golan disengagement agreement in 1974 to Egypt's acceptance of the Camp David Accords, Syria participated in the U.S.–led peace process. In 1975, Asad made his readiness for peace explicit in a number of statements and, for the first time, conceded that a settlement would have to be formalized with a peace treaty. In 1976, Syria backed a UN Security Council resolution calling for Israel's withdrawal from the occupied territories in return for guarantees of the "sovereignty, territorial integrity, and political independence of all states in the area" and of "their right to live in peace within secure recognized borders." Six years later, Syria also agreed to King Fahd's Arab League peace plan in which the Arabs effectively stated their acceptance of Israel (although not clearly enough from Israel's point of view).

Syria has also made its terms for entering negotiations reasonably clear: It seeks a settlement based on UN resolutions 242 and 338 and will offer peace in exchange for Israel's withdrawal to the 1967 lines. To be sure, Syria is unlikely to accept anything less than a return of the Golan Heights and a resolution of the Palestinian problem, either through the creation of an independent Palestinian state in the West Bank and the Gaza Strip or of a Jordanian-Palestinian confederation. Asad's vision of peace has evolved subtly over the past twenty years, partly through force of circumstance. At first, he believed that a settlement could be achieved through a UN accord, rather than through state-to-state peace treaties. The end of belligerency, however, would not automatically result in diplomatic or trade relations, which Asad considered the right of sovereign states to pursue as they wished. This fell far short of the full peace settlement and direct negotiations sought by Israel. Over the years, Asad has edged closer to Israel's demand for a comprehensive settlement, although he still believes this could only be implemented in stages.

Syria, no less than Israel, has strong ideas about the most favorable and appropriate framework for negotiations, although its acceptance in mid-July 1991 of U.S. proposals for convening a peace conference indicated new flexibility over procedural matters. Ideally, it seeks an open-ended international conference in which the United Nations and the superpowers would play a role and the frontline states and the Palestinians are represented. Under such an umbrella, Syria would be willing to hold bilateral talks with Israel. Syria, like Israel, fears that unless the modalities of a peace conference are carefully worked out in advance it might be forced into an unfavorable settlement. Both believe that the structure of the peace conference will shape the outcome of negotiations and that matters of procedure and substance are inseparable. Essentially, Syria calculates that as a participant in an international conference in which the United Nations and the superpowers play a role, it would have a better chance to recover the Golan Heights and more leverage than in some other forum. Israel opposes such a conference for precisely this reason and believes that its interests would be best served in separate bilateral negotiations with each Arab state. The Asad regime also has to consider its domestic constituency: If it were to make a separate deal with Israel over the Golan Heights, ignoring the Palestinian problem, it might sacrifice whatever legitimacy it still has. An international conference of the sort he envisions would provide Asad with cover and make it easier for him to make concessions.

Despite their mutual antagonism, Syria and Israel have shown that they can interact prudently and rationally. The 1974 Golan disengagement agreement, which Syria has scrupulously observed, set an important precedent. Similarly, their tacit understanding over Syria's intervention in Lebanon in 1976 revealed their shared desire for stability and their wish to avoid an unwanted confrontation. More recently, Asad's determination not to be drawn into a war with Israel, even if the latter had chosen to respond to Iraq's Scud missile attacks with force, demonstrated once again that—notwithstanding his pan-Arabist rhetoric—Syria's national security is his primary concern. Asad plays his cards carefully and thoughtfully: He is a realist and a pragmatist more than an ideologue. He will do business with his adversaries and has shown that he can keep his word. Furthermore, he can deliver Syria. Although his regime has a narrow sectarian base and a precarious legitimacy, his notion of what constitutes an acceptable settlement seems to be rooted in a Syrian consensus (insofar as popular views can be gauged in such a repressive state). A comprehensive peace settlement with Israel would, if it satisfied Syrian interests, outlive Asad, just as Egypt's settlement with Israel survived Sadat's assassination.

Although the opportunity to negotiate a lasting peace exists, diplomacy cannot advance very far without a change of attitude on both sides. For Israel to return the territories it took in 1967, it must believe that such a move would enhance, rather than threaten, its security. As things stand, most Israelis believe their security is better served by holding on to the occupied territories. If Syria wants to recover the Golan Heights, it must offer Israel unambiguous reassurances of its peaceful intentions. Israel is unlikely to relinquish the Golan Heights unless Syria agrees to their demilitarization. Asad would probably be willing to concede this, despite his position so far that he would only agree to do so if an equivalent area of Israel was demilitarized. Syria must lay to rest lingering Israeli fears that its irredentist goals extend far beyond the Golan Heights to the liberation of all of Palestine. Decades of bellicose rhetoric are etched in Israel's collective memory and feed deep-seated fears about its very survival. Syria must also end its support for rejectionist Palestinian groups: Israelis must see that Asad's left and right hands are doing the same thing. Many Israelis have an entirely appropriate concern about the autocratic nature of the Asad regime and are apprehensive about signing a peace treaty with a country whose basic direction is determined by one man. Although Asad is not going to liberalize Syria's political system to assuage the fears of Israelis (any more than he will do so to please Syrians), he has the power to normalize diplomatic relations with Israel and negotiate economic cooperation, cultural exchanges, arms control, and water-sharing agreements. Once agreed upon, such a comprehensive settlement would not be easy to renounce.

But Syria cannot make concessions without a sign that Israel will reciprocate. If Syrians are to abandon their dreams of Arab nationalism and a Greater Syria, Israelis must give up their dreams of a Greater Israel. They must make it clear that the Golan Heights, the West Bank, and the Gaza Strip are not irrevocably lost to the Arabs. An opinion poll conducted after the gulf war revealed that 83 percent of Israelis believe that negotiations with Syria should be launched without preconditions. A smaller number—49 percent—accept the principle of trading territories for peace.[1] Israel's policies in the occupied territories, particularly under the Likud's leadership, have given the Arabs little reason to believe it is willing to relinquish territory. Indeed, the Likud government's steadfast opposition to returning the occupied territories must be considered a primary obstacle to peace. As recently as January 1991, the Israeli government forecast a fourfold increase of the Jewish population in the occupied territories within two decades. Significantly, Qazrin, on the Golan Heights, had the highest planned growth rate of any settlement in all of Israel and the occupied territories, with its population expected to grow from 3,000 to 30,000 by the year 2010.[2] In March 1991, on the eve of a visit by Secretary of State Baker, Israel announced that 1,000 additional housing units would be built on the Golan Heights. The previous month, Prime Minister Shamir dismissed reports that Israel might agree to the demilitarization of the Golan Heights, saying they had "no basis whatsoever." A cable from Shamir's office to Jewish settlers on the Golan stated that "Israel has jurisdiction over the Golan Heights and there will be no change in that situation."[3] On March 10, 1991, Dov Shilansky, the Knesset chairman, said that the Golan Heights were an "integral part" of Israel and there was no possibility of discussing their future with the Syrians.[4] The same day, the minister of economy and planning, David Magen, stated that the Golan Heights "are not on the negotiating table. . . . They are under Israeli sovereignty."[5] Shortly thereafter, Yig'al Bibi of the National Religious Party said that his party had formulated "an unequivocal stand against any negotiations with Syria over the future of the Golan Heights" and indicated that NRP representatives in the cabinet and the Knesset would take action "to thwart any political initiative" concerning the Golan Heights' future. And Prime Minister Shamir stated that "the Golan Heights is [sic] not a subject for territorial negotiations. . . . [UN] Resolution 242 has nothing to do with the Golan."[6] On March 20, Moshe Arens, the defense minister, asserted that the Golan Heights were an "inseparable part" of Israel.[7] Two months later, Ariel Sharon, the minister of housing, vowed to double the number of Israelis living in the Golan Heights.[8] Opposition to a withdrawal from the Golan has also been expressed by Labor party leaders during this period: Yitzhak Rabin, the former defense minister, stated his belief that "even in the context of peace with Syria" Israel should not withdraw from the Golan Heights.[9] Even if one allows for a certain amount of political posturing in advance of a serious U.S. effort to revive the peace process and assumes that many more Israelis might be willing to concede territory if Syria were to use the "magic words" they want to hear, Israeli statements about the future of the Golan provide Syria with little incentive to enter into negotiations. If Israel has no intention of returning the Golan Heights, Syria can legitimately ask what there is to talk about. Arab fears that Israel is bent on territorial expansion are no less real than Israel's fears that the Arabs wish to see it eradicated. If Israel wants a durable peace, it must reassure Syria about its territorial ambitions by making the concrete concessions that alone can give Syria a stake in a settlement.

The regional and global costs of not pursuing peace are unacceptably high. If Syria is unable to recover the Golan Heights through peaceful means, it may eventually try to break the stalemate and regain them militarily. Syria would certainly be inviting disaster to take on Israel alone, and the reconstruction of a supporting Arab war coalition is unlikely, especially after the destruction of Iraq's military power. But if the past quarter-century is any guide, enormous changes in the Middle East's political landscape are bound to occur in the future, particularly if the region's foremost problems remain unaddressed. The fact that a Syrian-initiated war seems unlikely now does not mean that this will hold true indefinitely. If an Arab war coalition appeared to be forming, Syria might seize the opportunity to attack Israel, hoping the other Arab states would be drawn into the conflict and the superpowers forced to intervene and impose a satisfactory peace settlement. However, so long as Asad remains in power, such a move is unlikely: Asad is extremely cautious and has a firm grasp of Syria's strengths and limitations.

He also has few illusions about the likelihood of Arab support—the 1982 war, when Syria was left to fight Israel on its own, is still a bitter memory. Asad also has a keen understanding of the international political environment; he knows that the international community would not countenance a Syrian-initiated war and that Syria could expect to be punished, not rewarded, for an attack on Israel. He can no longer count on Soviet support, and after witnessing the response to Iraq's invasion of Kuwait, he will be less tempted than ever to exercise Syria's military options.

A more likely cause of war would be an Israeli preemptive strike against Syria in the face of a perceived military threat. Since there are no indications that the arms race in the region will end soon, it must be assumed that Israeli and Syrian anxiety over one another's increasingly sophisticated and destructive arsenal will grow. Syria is afraid that, with Iraq's military power destroyed, it will be singled out by Israel as the next Arab target. There are also any number of flashpoints in the Middle East that could ignite a war between Syria and Israel. The risks of miscalculation in Lebanon, where both countries are deeply involved in defending perceived vital security interests, remain high. Palestinian terrorist attacks on northern Israel and Israeli retaliatory strikes could, under certain conditions, trigger a confrontation. The explosive situation in the Israeli-occupied territories, where Palestinian human rights are violated on a regular basis, could also degenerate into a broader conflict.

NEW DANGERS AND OPPORTUNITIES

In the aftermath of the gulf war, there was a strong sense that a resolution of the Arab-Israeli conflict could no longer be deferred and that a new opportunity to achieve a lasting peace in the Middle East had to be seized, despite serious obstacles.

Initially, the crisis triggered by Iraq's invasion of Kuwait seemed to set back prospects for peace by exposing the immense divide between Israelis and Palestinians. By the war's end, many Israelis were more reluctant than ever to participate in an international peace conference. They were convinced that Palestinian support for Saddam Hussein demonstrated why Israel should not withdraw from the occupied territories and permit the establishment of a Palestinian state. In addition, the Palestinians lost some of the sympathy they had earned around the world: Yasir Arafat and the PLO were among the war's biggest losers, further complicating the question of who would represent the Palestinians in peace talks. Iraq's missile attacks, which Syria dismissed as "theatrical," accentuated many Israelis' feelings of vulnerability and reinforced their belief that the main threat to their existence came from the Arab states, not the Palestinians.

But in many other respects, Iraq's defeat presented an opportunity to advance the cause of peace in the region. The United States found itself well positioned to harness the international energies it had mobilized in the gulf crisis to resolve the Arab-Israeli conflict once and for all. There was a strong expectation that Washington, having become so deeply involved in the Middle East, would seize the chance to address the main source of regional instability. The coalition victory against Iraq was widely viewed as a "defining moment" in the region's history. The war reshuffled the cards, perhaps more thoroughly than at any time in 40 years. Never before have moderate Arab regimes held the upper hand in the region so decisively and been so willing to work openly with the United States, despite its continued support for Israel. Although U.S. power and prestige are at their peak in some parts of the region, it is widely understood that the United States' political capital could be quickly dissipated if it does not move to resolve the Arab-Israeli dispute with the same vigor and sense of purpose it brought to bear in securing Iraq's withdrawal from Kuwait.

The Middle East has entered a period of fluidity and uncertainty, a time in which both opportunities and dangers have multiplied. The PLO's embrace of a two-state solution, a realist regime in Syria that has, however reluctantly, accepted the existence of Israel, an Egyptian-Israeli peace treaty that has withstood the test of time, and the mobilization of much of the Arab world in defense of the status quo against Iraq are all indicators that the Arabs share with Israel an interest in putting an end to regional conflict. If new hopes for peace are not fulfilled, they will surely give way to an even deeper despair. The challenge is formidable: The United States, having won a war, sees that it has an opportunity to use its enhanced power and influence in the region to arrange peace talks, but it knows that it must act quickly, while its prestige is at its zenith and before old attitudes and patterns reassert themselves.

Despite the steadfast refusal of the United States and its coalition partners to link a resolution of the Persian Gulf crisis with a resolution of the Arab-Israeli conflict, it was universally understood that the United States would, after the war, direct its energies to reviving the peace process. Immediately after Iraq's defeat, President Bush made it clear that solving the region's problems was high on his agenda. In an address before a joint session of Congress on March 7, he reassured the world that the U.S. commitment to peace in the Middle East did not "end with the liberation of Kuwait" and pledged that efforts to find solutions to the region's problems would proceed "with new vigor and determination." He added: "The time has come to put an end to the Arab-Israeli conflict."

If the United States fails to address the Israeli occupation of Arab lands, the Arab regimes allied with Washington during the gulf war may ultimately find this association a liability. There is a widespread perception throughout the Arab world that the United States, which acted so quickly and decisively to end Iraq's occupation of Kuwait, has been unwilling to use its power and influence to reverse the Israeli occupation of conquered Arab lands. Many in the region also interpret the humiliation of Saddam Hussein and the destruction of Iraq's military power primarily in terms of the Arab-Israeli balance of power. The residue of bitterness and resentment "on the street" in some parts of the Arab world over Iraq's defeat should not be underestimated: It will probably grow if U.S. policy is perceived to be inconsistent. The United States will be under pressure from its Arab allies to demonstrate that the coalition was not fighting a surrogate war for Israel and that it cares about their grievances, the foremost of which remains the continued Israeli occupation of Arab land. Without an Arab-Israeli peace settlement, a new U.S.–sponsored security system in the region will be unlikely to endure. But if the Arab states in the anti-Iraq coalition have expectations about new U.S. obligations to them, the reverse is also true. Washington has never been so well positioned to press its Arab allies to make conciliatory, confidence-building gestures toward Israel.

The Arabs are not alone in expecting favors from the United States. Israel clearly hoped that after the war Washington would reward it for its restraint in the face of Iraqi provocations, possibly by not pressing it to make concessions to the Palestinians. For its part, the United States, in responding decisively to Iraq's invasion of Kuwait, in destroying Saddam Hussein's military power, and in deploying Patriot missiles in Israel's defense, hoped that Israel would have greater confidence in the U.S. commitment to its security and would, as a result, be more flexible in the peace process. The destruction of Iraq's military might has dramatically altered the balance of power in the region. Israel's military superiority is, by any objective standard, greater than it has ever been: The threat of an attack from the east has been all but eliminated.

U.S. POLICY AND THE PEACE PROCESS

The hurdles Secretary of State Baker encountered in arranging an Arab-Israeli peace conference following the gulf war underscored that it is not within Washington's power to bring peace to the Middle East if the main parties to the dispute prefer the status quo to a settlement that requires them to make substantial and painful compromises. Nevertheless, the United States has a vital role to play in facilitating peace in the region. Whether Israel and the Arabs are ultimately able to bridge the chasm that separates them still depends to some extent on how much energy the United States is willing to invest as a mediator. While Washington cannot impose peace on a region that is not ready for it and must steer a delicate course if it is to maintain the trust of those most centrally involved in the dispute, no one can seriously argue that the United States has yet used its full power to bring about a settlement based on the principle of exchanging territory for peace—a goal that six consecutive U.S. presidents have nominally supported since 1967. This is not to underestimate the practical limits to the United States' influence in the region: U.S. presidents have generally been reluctant to exert pressure on Israel when the Jewish state has the overwhelming support of Congress, and the United States has little leverage over Syria, except indirectly through Saudi Arabia, Egypt, and, now, the Soviet Union.

The U.S. peace initiative following the gulf war contained many of the external ingredients necessary for a diplomatic breakthrough: It aimed at achieving a comprehensive, region-wide settlement through a two-track approach that would simultaneously resolve the conflict between Israel and the Arab states and address the Palestinian problem; it sought the widest possible participation within the region and included Syria from the outset as a key player; it involved the Soviet Union and envisioned some role for the United Nations and the European Community; it sought some sort of balance between the Arabs' desire for an international conference and Israel's insistence on direct bilateral talks; and it recognized the importance of linking a settlement to arms control and water-sharing agreements, as well as to regional security arrangements. By late summer the initiative had brought the main parties closer than ever before to taking the final, difficult plunge. U.S. policy is on the right track. But in the Middle East, pessimists are rewarded for their predictions more often than optimists. Despite many encouraging signs that a historic breakthrough was possible, past experience tells us how easily the peace process can be derailed. The obstacles to a comprehensive peace agreement will remain formidable even if a peace conference is convened. If this latest, and most promising, U.S. peace initiative ultimately fails, what can the United States do?

First, Washington must continue to make it clear that it seeks a comprehensive settlement based on an Israeli withdrawal from occupied Arab territories, a resolution of the Palestinian problem, and full Arab recognition of Israel. President Bush did just that in a speech before Congress on March 7 when he stated:

A comprehensive peace must be grounded in United Nations Security Council Resolutions 242 and 338 and the principle of territory for peace. This principle must be elaborated to provide for Israel's security and recognition, and at the same time for legitimate Palestinian political rights. Anything else would fail the twin tests of fairness and security.

In the long run, this land-for-peace formula, embodied in UN Resolution 242, which has almost universal international backing, is the only approach that addresses the concerns of all parties and therefore has a chance of succeeding. Implementing the key UN resolutions will require difficult concessions from Israel and major political concessions from the Arabs, but as Bush observed, "By now, it should be plain to all parties that peacekeeping in the Middle East requires compromise." He noted: "We have learned in the modern age, geography cannot guarantee security and security does not come from military power alone." Since Israel's policy of expropriating land and building new settlements in the occupied territories seriously complicates peace-making efforts and is designed in part to make the eventual return of these lands to Arab control more difficult (if not impossible), the United States must be more vocal and vigorous in its opposition to this policy. This is an urgent matter. If Washington permits Israel's creeping annexation of the occupied territories to proceed unchecked, it will be confronted with a far more difficult problem to resolve in the future. The United States should press Israel to freeze new settlement activity in the occupied territories in order to improve the climate for a land-for-peace deal, which will be difficult to engineer while mutual suspicion and fear run so high. But that is not enough. The United States should also press both sides to take a number of confidence-building steps. Israel should be encouraged to release Palestinian prisoners, reopen Palestinian universities, and observe human rights in the occupied territories. In turn, the Arabs should be pressed to end their economic boycott, which stands as a powerful symbol of their nonrecognition, and to reassure Israel that any peace treaty it signs will not simply be a paper agreement that still leaves it ostracized within the region.

Second, although the dispute between Israelis and Palestinians constitutes the heart of the Arab-Israeli problem, the United States must continue to involve Syria fully in its efforts to resolve the conflict. There is no way to get around the fact that Syria is a major party to the dispute with legitimate interests in its outcome. Without its involvement, there can be no real or lasting peace. Historically, the United States and Syria have each held the other partly responsible for the failure of the peace process. From Washington's perspective, Syria has not demonstrated sufficient interest in pursuing peace in the past and has dismissed out of hand or obstructed a variety of U.S. diplomatic initiatives, insisting that it would only participate in an international conference convened under UN auspices. Recent American administrations have viewed Syria as intransigent and rejectionist and as an obstacle to peace in the region. There is certainly some truth to the charge that Asad has been stubborn and inflexible about the way in which the peace process should proceed, although he would claim that he was only being consistent and principled. Asad is not a risk-taker, willing to explore any avenue to peace and ready to participate in an open-ended process with ill-defined parameters. If the music is not right, he will sit out the dance. From Damascus's perspective, it is the United States that historically has lacked a sufficient commitment to peace in the Middle East by avoiding a comprehensive settlement that entailed substantial Israeli territorial concessions, accorded the Palestinians their national rights, and, most important, included Syria. There is also some truth to this charge. The United States helped sponsor UN Resolution 242, which expresses the international consensus on a peaceful settlement, but from Damascus's vantage it has not pressed hard for its implementation. In addition, by promoting separate agreements that have left Syria out, the United States has allowed Asad to think that he has little to gain from supporting the peace process and much to gain by obstructing it. Despite the mutual recriminations, the United States and Syria need one another's help in resolving some of the region's main problems. Recognition of this reality has grown in recent years, with the United States giving Syria an important role in its efforts to revive the peace process after the gulf war.

If U.S. efforts to convene an international conference fail, or if negotiations between Israel and Syria reach an impasse, Washington may once again be tempted to seek separate bilateral talks between Israel and a joint Jordanian-Palestinian delegation. While no avenue to peace should be ignored, such a plan would probably be no more successful now than in the past. To be sure, much has changed in the region since the last time the "Jordanian option" was pursued. In particular, King Hussein, the PLO leadership, and many Palestinians in the occupied territories seem eager in the aftermath of the gulf war to consider almost every offer placed before them. But the possibility that Syria would try to sabotage a separate deal remains acute. No one really knows if Syria could successfully derail peace talks that excluded it, especially if all of the other key Arab states supported such negotiations, but the record suggests it will energetically and ruthlessly defend its interests. Some have argued that Syria's power in the Levant is exaggerated. That may be so, but the Jordanians and Palestinians cannot ignore the fact that Syria is a prominent Arab power in the immediate region. If anything, the defeat of Iraq, which they looked to for protection from Syria as well as from Israel, has increased their vulnerability to Damascus's pressure. Bypassing Syria might work, but involving it as a central partner in the peace process makes it easier for Arab states to participate. Ultimately, including Syria in an effort to reach a comprehensive peace on all fronts will be a more productive policy, whatever the frustrations it may entail in the short run.

Third, irrespective of the domestic situation within the Soviet Union, the United States must continue to involve Moscow directly and centrally in efforts to resolve the Arab-Israeli conflict, as it has done very effectively since the end of the gulf war. Historically, the United States tended to view the Middle East primarily as an arena of superpower rivalry and to interpret local issues in terms of the East-West conflict. This was counterproductive and detrimental to the peace process. Because Washington was determined to prevent Moscow from having a role in Middle East diplomacy, the Soviets had no incentive to cooperate in solving the conflict and no reason to pressure Syria and the PLO in ways that would have served the interests of peace. Nixon (at least initially) and Reagan both believed that Syria's interests could be ignored because of their overriding concern with containing the Soviet Union and undermining its clients.

With the end of the Cold War, the United States has no good reason to exclude the Soviet Union from the peace process and excellent reasons to give it a stake in its success. The dispute between Arabs and Israelis is too complex for Washington to resolve on its own, as the record clearly shows, and there are ways in which Moscow is uniquely situated to advance the peace process. Most obviously, while the United States has almost no direct leverage over Syria, the Soviet Union can, if it is so inclined, prod it to be more flexible. However, the Asad regime will not let itself be dictated to by its superpower patron if its vital interests are at stake any more than Israel will comply with U.S. wishes in the same circumstances. So long as the Soviet Union remains the main supplier of weapons to Syria, it will have influence in Damascus. Gorbachev has told Syria that Israel's interests must be taken into account, and he has made it clear that the Soviet Union would not support any attempt to reclaim the Golan Heights through military action. Israel now has far less reason to fear that Soviet participation in the peace process would be to its detriment. Moscow has demonstrated its commitment to playing a constructive role in the region and has expressed its desire to normalize relations with Jerusalem. In particular, opening the door for millions of Soviet Jews who may wish to emigrate to Israel over the next few years has improved relations between the two countries and shifted thinking in Israel about the Soviet Union's potential contribution to the peace process. The first visit by a Soviet foreign minister to Israel in May 1991 underscored how dramatically different a role the Soviet Union is now playing in the region.

Today, neither the United States nor the Soviet Union has as much reason to take sides in regional conflicts. Superpower cooperation in the gulf crisis provided conclusive evidence of this trend and underlined the enormous advantages of multilateral approaches to solving regional disputes. Making it clear that the United States and the Soviet Union are in substantial agreement about the peace process and that both favor a settlement based on the implementation of UN resolutions 242 and 338 and the exchange of territory for peace sends a powerful signal to the main parties in the dispute. A joint stance by the superpowers puts more pressure on Israel and Syria to reach a compromise, but it also offers both of them the reassurances they need to risk negotiations. Growing cooperation between the United States and the Soviet Union makes an effective joint superpower guarantee of a peace settlement more feasible than ever before.

The degree to which the United States should involve the United Nations and the European Community in resolving the dispute is more problematical. Washington's desire to play the dominant role in the Middle East has led it in the past to give little encouragement to European diplomatic initiatives and to downplay the United Nations as a forum for resolving the dispute. If the "new world order" is to have any meaning at all, the responsibility for bringing peace to the region must be broadened, not narrowed. Furthermore, the participation of the United Nations in the gulf crisis emphasized the advantages for the United States of acting multilaterally and within the context of a worldwide consensus. The apparent strengthening of the United Nations as a hub of the new world order gives greater reason than ever before to believe that global solutions to regional problems can be devised and enforced. To the extent that the international community can speak with one voice about what kind of peace it believes is fair and reasonable, the harder it will be for Israel and the Arabs to avoid a settlement based on real compromises and the more secure they may feel about taking the necessary risks. But there is a difference between what may be desirable in principle and what may be practical in a less than ideal world. Israel is as opposed to the United Nations playing a major role in resolving the dispute as Syria is in favor of it, in both cases for understandable reasons. The former sees the United Nations as an unsympathetic and untrustworthy body that is dominated by its adversaries. The latter, by contrast, sees the United Nations as a source of international legitimacy for its position and as a useful instrument to further its goals. Significantly, disagreement between the two countries over what the United Nations' role should be in a peace conference was the main stumbling block to U.S. efforts to arrange direct talks after the gulf war. Nevertheless, the United States should continue to search for a formula that does not exclude the United Nations from the peace process.

Fourth, the United States must avoid the temptation to disengage from the peace process if its post–gulf war peace initiative flounders. Nor should the United States let itself be sidetracked by endless procedural wrangling, as apparently happened during Baker's visits to the Middle East after the war. A bold and dramatic gesture by President Bush, such as publicly inviting the main parties to a conference in Washington, could provide just the right amount of pressure and momentum to reinvigorate the peace process. In addition, if Bush decided, in spite of the risk of failure, to involve himself personally in the peace process and invested his full authority in brokering a compromise, it could break the logjam and produce a settlement. Jimmy Carter understood that a successful peace settlement could not dispense with the personal commitment of the president. From the time Kissinger began his shuttle diplomacy, the Syrians insisted that only a vigorous U.S. effort could achieve a settlement. Many Israelis feel the same way: Abba Eban once lamented that the United States "pays lip-service to peace, encouraging the parties directly involved to enter into 'direct negotiations.' Yet . . . such talks [can] bear no fruit without active outside involvement. Meanwhile, American inaction lends support to the rejectionist fronts in both the Arab world and Israel."[10] It is only when the United States has played a vigorous mediating role, as under Nixon and Carter, that it has brokered diplomatic breakthroughs. The gap between the Arabs and the Israelis is wide, but it is precisely in such cases that third-party mediation is most essential. Neither side can make concessions unless there is a powerful third party able to communicate with both—one that is capable of using both carrots and sticks, making sure negotiations do not break down, and giving the security and political guarantees needed for the parties to take the risks involved. The United States is still uniquely situated to play this role.

Fifth, if there is to be peace and stability in the Middle East, the United States and the other major powers must commit themselves to ending a dangerous and expensive local arms race. The number of weapons in the region is so excessive, and their nature so destructive, that they can no longer be considered merely a symptom of conflict or a means of deterring aggression: They have themselves become a source of tension and an invitation to war. One of the main goals in the war against Iraq was to destroy some of the $50 billion in arms it had purchased from 24 countries in the 1980s. The Middle East is today the world's largest importer of arms, buying over a third of all weapons imports and half of all third world weapons imports. Six of the ten leading arms importing countries are in the Middle East: Saudi Arabia, Iraq, Israel, Syria, Libya, and Egypt. Saudi Arabia and Iraq alone accounted for 30 percent of third world arms purchases between 1981 and 1989, spending almost $100 billion between them. The United States and the Soviet Union are the source of over half of the Middle East's arms imports and thus bear a special responsibility to control the flow of weapons. While there are, in fact, many concurrent arms races in the region, they are clearly synergistic and impossible to separate. It is imperative that this arms race be controlled. The United States can begin by resisting the temptation, which will be strong in the wake of the gulf war, to heavily arm its allies, who will undoubtedly want to obtain some of the weapons they saw displayed with such effectiveness against Iraq. However, there seems little chance the United States or any other power will significantly restrict conventional arms sales to the region. Immediately after the end of the gulf war, the Bush administration asked Congress to approve the sale of 46 F-16 fighter jets, worth $1.6 billion, to Egypt, and indicated that it was considering selling $18-billion worth of arms to Saudi Arabia, the United Arab Emirates, Bahrain, Egypt, and Turkey.[11] Israel will certainly seek to preserve its superiority over any likely combination of Arab states, and Syria will inevitably struggle to keep up with Israel. Unfortunately, the gulf war will probably accelerate the arms race in the region, despite all the lofty rhetoric about the need to control arms sales: Geopolitical and commercial considerations will once again win out over common sense. Some analysts have advocated that the United States put pressure on the Soviet Union to reduce arms shipments to Syria, but the Soviets have made it clear that such restraint on their part must be matched by reduced U.S. arms deliveries to Israel—something that no U.S. administration is likely to agree to. However, jointly scaling down military aid to the region would reduce the danger of war and send the message to both sides that they cannot achieve their goals by military force. Realistically, arms control measures will not work unless they are coupled with a resolution of the conflicts that create the demand for weapons in the first place. The issues of peace, security, and arms control in the region are inseparable and must, therefore, be dealt with simultaneously and multilaterally.

•

It has been fashionable in some quarters recently to argue that Syria is in decline, that it need not be considered in the peace process, and that its presumed opposition to peace can and should be contained and neutralized. The problem with this argument is that it grossly underestimates Syria's ability to defend its vital interests and neglects both its significant political influence within the Levant and its pivotal role in the Arab-Israeli conflict. Syria's role in the gulf crisis should lay to rest the notion that Damascus does not count in the wider Middle Eastern arena. In the long run, it will be more productive to involve Syria centrally in the peace process, as the Bush administration has recently tried to do, and strive for a comprehensive settlement that includes, rather than excludes, this key frontline state.

APPENDIX

RESOLUTION 242:

THE SECURITY COUNCIL,

Expressing its continued concern with the grave situation in the Middle East,

Emphasizing the inadmissibility of the acquisition of territory by war and the need to work for a just and lasting peace in which every state in the area can live in security,

Emphasizing further that all member states in their acceptance of the Charter of the United Nations have undertaken a commitment to act in accordance with Article 2 of the Charter.

1. Affirms that the fulfilment of Charter principles requires the establishment of a just and lasting peace in the Middle East which should include the application of both the following principles:

(i) Withdrawal of Israel armed forces from territories occupied in the recent conflict;

(ii) Termination of all claims or states of belligerency and respect for and acknowledgement of the sovereignty, territorial integrity and political independence of every state in the area and their right to live in peace within secure and recognized boundaries free from threats or acts of force.

2. Affirms further the necessity (a) for guaranteeing freedom of navigation through international waterways in the area; (b) for achieving a just settlement of the refugee problem; (c) for guaranteeing the territorial inviolability and political independence of every state in the area, through measures including the establishment of demilitarized zones;

3. Requests the Secretary General to designate a special representative to proceed to the Middle East to establish and maintain contacts with the states concerned in order to promote agreement and assist efforts to achieve a peaceful and accepted

settlement in accordance with the provisions and principles in this resolution;

4. Requests the Secretary General to report to the Security Council on the progress of the efforts of the special representative as soon as possible.

RESOLUTION 338:

THE SECURITY COUNCIL,

1. Calls upon all parties to the present fighting to cease all firing and terminate all military activity immediately, no later than 12 hours after the moment of the adoption of this decision in the positions they now occupy;

2. Calls upon the parties concerned to start immediately after the cease-fire the implementation of Security Council Resolution 242 in all of its parts;

3. Decided that immediately and concurrently with the cease-fire, negotiations start between the parties concerned under appropriate auspices aimed at establishing a just and durable peace in the Middle East.

NOTES

CHAPTER 2

1. Moshe Ma'oz, *Asad: The Sphinx of Damascus* (New York: Weidenfeld & Nicolson, 1988), p. ix.
2. Patrick Seale, *Asad: The Struggle for the Middle East* (Berkeley: University of California Press, 1988), p. 493.
3. Syria's population is among the most religiously and ethnically diverse in the Middle East. According to one estimate, roughly 85 percent of all Syrians are Arabic-speaking and some 70 percent are Sunni Muslim, but these two categories are not completely congruent and Arabic-speaking Sunni Muslims account for less than 60 percent of the total population. The religious and ethnic minorities that comprise 40 percent of Syria's population are diverse. Although 85 percent of all Syrians are Muslim and almost all the rest are Christian, both communities are subdivided into many sects. Among the former, the main minorities are the Alawis (11.5 percent), Druzes (3 percent) and Isma'ilis (1.5 percent), all of whom are Arabic-speaking splinter Shiite groups. The largely Arab Christians are divided among a large number of denominations, with the Greek Orthodox the largest (4.7 percent). The main ethnic minorities, among whom Arabic is now widely used, are the Kurds (8.5 percent), Armenians (4 percent), Turcomans (3 percent), and Circassians (under 1 percent). Of these, all but the Christian Armenians are Sunni Muslim. The geographical distribution of the various religious and ethnic communities has emphasized their social differences, accentuated regional cleavages, and impeded national integration. Whereas many of the minorities are scattered, the so-called compact minorities constitute a local majority in particular parts of the country: the Alawis in the mountainous coastal provinces of Ladhiqiyah and Tartus in the northwest, the Druzes in al-Suwayda' in the southwest, the Kurds in parts of Hasakah in the northeast, and the Isma'ilis to the east of Hamah. Sunnis form a majority in all of the large cities and in every province except the three dominated by Alawis and Druzes. Historically, the Alawis and Druzes, whom many Sunnis persecuted as heretics, resisted the imposition of outside authority and enjoyed a large measure of autonomy in their impoverished mountain redoubts. The French exploited these sectarian differences and relied heavily on divide-and-rule policies during their colonial mandate over Syria between the two world wars, recruiting minorities in disproportionate numbers into their local militias and establishing separate mini-states for the Alawis and Druzes. This left a legacy of mistrust between the Sunni Arab majority, who led the country to independence and dominated the state's political institutions, and the peripheral minorities, who felt excluded and ignored.
4. Seale, *Asad*, p. 441.

5. Michael Van Dusen, "Syria: Downfall of a Traditional Elite," in Frank Tachau, ed., *Political Elites and Political Development in the Middle East* (Cambridge, Mass.: Schenkman, 1975), pp. 115–55.

6. The Ba'th party's precise origins have been a matter of dispute among its members, who disagree about the relative contributions of Michel Aflaq, Salah al-Din Bitar, and Zaki Arsuzi as founding fathers. Since 1963, Syrian Ba'thists have given far more weight to Arsuzi, an activist Alawi intellectual from Alexandretta, who is credited with attracting a large number of Alawi youth from the Ladhiqiyah region into the party. However, throughout the 1950s and early 1960s the Ba'th was dominated both intellectually and organizationally by Aflaq and Bitar. Part of the dispute about the party's genesis reflects the early Ba'thi movement's diversity and disorganization: At the outset, there were in fact two Ba'thi groups, one led by Arsuzi, the other by Aflaq and Bitar. Arsuzi subsequently accused Aflaq and Bitar of stealing the name Ba'th (some of his supporters went even further, charging Aflaq with pilfering his ideas too). Not until 1947 did the two groups merge under Aflaq and Bitar's leadership. For the party's history, see John F. Devlin, *The Ba'th Party: A History from Its Origins to 1966* (Stanford: Hoover Institution Press, 1976) and Kamel S. Abu Jaber, *The Arab Ba'th Socialist Party* (Syracuse, N.Y.: Syracuse University Press, 1966).

7. Seale, *Asad*, p. 30.

8. The constitution is reprinted in full in Devlin, *Ba'th Party.*

9. Gordon Torrey, *Syrian Politics and the Military, 1945–1958* (Columbus: Ohio State University Press, 1964), p. 45.

10. Patrick Seale, *The Struggle for Syria: A Study of Post-War Arab Politics, 1945–1958* (London: Oxford University Press, 1965), p. 37.

11. Alasdair Drysdale, "The Syrian Armed Forces in National Politics: The Role of the Ethnic and Geographic Periphery," in Roman Kolkowicz and Andrzej Korbonski, eds., *Soldiers, Peasants, and Bureaucrats* (London: Allen & Unwin, 1982).

12. The best accounts of the Ba'th's ascent to power and the early years of the regime are in Itamar Rabinovich, *Syria Under the Ba'th: The Army-Party Symbiosis* (New York: Halstead Press, 1972) and Nikolaos van Dam, *The Struggle for Power in Syria: Sectarianism, Regionalism, and Tribalism in Politics, 1961–1980* (London: Croom Helm, 1981).

13. *Human Rights in Syria* (New York: Human Rights Watch, 1990), pp. 29–31.

14. Seale, *Asad*, p. 341.

15. Raymond A. Hinnebusch, *Authoritarian Power and State Formation in Ba'thist Syria: Army, Party, and Peasant* (Boulder, Col.: Westview Press, 1990), pp. 166–90.

16. Seale, *Asad*, p. 175.

17. *Human Rights in Syria*, p. 32.

18. Ibid., p. 164.

19. Seale, *Asad*, pp. 180–81.

20. Hanna Batatu, "Some Observations on the Social Roots of Syria's Ruling Military Group and the Causes for Its Dominance," *Middle East Journal*, vol. 35, no. 3 (1981), pp. 331–44.

21. Ma'oz, *Asad*, pp. 62–67.

22. Martin Kramer, "Syria's Alawis and Shi'ism," in Martin Kramer, ed., *Shi'ism, Resistance, and Revolution* (Boulder, Col.: Westview Press, 1987), pp. 245–49.
23. Van Dam, *Struggle for Power in Syria*, p. 114.
24. Seale, *Asad*, p. 456.
25. Foreign Broadcast Information Service, *Near East and South Asia* (hereafter cited as FBIS), April 9, 1981, p. G11.
26. For accounts of the Hamah massacre, see *Report from Amnesty International to the Government of the Syrian Arab Republic* (London: Amnesty International, 1983) and Thomas L. Friedman, *From Beirut to Jerusalem* (New York: Doubleday, 1989), pp. 76–105. The Asad regime's mounting difficulties in the 1970s and early 1980s, which culminated in the Hamah massacre, are more fully discussed in Alasdair Drysdale, "The Asad Regime and Its Troubles," *Merip Reports*, no. 112 (November–December 1982), pp. 3–11.
27. FBIS, March 31, 1980, p. H4.
28. Seale, *Asad*, pp. 334–35.
29. Alasdair Drysdale, "The Succession Question in Syria," *Middle East Journal*, vol. 39, no. 2 (1985), pp. 246–57.
30. Seale, *Asad*, p. 440.
31. FBIS, March 8, 1990, p. 32.
32. FBIS, February 28, 1990, p. 45.
33. FBIS, May 8, 1990, p. 29.
34. FBIS, February 28, 1990, p. 45.
35. FBIS, May 17, 1990, p. 27.
36. FBIS, June 12, 1990, pp. 38–39.
37. FBIS, May 17, 1990, p. 27.
38. FBIS, March 9, 1990, pp. 29–30.
39. FBIS, May 17, 1990, pp. 27–28.
40. Milton Viorst, "The Shadow of Saladin," *New Yorker*, January 8, 1990, pp. 54–57.
41. See John Devlin, *Syria: Modern State in an Ancient Land* (Boulder, Col.: Westview Press, 1983) and Kais Faro, "The Syrian Economy under the Assad Regime," in Moshe Ma'oz and Avner Yaniv, eds., *Syria under Assad: Domestic Constraints and Regional Risks* (New York: St. Martin's Press, 1986), pp. 36–68.
42. Economist Intelligence Unit (hereafter cited as EIU), *Syria*, no. 3 (1990), p. 3. *Middle East Economic Digest* (hereafter cited as MEED), February 1, 1991, p. 22.
43. *Foreign Economic Trends and Their Implications for the United States: Syria* (Washington, D.C.: International Trade Administration, U.S. Department of Commerce, October 1989).
44. EIU, *Syria*, no. 1 (1990), p. 17.
45. Patrick Clawson, *Unaffordable Ambitions: Syria's Military Buildup and Economic Crisis*, Policy Papers No. 17 (Washington, D.C.: Washington Institute for Near East Policy, 1989), pp. 1–18.
46. EIU, *Syria*, no. 2 (1990), pp. 11–12.
47. Clawson, *Unaffordable Ambitions*, p. 1.
48. Ibid., p. 17.
49. EIU, *Syria*, no. 2 (1990), p. 17.

50. MEED, September 8, 1989, p. 7.
51. MEED, January 18, 1991, p. 19.
52. MEED, December 21, 1990, p. 19.
53. "Breathing through the Lebanese Lung," *The Middle East*, March 1990, p. 46.
54. MEED, February 16, 1990, p. 33.
55. MEED, March 16, 1990, p. 31.
56. MEED, February 23, 1990, p. 5.
57. EIU, *Syria*, no. 2 (1990), p. 4.
58. Clawson, *Unaffordable Ambitions*, p. 2.

CHAPTER 3

1. Michael Hudson, *Arab Politics: The Search for Legitimacy* (New Haven, Conn.: Yale University Press, 1977), p. 257.
2. Fouad Ajami, *The Arab Predicament: Arab Political Thought and Practice Since 1967* (Cambridge: Cambridge University Press, 1981), p. 124.
3. Ma'oz, *Asad*, p. 182.
4. FBIS, August 10, 1988, p. 38.
5. Bernard Lewis, *The Middle East and the West* (New York: Harper & Row, 1964), p. 94.
6. Seale, *Struggle for Syria*, p. 130.
7. Eliezer Be'eri, *Army Officers in Arab Politics and Society* (New York: Praeger, 1970), p. 151.
8. *King Henry the Sixth, Part III*, Act III, sc. iii.
9. Raymond A. Hinnebusch, "Revisionist Dreams, Realist Strategies: The Foreign Policy of Syria," in B. Korany and A. E. Hillal Dessouki, eds., *The Foreign Policies of Arab States* (Boulder, Colo.: Westview Press, 1984), p. 289.
10. FBIS, August 15, 1990, p. 44.
11. FBIS, August 17, 1990, p. 50.
12. For a discussion of the Greater Syria concept, see Daniel Pipes, *Greater Syria: The History of an Ambition* (New York: Oxford University Press, 1990).
13. FBIS, March 24, 1980, p. H5.
14. FBIS, March 26, 1981, p. H15.
15. FBIS, April 27, 1981, p. H4.
16. *New York Times*, December 4, 1983, p. A4.
17. *The Nation*, October 1, 1983, p. 269.
18. FBIS, August 6, 1985, p. H2.
19. Martha Neff Kessler, *Syria: Fragile Mosaic of Power* (Washington, D.C.: National Defense University Press, 1987), p. 71.
20. FBIS, December 18, 1989, p. 48.
21. FBIS, December 27, 1989, p. 36.
22. Fuad Jabber, "The Palestinian Resistance and Inter-Arab Politics," in William Quandt, ed., *The Politics of Palestinian Nationalism* (Berkeley: University of California Press, 1973), pp. 157–216; Moshe Ma'oz and Avner Yaniv, "On a Short Leash: Syria and the PLO," in Ma'oz and Yaniv, eds., *Syria under Assad*, pp. 192–96; Aaron D. Miller, "Syria and the Palestinians,"

Middle East Insight, vol. 4, no. 2 (June/July 1985), pp. 3–9; Yezid Sayigh, "Understanding Palestinian-Arab Relations: The Interventionists," *Middle East International,* no. 297 (April 3, 1987), pp. 17–18.

23. This analysis is based on "Speech Delivered by Comrade Hafiz al-Asad before a General Plenum of Local Government Councils," Damascus, July 20, 1976; Adeed Dawisha, *Syria and the Lebanese Crisis* (London: Macmillan, 1980); and Naomi J. Weinberger, *Syrian Intervention in Lebanon: The 1975–1976 Civil War* (New York: Oxford University Press, 1986).

24. Adeed Dawisha, "Syria in Lebanon: Asad's Vietnam?" *Foreign Policy,* no. 33 (Winter 1978–1979), pp. 135–50.

25. Itamar Rabinovich, *The War for Lebanon* (Ithaca, N. Y.: Cornell University Press, 1984), p. 190; Tabitha Petran, *The Struggle for Lebanon* (New York: Monthly Review Press, 1987), pp. 313–83.

26. FBIS, February 22, 1990, p. 1.

27. FBIS, May 8, 1990, p. 27.

28. FBIS, August 8, 1990, p. 50.

29. Elie Chalala, "Syria's Support of Iran in the Gulf War: The Role of Structural Change and the Emergence of a Relatively Strong State," *Journal of Arab Affairs,* vol. 7 (1988), p. 110.

30. *Washington Post,* May 3, 1985, p. A28, as quoted in Kessler, *Syria,* p. 88.

31. Cited in Ma'oz, *Asad,* p. 156.

32. Seale, *Asad,* p. 357.

33. Yair Hirschfeld, "The Odd Couple: Ba'thist Syria and Khomeini's Iran," in Ma'oz and Yaniv, eds., *Syria under Assad,* pp. 105–24.

34. Tehran radio commentary, quoted in *Middle East International,* January 5, 1990, p. 4.

CHAPTER 4

1. Avner Yaniv, "Syria and Israel: The Politics of Escalation," in Ma'oz and Yaniv, eds., *Syria under Assad,* pp. 158–62.

2. Seale, *Struggle for Syria,* pp. 254–55.

3. Avraham Ben Tzur, *The Syrian Baath Party and Israel* (Givat Haviva, Israel: Center for Arab and Afro-Asian Studies, 1968).

4. Quoted in David Hirst, *The Gun and the Olive Branch* (London: MacDonald & Co., 1978), p. 216. The concentration of tanks was later acknowledged by Israeli chief of operations Ezar Weizman in the Israeli weekly *Ot,* June 1, 1972 (cited in Hirst, p. 215).

5. Yoram Peri, *Between Battles and Ballots: Israel's Military in Politics* (New York: Cambridge University Press, 1983), pp. 244–51; Charles Smith, *Palestine and the Arab-Israeli Conflict* (New York: St. Martins Press, 1988), p. 200. Dayan was long distinguished as a leading hawk. He is quoted in the diaries of Moshe Sharett as arguing very early on that Israel "must adopt the method of provocation . . . and . . . hope for a new war with the Arab countries—so that we may finally get rid of our troubles and acquire space" (quoted in Jonathan Randall, *Going All the Way: Christian Warlords, Israeli Adventurers, and the War in Lebanon* [New York: Vintage Books, 1984], p. 194).

6. Quotation cited in Yaniv, "Syria and Israel," p. 165.

7. Smith, *Palestine and the Arab-Israeli Conflict*, pp. 208–10, 229–30. See also William W. Harris, *Taking Root: Israeli Settlements in the West Bank, the Golan, and Gaza-Sinai, 1967–1980* (New York: John Wiley & Sons, 1980).

8. Yair Evron, *War and Intervention in Lebanon: The Israeli-Syrian Deterrence Dialogue* (Baltimore: Johns Hopkins University Press, 1987), pp. 183–84, 197.

9. Avner Yaniv, "Alliance Politics in the Middle East: A Security Dilemma Perspective," in Aurel Braun, ed., *The Middle East in Global Strategy* (New York: Westview Press, 1987), pp. 141–43.

10. The military analysis of the war relies on Martin van Creveld, *Military Lessons of the Yom Kipper War: Historical Perspectives*, The Washington Papers, vol. 3, no. 24 (Beverly Hills, Cal.: Sage Publications, 1975); Seale, *Asad*, pp. 207–21; P. R. Chari, "Military Lessons of the Arab-Israeli War of 1973," *Institute for Defense Studies and Analysis Journal* (New Delhi) [April–June 1976]; Riad Askar, "The Syrian and Egyptian Campaigns, *Journal of Palestine Studies*, vol. 14 (1974), pp. 15–33; Charles Wakebridge, "The Syrian Side of the Hill," *Military Review*, vol. 56 (February 1976), pp. 20–30.

11. Wakebridge, "Syrian Side of the Hill," p. 27.

12. FBIS, May 8, 1990, p. 31.

13. Henry A. Kissinger, *Years of Upheaval* (Boston: Little, Brown & Company, 1982), pp. 1046, 1067.

14. *Newsweek*, June 10, 1974, p. 34.

15. Interview with Arnaud de Borchgrave, *Newsweek*, March 3, 1975, p. 35.

16. Noam Chomsky, *The Fateful Triangle: The United States, Israel and the Palestinians* (Boston, Mass.: South End Press), p. 67.

17. "Statement of the National Leadership on the Activities of the 12th National Congress of the Arab Socialist Ba'th Party," Damascus, 1975.

18. Cyrus Vance, *Hard Choices: Critical Years in America's Foreign Policy* (New York: Simon & Schuster, 1983), p. 170; William Quandt, *Decade of Decisions: American Policy Toward the Arab-Israeli Conflict, 1967–1976* (Berkeley: University of California Press, 1977), pp. 138–39.

19. Kissinger, *Years of Upheaval*, p. 1054; Edward R. F. Sheehan, "How Kissinger Did It: Step By Step in the Middle East," *Foreign Policy*, no. 22 (1976), reprinted in Jeffrey Z. Rubin, ed., *Dynamics of Third Party Intervention: Kissinger in the Middle East* (New York: Praeger, 1981), p. 68.

20. Smith, *Palestine and the Arab-Israeli Conflict*, p. 253.

21. Cited in Itamar Rabinovich, "Israel, Syria, and Jordan," paper presented at the Council on Foreign Relations, New York City, October 1989, p. 6.

22. Jimmy Carter, *The Blood of Abraham: Insights into the Middle East* (Boston: Houghton-Mifflin, 1985), p. 72.

23. *New York Times*, August 21, 1977; Vance, *Hard Choices*, pp. 171, 177–78.

24. Evron, *War and Intervention*, pp. 54, 203.

25. Ibid., pp. 54–66.

26. Seale, *Asad*, p. 302; Carter, *Blood of Abraham*, pp. 73–74.

27. Randall, *Going all the Way*, pp. 312–14.

28. Ze'ev Schiff and Ehud Ya'ari, *Israel's Lebanon War* (New York: Simon & Schuster, 1984), pp. 38–40.

29. Evron, *War and Intervention*, pp. 84, 106; Randall, *Going all the Way*, pp. 228–29.
30. Rabinovich, *War for Lebanon*, p. 104.
31. Evron, *War and Intervention*, pp. 54–66; Itamar Rabinovich, "Controlled Conflict in the Middle East: The Syrian-Israeli Rivalry in Lebanon," in Gabriel Ben Dor, ed., *Conflict Management in the Middle East* (Lexington, Mass.: Lexington Books, 1987), pp. 100–101.
32. Evron, *War and Intervention*, pp. 83–93.
33. Ibid., pp. 25–27; Randall, *Going all the Way*, pp. 186–92; Rabinovich, *War for Lebanon*, pp. 162–63.
34. Schiff and Ya'ari, *Israel's Lebanon War*, pp. 31–35.
35. Ronald J. Young, *Missed Opportunities for Peace: U.S. Middle East Policy, 1981–1986* (Philadelphia: American Friends Service Committee, 1987), p. 16.
36. Schiff and Ya'ari, *Israel's Lebanon War*, p. 70.
37. Ofira Selektar, "Israel's Menachem Begin," in Barbara Kellerman and Jeffrey Z. Rubin, eds., *Leadership and Negotiation in the Middle East* (New York: Praeger, 1988), p. 43; Randall, *Going all the Way*, p. 244; Schiff and Ya'ari, *Israel's Lebanon War*, p. 39.
38. Schiff and Ya'ari, *Israel's Lebanon War*, pp. 14, 43.
39. Schiff and Ya'ari, *Israel's Lebanon War*, pp. 42–43, 53, 61, 112–13; Rabinovich, *War for Lebanon*, p. 101.
40. Evron, *War and Intervention*, pp. 84, 106–11; Randall, *Going all the Way*, pp. 228–29, 251–52; Rabinovich, *War for Lebanon*, pp. 121–33.
41. George Ball, *Error and Betrayal in Lebanon* (Washington, D.C.: Foundation for Middle East Peace, 1984), p. 29.
42. Joseph Kraft, *Washington Post*, March 16, 1982, p. A23, reporting on Israeli thinking about the possible outcome of the proposed invasion.
43. Schiff and Ya'ari, *Israel's Lebanon War*, p. 117.
44. Ibid., pp. 151–80; Seale, *Asad*, pp. 376–90.
45. *New York Times*, May 11, 1983, p. A9.
46. *New York Times*, May 10, 1983, p. A24.
47. Meir Zamir, "The Emergence of Syria?" in Braun, ed., *The Middle East in Global Strategy*, pp. 54–55.
48. Quoted in Rabinovich, *War for Lebanon*, p. 149.
49. Saadia Touval, "Commentary," in Kellerman and Rubin, eds., *Leadership and Negotiation*, p. 235.
50. Seale, *Asad*, p. 345.
51. Evron, *War and Intervention*, pp. 192–93.
52. David Bar-Illan, "Can Israel Withdraw? No!," *Commentary*, April 1988, pp. 33–38.
53. Carter, *Blood of Abraham*, p. 54.
54. Interview with Yahya Sadowski, *MEAG Perspective*, November-December 1986.
55. FBIS, May 8, 1990, p. 31.
56. Carter, *Blood of Abraham*, p. 71.
57. William Quandt, "The Uprising: Breaking a Ten Year Deadlock," *American-Arab Affairs*, no. 27 (Winter 1988/1989), p. 19.

58. *Al-Qabas,* December 9, 1989, cited in FBIS, December 11, 1989, p. 52.
59. Evron, *War and Intervention,* p. 188.
60. Ibid., p. 193.
61. *Jerusalem Post Magazine,* September 10, 1982.
62. Clawson, *Unaffordable Ambitions,* pp. 3–5; Aharon Levron, "Syria's Military Strength and Capability," *Middle East Review,* vol. 19 (Spring 1987), pp. 5–15; International Institute for Strategic Studies, *The Military Balance, 1989–1990* (London, 1990); Kessler, *Syria,* pp. 114–15.
63. The two sources differ on military manpower, with Gazit putting the size of Syrian forces at 730,000 (reserves of 340,000) and combat aircraft at 650, as opposed to the IISS figure of 448.
64. Levron, "Syria's Military Strength," p. 6; Cynthia Roberts, "Soviet Transfer Policy and the Decision to Upgrade Syrian Air Defenses, *Survival* (July-August, 1983), pp. 134–64.
65. Yezid Sayigh, "The Middle East Strategic Balance," *Middle East International,* June 22, 1990, p. 15.
66. Kessler, *Syria,* p. 110; Zeev Ma'oz, "The Evolution of Syrian Power, 1948–1984," in Ma'oz and Yaniv, eds., *Syria under Assad,* pp. 73–75.
67. Kessler, *Syria,* pp. 119–20.
68. Ibid., pp. 115–16, 122–24; Yehosha Raviv, "Arab-Israeli Military Balance," *Jerusalem Quarterly,* vol. 18 (Winter 1981), pp. 137–38.
69. Mark Heller, Dov Tamari, and Zeev Eitan, *The Middle East Military Balance, 1983* (Tel Aviv: Jaffee Center for Strategic Studies, 1984); Seale, *Asad,* p. 206.
70. Ball, *Error and Betrayal,* pp. 107–108; Raviv, "Arab-Israeli Military Balance," pp. 124, 136.
71. Ma'oz, "Evolution of Syrian Power," pp. 77–81.
72. Including during a recent trip by Jimmy Carter and during a visit by the Council on Foreign Relations' delegation mission headed by Cyrus Vance (out of which this study grew).
73. *Minneapolis Star-Tribune,* June 17, 1990, p. 21A.
74. Kenneth W. Stein, "Texture of the Middle East Peace Process," *Middle East Insight,* vol. 7, nos. 2–3 (1990), p. 86.

CHAPTER 5

1. Efraim Karsh, *The Soviet Union and Syria: The Asad Years* (New York: Routledge, 1988), p. 1.
2. Ibid., p. 54.
3. Ibid., p. 62.
4. Seale, *Asad,* p. 359.
5. Pedro Ramet, *The Soviet-Syrian Relationship Since 1955: A Troubled Alliance* (Boulder, Colo.: Westview Press, 1990), p. 149.
6. Seale, *Asad,* p. 399.
7. See John P. Hannah, *At Arms Length: Soviet-Syrian Relations in the Gorbachev Era* (Washington, D.C.: Washington Institute for Near East Policy, 1989).
8. FBIS, February 24, 1989, pp. 12–19.
9. Karsh, *Soviet Union and Syria,* p. 92.

10. *Boston Globe*, September 19, 1989, p. 7.
11. *Washington Post*, November 20, 1989, pp. A1, A28.
12. FBIS, November 24, 1989, pp. 52–54.
13. FBIS, June 1, 1990, p.16.
14. Speech by President Asad, FBIS, March 9, 1990, p. 33.
15. FBIS, February 9, 1990, p. 49.
16. Ramet, *Soviet-Syrian Relationship*, p. 231.
17. Ibid., p. 237.
18. FBIS, March 9, 1990, p. 34.
19. FBIS, May 17, 1990, pp. 28–29.
20. FBIS, February 8, 1990, p. 44.
21. FBIS, May 1, 1990, p. 20.
22. FBIS, May 2, 1990, p. 17.
23. FBIS, May 3, 1990, p. 44.
24. Kessler, *Syria* (unpublished update, 1989), p. 2.
25. Seale, *Struggle for Syria*, especially, pp. 283–306; Douglas Little, "Cold War and Covert Action: The United States and Syria, 1945–1958," *Middle East Journal*, vol. 44 (1990), pp. 51–75.
26. Smith, *Palestine and the Arab-Israeli Conflict*, pp. 200–202.
27. Ball, *Error and Betrayal in Lebanon*, pp. 93–94.
28. Ben Tzur, *Syrian Baath Party and Israel.*
29. Quandt, *Decade of Decisions*, pp. 79–80.
30. Smith, *Palestine and the Arab-Israeli Conflict*, p. 226.
31. Alan Dowty, "The United States and the Syrian-Jordanian Confrontation of 1970," *Jerusalem Journal of International Relations*, vol. 3 (1978), pp. 179–82.
32. Quandt, *Decade of Decisions*, 129.
33. Smith, *Palestine and the Arab-Israeli Conflict*, pp. 228–29; Quandt, *Decade of Decisions*, pp. 128–64.
34. Quandt, *Decade of Decisions*, pp. 208–209.
35. Ibid., pp. 219–20; Kissinger, *Years of Upheaval*, p. 1057.
36. Quandt, *Decade of Decisions*, p. 248; Sheehan, "How Kissinger Did It," pp. 60–67.
37. Seale, *Asad*, pp. 249–50.
38. Kissinger, *Years of Upheaval*, pp. 941–45, 947–56, 963, 976–77, 1032, 1069, 1071, 1078, 1088; Quandt, *Decade of Decisions*, p. 242.
39. Sheehan, "How Kissinger Did It," p. 83; Kissinger, *Years of Upheaval*, pp. 786–87.
40. Sheehan, "How Kissinger Did It," pp. 87–89.
41. Ibid., p. 88.
42. George Ball, *Diplomacy for a Crowded World: An American Foreign Policy* (Boston: Little, Brown, 1976), p. 145.
43. Ball, *Diplomacy*, pp. 133–52; Roger Fisher, "Playing the Wrong Game?" in Rubin, ed., *Dynamics of Third Party Intervention*, pp. 95–121.
44. Quandt, *Decade of Decisions*, p. 267.
45. Seale, *Asad*, p. 273; Randall, *Going All the Way*, pp. 178, 184.
46. Matti Golan, *The Secret Conversations of Henry Kissinger* (New York: Quadrangle Books, 1976); Sheehan, "How Kissinger Did It"; Seale, *Asad*, pp. 226–49; Quandt, *Decade of Decisions*, pp. 207–300; I. William Zartman,

"Explaining Disengagement," in Rubin, ed., *Dynamics of Third Party Intervention*, pp. 148–67.

47. Carter, *Blood of Abraham;* Cyrus Vance, *Hard Choices*, pp. 159–255.

48. Carter, *Blood of Abraham*, pp. 63–84.

49. Ismail Fahmy, *Negotiating for Peace in the Middle East* (Baltimore: Johns Hopkins University Press, 1983), p. 196.

50. Vance, *Hard Choices*, pp. 213–55; Carter, *Blood of Abraham*, p. 204.

51. Talcott Seelye, *U.S.-Arab Relations: The Syrian Dimension* (Portland, Ore.: Portland State University and National Council on U.S.–Arab Relations, 1985), pp. 12–13.

52. *Christian Science Monitor*, September 14, 1981, p. 24.

53. Betty Glad, "The United States' Ronald Reagan," in Kellerman and Rubin, eds., *Leadership and Negotiation*, pp. 212–23; Randall, *Going All the Way*, p. 252; Rabinovich, *War for Lebanon*, p. 91.

54. Randall, *Going All the Way*, pp. 195, 204, 207–08.

55. Ibid., pp. 210, 216; Carter, *Blood of Abraham*, p. 97; Evron, *War and Intervention*, p. 78.

56. Rabinovich, *War for Lebanon*, p. 148; Schiff and Ya'ari, *Israel's Lebanon War*, p. 70.

57. Schiff and Ya'ari, *Israel's Lebanon War*, pp. 73–77; Young, *Missed Opportunities*, pp. 31, 35.

58. Rabinovich, *War for Lebanon*, pp. 91–92, 146; Schiff and Ya'ari, *Israel's Lebanon War*, pp. 31, 73–75; Glad, "The United States' Ronald Reagan," pp. 212–14.

59. Yair Evron, "Washington, Damascus, and the Lebanon Crisis," in Maoz and Yaniv, eds., *Syria under Assad*, p. 218.

60. Seale, *Assad*, p. 390.

61. Seelye, *U.S.-Arab Relations*, pp. 12–13; Schiff and Ya'ari, *Israel's Lebanon War*, pp. 152–55, 202–03; Randall, *Going All the Way*, p. 252; Seale, *Asad*, pp. 384–90.

62. Schiff and Ya'ari, *Israel's Lebanon War*, p. 293.

63. Rabinovich, *War for Lebanon*, pp. 183–85; Bernard Gwertzman, *New York Times*, May 1, 1983.

64. Carter, *Blood of Abraham*, p. 100.

65. Young, *Missed Opportunities*, p. 60; Seale, *Asad*, p. 407; Seelye, *U.S.-Arab Relations*, pp. 7–8.

66. Leslie Gelb, *New York Times*, October 31, 1982, p. 20.

67. *International Herald Tribune*, November 5, 1983, p. 2.

68. Bernard Gwertzman, *New York Times*, July 7, 1983, p. A7; William Quandt, "Reagan's Lebanon Policy: Trial and Error," *Middle East Journal*, vol. 38 (1984), pp. 245–70.

69. *New York Times*, October 23, 1983, p. E1.

70. *Jerusalem Post*, January 4, 1985.

71. Seelye, *U.S.-Arab Relations*, p. 10; Seale, *Asad*, p. 416.

72. Rabinovich, *War for Lebanon*, p. 186.

73. Schiff and Ya'ari, *Israel's Lebanon War*, p. 293.

74. Randall, *Going All the Way*, p. 292; Seale, *Asad*, p. 417.

75. Glad, "United States' Ronald Reagan," pp. 220–21; Carter, *Blood of Abraham*, p. 148; Randall, *Going All the Way*, p. 293; Young, *Missed Opportunities*, pp. 56–57.
76. Carter, *Blood of Abraham*, p. 81.
77. Seale, *Asad*, pp. 473–74.

CHAPTER 6

1. *Yedi'ot Aharonot*, March 8 and 11, 1991, cited in FBIS, March 14, 1991, p. 31.
2. FBIS, January 17, 1991, p. 38.
3. FBIS, February 14, 1991, p. 27.
4. FBIS, March 11, 1991, p. 50.
5. Ibid.
6. FBIS, March 19, 1991, p. 26.
7. FBIS, March 21, 1991, p. 21.
8. *Boston Globe*, May 22, 1991, p. 15.
9. FBIS, April 9, 1991, p. 46.
10. *New York Times*, April 7, 1985.
11. *New York Times*, March 8, 1991, p. A8.

BIBLIOGRAPHY

Amnesty International. *Report from Amnesty International to the Government of the Syrian Arab Republic.* London: Amnesty International, 1983.

Batatu, Hanna. "Some Observations on the Social Roots of Syria's Ruling Military Group and the Causes for Its Dominance." *Middle East Journal,* vol. 35, no. 3 (1981), pp. 331–44.

Carter, Jimmy. *The Blood of Abraham: Insights into the Middle East.* Boston: Houghton Mifflin, 1985.

Clawson, Patrick. *Unaffordable Ambitions: Syria's Military Buildup and Economic Crisis.* Policy Papers, no. 17. Washington, D.C.: The Washington Institute for Near East Policy, 1989.

Cobban, Helena. *The Superpowers and the Syrian-Israeli Conflict: Beyond Crisis Management.* The Washington Papers, no. 149. New York: Praeger with The Center for International Studies, Washington, D.C., 1991.

Dawisha, Adeed. "Syria Under Asad, 1970–1978: The Centres of Power." *Government and Opposition,* vol. 13, no. 3 (Summer 1978), pp. 341–54.

———. *Syria and the Lebanese Crisis.* London: Macmillan, 1980.

Devlin, John. *The Ba'th Party: A History from Its Origins to 1966.* Stanford: Hoover Institution Press, 1976.

———. *Syria: Modern State in an Ancient Land.* Boulder, Colorado: Westview Press, 1983.

Drysdale, Alasdair. "Ethnicity in the Syrian Officer Corps: A Conceptualization." *Civilisations,* vol. 29, no. 3/4 (1979), pp. 359–73.

———. "The Syrian Political Elite, 1966–1976: A Spatial and Social Analysis." *Middle Eastern Studies,* vol. 17, no. 1 (1981), pp. 3–30.

———. "The Asad Regime and its Troubles." *MERIP Reports,* vol. 12, no. 9, (1982), pp. 3–11.

———. "The Succession Question in Syria." *Middle East Journal,* vol. 39, no. 2 (1985), pp. 246–62.

233

Evron, Yair. *War and Intervention in Lebanon: The Israeli-Syrian Deterrence Dialogue.* Baltimore: Johns Hopkins University Press, 1987.

Hanna, John P. *At Arms Length: Soviet-Syrian Relations in the Gorbachev Era.* Policy Papers, no. 18. Washington, D.C.: The Washington Institute for Near East Policy, 1989.

Hinnebusch, Raymond A. "Revisionist Dreams, Realist Strategies: The Foreign Policy of Syria." In *The Foreign Policies of Arab States,* edited by Bahgat Korany and Ali Dessouki, pp. 283–322. Boulder, Colorado: Westview Press, 1984.

———. "Syrian Policy in Lebanon and the Palestinians." *Arab Studies Quarterly,* vol. 8, no. 1 (1986), pp. 1–20.

———. "Egypt, Syria, and the Arab State System." In *The Arab-Israeli Conflict: Two Decades of Change,* edited by Yehuda Lukas and Abdalla Battah, pp. 182–90. Boulder, Colorado: Westview Press, 1988.

———. *Authoritarian Power and State Formation in Ba'thist Syria: Army, Party, and Peasant.* Boulder, Colorado: Westview Press, 1989.

Hopwood, Derek. *Syria, 1945–1986: Politics and Society.* London: Unwin Hyman, 1988.

Human Rights Watch. *Human Rights in Syria.* New York: Human Rights Watch, 1990.

Karsh, Efraim. *The Soviet Union and Syria: The Asad Years.* New York: Routledge, 1988.

Kessler, Martha Neff. *Syria: Fragile Mosaic of Power.* Washington, D.C.: National Defense University Press, 1987.

Khoury, Philip. *Syria and the French Mandate: The Politics of Arab Nationalism, 1920–1945.* Princeton, New Jersey: Princeton University Press, 1987.

Kissinger, Henry. *Years of Upheaval.* Boston: Little, Brown and Company, 1982.

Ma'oz, Moshe. *Asad: The Sphinx of Damascus.* New York: Weidenfeld & Nicolson, 1988.

——— and Yaniv, Avner, eds. *Syria under Assad: Domestic Constraints and Regional Risks.* New York: St. Martins Press, 1986.

Petran, Tabitha. *Syria.* London: Ernest Benn, 1972.

Picard, Elizabeth. "Arab Military in Politics: From Revolutionary Plot to Authoritarian State." In *Beyond Coercion: The Durability of the Arab State*, edited by Adeed Dawisha and I. William Zartman, pp. 116–46. London: Croom Helm, 1988.

Pipes, Daniel. *Greater Syria: The History of an Ambition*. New York: Oxford University Press, 1990.

Quandt, William. *Decade of Decisions: American Policy Toward The Arab-Israeli Conflict, 1967–1976*. Berkeley: University of California Press, 1977.

Rabinovich, Itamar. *Syria under the Ba'th, 1963–1966: The Army-Party Symbiosis*. New York: Halstead Press, 1972.

———. *The War for Lebanon*. Ithaca, New York: Cornell University Press, 1985.

Ramet, Pedro. *The Syrian-Soviet Relationship Since 1955: A Troubled Alliance*. Boulder, Colorado: Westview Press, 1990.

Randall, Jonathan. *Going All the Way: Christian Warlords, Israeli Adventurers and the War in Lebanon*. New York: Vintage Books, 1984.

Roberts, David. *The Ba'th and the Creation of Modern Syria*. London: Croom Helm, 1987.

Sadowski, Yahya M. "Patronage and the Ba'th: Corruption and Control in Contemporary Syria." *Arab Studies Quarterly*, vol. 9, no. 4 (1987), pp. 442–61.

Schiff, Zeev and Ya'ari, Ehud. *Israel's Lebanon War*. New York: Simon & Shuster, 1984.

Seale, Patrick. *The Struggle for Syria: A Study of Post-War Arab Politics*. London: Oxford University Press, 1965.

———. *Asad: The Struggle for the Middle East*. Berkeley: University of California Press, 1988.

Sheehan, Edward. "How Kissinger Did It: Step By Step in the Middle East." *Foreign Policy*, no. 22 (Spring 1976).

Tibawi, A. L. *A Modern History of Syria*. London: Macmillan, 1969.

Torrey, Gordon. *Syrian Politics and the Military, 1945–1958*. Columbus, Ohio: Ohio State University Press, 1964.

Van Dam, Nikolaos. *The Struggle for Power in Syria: Sectarianism, Regionalism and Tribalism in Politics, 1961–1980*. London: Croom Helm, 1981.

Vance, Cyrus. *Hard Choices: Critical Years in America's Foreign Policy.* New York: Simon & Schuster, 1983.

Van Dusen, Michael. "Downfall of a Traditional Elite." In *Political Elites and Political Development in the Middle East,* edited by Frank Tachau, pp. 115–55. Cambridge, Massachusetts: Schenkman, 1975.

Weinberger, Naomi J. *Syrian Intervention in Lebanon: The 1975–76 Civil War.* New York: Oxford University Press, 1986.

INDEX

74–75; Iranian-Syrian alliance and, 94; Israeli domination of Lebanon, fight against, 126–28; Lebanon reconstruction efforts of 1980s, 82–84; Maronite forces, Syrian support for, 76, 77–78; Maronite-Syrian conflicts, 78–79; peacekeeping role for Syria, 77–78; PLO expulsion from Lebanon, 80–81; Syrian hegemony, institutionalization of, 84; Syrian-PLO alliance against Israel and, 79–80; trade, 49

Lebanon: Arab East alliance, 117–18; Greater Syria and, 60; Iraqi role in, 67; Israeli invasion of 1982, 80, 123–28, 190–93; Israeli-Syrian conflict over, 119–29; PLO in, 75, 76–77, 78, 79–81, 119–20, 123, 125; Soviet-Syrian relations, impact on, 156, 158–60; U.S. policy toward, 127, 189–93, 196–97; Zahlah missile crisis, 121–22, 189. *See also* Lebanese-Syrian relations

Liberation ideology, 15

Libya, 108, 137

Magen, David, 205
Makhluf, Adnan, 28
Maronites, 76, 77–79, 82–84, 121–22
Meir, Golda, 113
Mubarak, Hosni, 65, 66–67, 170
Muslim Brotherhood, 33, 34, 42, 70, 94, 95
Muslim fundamentalism, 41, 94–95

Nasser, Gamal Abdel, 100, 101, 178
Nassif, Mu'in, 29
National Alliance for the Liberation of Syria, 42–43
National Front for the Salvation of Syria (NFSS), 43
National Progressive Front coalition, 26–27, 39, 40
New York Times, 126
Nixon, Richard M., 155, 177, 178, 180, 181, 182, 214

October War of 1973, 103–8; disengagements following, 108–10, 114, 181–82, 183–84; Soviet-Syrian relations and, 154–55; Syria's relations with Arab countries and, 63–64, 69; U.S. response, 109–10, 179–80

Oil production, 49–50

Palestine Liberation Organization (PLO): Arab East alliance, 117–18; Arab solidarity in peace process, 145–46; "Black September" crisis, 178; Israeli invasion of Lebanon and, 123, 125; Jordan and, 69; in Lebanon, 75, 76–77, 78, 79–81, 119–20, 123, 125; as legitimate representative of Palestinian people, 111; Soviet-Syrian relations and, 160; Syria, relations with, 73, 74, 79–82, 134–35; United States, dialogue with, 197–98

Palestine National Salvation Front (PNSF), 74, 81

Palestinians, 111, 112; Greater Syria and, 60; *intifadah,* 81, 133; Jordan, proposed federation with, 71–72; Persian Gulf War and, 207–8; Shamir/Baker Plan and, 133–34; Syria, relations with, 72–74; Syrian notion of Palestinian rights, 134–35. *See also* Palestine Liberation Organization

Pan-Arabism, 15; Ba'th party and, 58; decline of, 56–57; as ideology for Asad regime, 57–58; partition of Arab world and, 55–56; Syrian tradition of, 54–55, 57

Partition of Arab world, 55–56

Peace process: Arab solidarity and, 145–46; arms race, need to end, 217–19; Asad regime's policy on, 5–6, 52–53; Asad's ability to deliver Syria, 203–4; comprehensive settlement, U.S. insistence on, 211–12; concessions necessary from Israel and Syria, 204–6;